# Donor Girl

## Lilli D. Adams

Donor Girl

**Printed by Create Space**

**First published in the United States of America 2009.**

**Copyright Lilli D. Adams, 2009**
**All rights reserved.**


**ISBN:  IS N 978-1449568399**

# Donor
# Girl

Donor Girl

# Prologue

Hypochondriacs should probably not volunteer to give up body organs. After all, by definition, a hypochondriac is "a person abnormally concerned about his or her health." Of course, then you would have to define "abnormally." Isn't it normal to be concerned about your health? If I weren't concerned about my health, would I have been healthy enough to donate a kidney? Or would I have been one of the many people flagged for health issues? I guess what I mean is, if you are the type of person who gets a leg cramp and immediately thinks "amputation," chances are you are going to worry about living without an organ. If every time you see too much hair in the brush and think "I need Rogaine" (worse yet, if you are female), you might want to reconsider organ donation. Just my opinion.

If you are on the OCD side of things, it might be a good idea not to consider parting with an organ. By definition, OCD is **"Obsessive-compulsive disorder:** A psychiatric disorder characterized by obsessive thoughts and compulsive actions, such as cleaning, checking, counting, or hoarding." While I can identify with some of this, I assure you I will never be accused of being obsessive or compulsive about cleaning. Ask my parents, sister, college roommate or husband, and they will confirm this.

However, if you can't sleep because you're lying awake obsessing over the time you said something really rude to the woman behind the counter at the drugstore when you were 12, you might be a little too obsessive to donate an organ. Do you check 8 times to make sure you turned off the iron? Do you worry that you left the water running in the sink? Do you know for sure you didn't turn off the stove even though you checked it over and over and over again? If so, you might be a little too OCD to consider organ donation.

# Donor Girl

I am neither a hoarder nor a cleaner, but I have struggled with other OCD traits. My dad just defined me as "a weird kid." That was before everything weird about me had a disorder to go with it. My dad figured it was best "fixed" by mercilessly teasing me, often in front of others. While I wouldn't necessarily recommend this style of humiliation as a cure for OCD, let me assure you that it did fix the problem, or at least caused it to go into hiding full time.

So, I'm an OCD hypochondriac who donated an organ. Why did I do this? Most OCD/hypochondriac personalities are also Type A personalities; and Type A personalities *fix* things. Granted, we tend to be irritable, angry and impatient; but in fairness, we also fix things. If something is broken, we fix it. We try to do this for friends, family, relationships, work. In my case, it was broken kidneys that needed fixing.

Did I obsess over the decision to donate a kidney? Yes. Do I still obsess over this decision? Sometimes, but strangely, not often. Is it possible to be a worrier, a worst case scenario person, or a hypochondriac and still donate a body organ without driving yourself crazy? Apparently it is, because I did. And so far, they have not tied me up in a pretty white jacket and sat me in a padded room with crayons. I must confess, however, that my family remains shocked that I passed the psychological portion of the testing.

My counselor told me, "You may be the most self-aware person I've ever met. Usually that works against people. But it seems to work for you." I'm still not sure how to respond to that.

# September 2006

In September of 2006, at 41 years of age, I was a full-time career woman. I'd been in the country music industry for 22 years, starting in radio at 19 and moving to the record business at 30. I had been married for 17 years, had a cat and two dogs, and no children. As a record promoter, I was on the road a fair amount of time and liked the fact that my responsibilities were limited to work and my husband. After all, my husband was self-sufficient and could take care of the pets when I was gone.

I am often asked,"So you're a record producer?"

I always answer, "No, a record promoter."

Then I hear, "What's the difference?"

I answer, "Potentially millions of dollars per year."

Most people don't really know what a record promoter does. All they know is I get to attend awards shows, go backstage at concerts and travel on tour buses; not to mention planes, trains and automobiles. I'm often envied for the glamorous lifestyle I supposedly lead. I remember another promoter calling me once and saying, "I'm at a sausage fair. I'm standing in a field at a sausage fair. I'm living the glamorous life!" That pretty much sums it up.

A record promoter has the rather thankless job of calling radio stations across the country to get them to play their label's songs. If it works, and the song becomes a hit, the credit usually goes to the songwriter, singer and producer. If the song doesn't become a hit, the blame usually goes to the promotions staff. It's a rare occasion when the music industry gives credit to the promotions

Donor Girl

team. And I'm pretty sure I've never heard the creative team say, "Wow, that song we produced/sang/wrote really must have sucked."

The music industry is an addiction, however. You literally feel addicted to the job. I always say it's a lot like being addicted to heroin; not that I have any idea what that is like. My description of a record promoter is as follows: The highs are high; the lows are low. It always takes more to reach a higher high. At some time we all figure we should get out, but we're addicted to the highs; and most of the time we just walk around strung out. I joke that I'm going to start a 12 step program for getting out of the music industry, but I'm going to charge and make millions.

The first step in promoting a song is to have an *amazing* song. It's true that it all starts with a song. On the NSAI (Nashville Songwriters Association International) building in Nashville is written their mantra: "It all begins with a song." That is probably the one truthful statement written in Nashville.

We have to have a talented artist with a great song, although a lot of people have great songs and great talent. However, without anyone taking songs to radio stations and convincing radio programmers to hear and play them, thousands of songs never get heard by the masses. When I was in radio, I had a VP of Promotions from Sony Music Nashville ask me, "What do you think is the hardest part of my job?" I replied, "Getting radio programmers to play your songs?" He said, "No, getting them to *listen* to my songs." I found that shocking. As a programmer of a radio station, I loved hearing new music. But I would later learn that getting programmers to listen to the music was very difficult. Just getting them to hear the music is the hardest part of the job. You are up against multitasking, lack of time, and, in some sad cases, pure apathy.

# Donor Girl

Of the hundreds of songs released in country music every year by record labels, there are roughly thirty that make it to #1. After all, there are only forty-nine charts per year and some songs stay at #1 for multiple weeks. So it's the Mount Everest of music to actually climb all the way to the highest point. I actually compare it to climbing Mount Everest, without the cold weather, pickax or crampons. When climbing Mount Everest, they set up base camp, which I liken to the Top 40 on the music chart. Then they climb up further to set up Camp One, which I liken to the Top 25. And so on up to the top of the mountain and to the top of the charts. Mountaineers may take offense to this since I've never climbed Mount Everest. To be fair, they've never tried to climb the charts!

As of 2006, I'd worked #1 hits and I'd worked failures and everything in between. While promoters give 100%+ of themselves to their artists and their music, always putting their needs second to their artists, I can't say we do it completely altruistically. After all, we have the opportunity to ride the coat tails of the rich and famous. We go through the backstage area with our laminate passes like we are a part of the show. In fact, if you've ever seen snow skiers that wear *all* their ski passes on their jackets as a way of saying, "I ski a lot!" you get the idea of our laminates. We could have last been on a big tour (say the George Strait tour) ten years ago, but we still have the laminate on our lanyard, along with our most current tour. We're funny that way. We get special parking and special access to the artist. We go to awards shows and dress up in long gowns and tuxes. We ride the tour buses, hang out with the band and singers, and live a life most only dream of. And we get paid fairly well to do it! Not so altruistic. Some of us are wannabe singers/songwriters/musicians, and some of us just got tired of being the nerd all the time and followed a dream. I fall more into the second category than the first.

Donor Girl

What most people don't realize is the fun part is only about 10% of our job. The other 90% consists of finding ways to convince Program Directors (PD's) to play our music. Thanks to former NY Governor Eliot Spitzer (no further comment necessary), our lives got even more difficult due to his crackdown on what he considered payola. While there was some payola going on, there were also a lot of honest dealings between records and radio. Yes, labels often offer to have their artists perform shows for radio listeners to gain exposure to the artists. The horror and shock of doing a concert for the masses! To add to the problems in our industry, downloading of music has cut CD sales by 20% per year. Luckily, our label is remaining successful!

That being said, we do have a very fun, albeit stressful, job. We work hard long hours and spend a lot of time away from our families and friends. We give up attending weddings, funerals, parties, holidays and anything else that might happen on a day when we have a concert we must attend. It's all about the job. We don't have time to focus too much energy on anything else.

I did, however, find a way to also have a personal life. Those that don't, find a very sad end to their career when they either get fired (which we all do eventually) or they retire. I'm a record promoter, but I'm also a Christian, wife, daughter, sister, aunt and friend. While my work takes a majority of my time and effort, if I had to put things in order of importance, work would not come first. God and family would definitely come first. I can't say the way I live my life has necessarily proven that, but I know what is in my heart. Who knew I'd end up having to prove it?

Donor Girl

# Why Write My Story?

I recently read a book called *Sick Girl* by Amy Silverstein about living with a transplanted heart for nearly 20 years. Naturally, the donor had to die in order to donate a heart, so the reader didn't have a chance to hear from the donor. Even if the person could have talked, the book wasn't about the donor; it was about the recipient. The author detailed the trials and tribulations of living a life with immunosuppressant drugs, pains, illnesses and frustrations. But at some point and time, there had been a living being that died in order for her to live. This wasn't the goal of the person who died, but it was the outcome. That person can't tell their story. They can't tell what it felt like to have a working body part taken out of them and put in another person so that they might live. There's a story there; the person just can't tell it. Did they have "organ donor" on their license? Did their family make the painful decision in the throes of heartbreak and mourning to offer the organs? There's a story there.

A few years ago I read a fiction book called *My Sister's Keeper* by Jodi Picoult. It dealt with a sister in need of a kidney and the sister that was supposed to donate. This was a variation on the real life story of the parents who decided to have another baby in hopes the child would be a bone marrow match for an older, ill child. This real life story was very controversial at the time, with strangers trying to get custody of the fetus to stop the parents from allowing her to be a donor. Personally, I believe this wasn't the decision for strangers to make. Parents that would go to that extreme measure to save a child would equally love and protect another child, and I always felt the "fetus" was going to be one lucky person. However, Jodi Picoult, in her fictionalized version, took it one step further. After the bone marrow successfully took and gave the older child a few healthy years, her kidneys started to fail. They were now looking to the younger child to donate a kidney. This

Donor Girl

took the debate to a new level; one that is unimaginable. For a prepubescent child to know her younger sibling was being asked to give up a body part so that she might live has to be painful beyond anything we can understand. For the younger child to have to make such a sacrifice is unconscionable. It is very rare for someone under age 18 to be a living organ donor. But it did bring about an interesting discourse.

To anyone who has ever wondered, "What do they do with bodies donated to science?" I recommend the book, *Stiff* by Mary Roach. The book follows cadavers donated to science for a multitude of purposes. This was one of the funniest books I've ever read, despite the rather macabre topic. While I didn't find it difficult to check "yes" on my driver's license to donate organs once I die, donating your entire body takes on a whole new element of soul searching. Prior to people willingly donating their bodies to science, medical schools and hospitals resorted to some very questionable means of obtaining bodies. Some had students dig up newly buried bodies. Some paid people to exhume bodies illegally. Some paid people to steal cadavers that had not yet been buried. Naturally, this had the horrible effect of people killing people to get money for their bodies. However, these extreme measures of obtaining cadavers for the purpose of learning how to heal is what has brought our medicine to the heights it's achieved. Without these cadavers to study, we'd be much farther behind in the knowledge of the human body. It wasn't their intent to donate themselves, but again, it was their outcome. For those that do donate their bodies, I have an enormous level of respect and have fought the odd desire to do it myself. After all, I won't need it. So far, I haven't been able to bring myself to take that final step. I thank God for those that do.

With all that I have read, what I've never seen is a book purely about donation from the perspective of the donor. And I never would have thought about it had I not chosen to be a living kidney donor for my sister's husband in October of 2006. However, I've

Donor Girl

learned through the telling of my story that people are not simply interested in hearing about my surgery; they are fascinated and ask a plethora of questions. And more than anything, I've realized that it makes them think about their own life decisions. Is this something I could do? Would I do it if called upon? I laugh at the number of times I've heard people say, "If I'd been you, I think my brother-in- law would have heard the words, 'You're going to die.'" And in all honesty, I've admitted to Dave that if it weren't for his children, Will and Kayla, he'd probably be on dialysis right now. Sorry dude, but have a seat and wait your turn. But there were children at stake and I think we amaze ourselves when called upon to do the ultimate, which is save a life, even if it could be at our own expense. Our soldiers do it every single day. God bless every one of them! And they don't get knocked out by an anesthesiologist or have a medical team assuring them they'll be ok. I don't think I could be a front line soldier, although I like to think if called upon I would. But I never thought I'd be a living organ donor either.

I thought about calling this book *Well Girl* as opposed to *Sick Girl*, or maybe *My Sister's Husband's Keeper*. But my sister suggested *Donor Girl*, which is funny since unbeknownst to her I referred to myself that way many times.

I've heard so many things since starting on a journey toward kidney donation. And it is a journey. I was not one of those people who read about someone altruistically donating a kidney to a stranger and felt a higher call to do the same. I've read about those people in magazines like *People*. They get a calling to be a living donor and follow through on it by contacting a transplant hospital and saying, "Hey, you have anybody there that is A Positive and needs a kidney? I have a spare." Not me! Shy of checking "yes" under organ donor on my driver's license, I had no plans to give up working body parts, at least not while I was still using them. I felt my body parts were quite happy living and working in my body. I never saw a "For Sale" sign on them, and they gave me absolutely

Donor Girl

no indication that they weren't happy right where they were. And selling them wasn't a legal option anyway.

In our country, you can't sell body parts...or can you? Think about this: A man can self stimulate into a cup in the hopes of donating a part of his body that creates a child. And he can get paid for it! But giving up a kidney to save a life, you can't legally get a penny. Hello? Who is making these rules?

I recently posed these questions in mixed company and one guy said, "Hell yeah, I'd be a sperm donor. I wish they had one of those where I live. I'd quit my day job and just donate all day long. There'd be hundreds of big-nosed, red-haired kids running all around this town."

Before I could stop laughing at him, a young twenty-one-year old guy said, "I tried that. I went to a sperm donation clinic. They turned me down. They said I looked too generic. They didn't want my sperm." I'm sure I have laughed harder in my life, but I'm not sure when. I have never known anyone to actually go to one of those clinics, much less be turned down for looking too normal. I couldn't stop laughing. I'm not sure he appreciated my laughter as he then said, "I'm not really over that yet." I think I laughed harder. Making it even funnier is he's a good-looking guy and goes to a prestigious college in Boston. He is attractive, intelligent and everything you'd expect a sperm bank to want. Yet he wasn't "ethnic enough." Go figure.

All joking aside, I hear they are considering making the selling of kidneys legal in the U.S. I don't know if it's true, but as a kidney donor, I don't think it's a good idea. There is only one reason someone should donate a kidney or any other body organ, and that's because they feel led to do it, not lured by money but by a higher calling. Whether that calling is God or family or friend or stranger, it doesn't matter. I just don't believe the calling should have anything to do with the almighty dollar. I believe what will happen is this. The rich will get organs, the poor will donate organs. The poor can't afford the health care and lifestyle needed to live healthily with one kidney the same way people of more resources can. So they will be in even worse health. I also believe the strict procedures currently followed in the process of organ donation will fall below standard. No, organ donation should not be a way to make money. It should only be done to save a life. If you can sell a body organ to make money, why can't you sell your body to make money? Aren't we splitting hairs here?

According to UNOS (the United Network for Organ Sharing), currently there are roughly 100,000 waiting list candidates for organs. From January to November of 2007, there were a little over 26,000 transplants from roughly 13,000 donors, both living and dead. The United States is the leader in transplants and has very strict guidelines for when organs can be transplanted, whether from a living donor or a cadaver donor.

In 2006, there were 14,755 deceased and living organ donors, 28,930 lifesaving organ transplants, 48,206 candidates added to the national transplant waiting list, and 6,368 people who died while waiting. **Source: http://unos.org/**

Sadly, in some countries, the medical profession actually steals people's kidneys in order to sell them to foreigners desperate enough to pay for a kidney. I can't tell you how many times people said, "Just have David go to Afghanistan. They're selling their kidneys for a few thousand dollars." Right. I'm going to entrust my brother-in-law, who is my sister's husband and the father of my niece and nephew, to the Afghanistan medical community with a paid-for kidney. I don't think so.

There has long been a hoax running through e-mails about people stealing kidneys in the U.S. A person is knocked out and wakes up in a tub of ice with an incision and missing a kidney. While this

Donor Girl

has been proven to be a hoax and no real life story of this in the U.S. has ever been documented, it *does* happen in other countries.

In 2008 there was a medical ring in New Delhi, India that involved doctors, nurses, hospitals and others who were stealing body organs from innocent victims and selling them to clients from all over the world. They would kidnap their victims, knock them out or lie, and after extracting a blood sample, take their kidneys. It is believed up to 500 were sold over a nine-year period before they were caught. Hearing about this touched me deeply. It's one thing to make a conscious decision to be an organ donor after going through all the medical testing, talking to a surgeon, and spending time with a counselor. It's quite another to wake up in a Third World country with your kidney stolen from you and your future uncertain. I was horrified.

One reason organ theft doesn't happen in our country is our medical system. It's not quite as easy as just taking a kidney and putting it into another person. While the "rumor" and "Internet hoax" of organ robbers comes up every so often, you can't just steal a person's kidney and give it to someone else without the medical community being involved. Organ donation requires an intense medical screening to make sure the kidney or organ will match. To steal a kidney would require our medical system being involved in something as horrific as black market stealing of organs. While there was a time that our medical profession "stole" cadavers to do research, theft of organs is simply not happening in the U.S.A. in this century.

So when people say, "I don't think I could donate an organ," how do I respond? By being honest: "I didn't either." Others have said, "I would only do it for a child." My niece and nephew are the closest things I have to my own children, and I did this for them. Some have said, "You're crazy." I somewhat agree. Some have said, "You're a hero." That makes me uncomfortable. And one, a pastor, said, "I feel like I'm in the company of a saint." He apparently hasn't spent time inside my head during a George Clooney or Richard Gere movie. I am definitely not a saint.

One of my favorite comments came from a program director of radio station WRNS who said, "That's the most idiotic, stupid, admirable thing I've ever heard of. You are one stupid chick, but you're my hero." I love that. And the funniest e-mail I received was when I told my friend Brandi about it.

Date: 6/22/2007 5:53:07 P.M. Eastern Daylight Time
From: Brandi
To: Lee

**HOLY COW, LEE!!!!!! You're donating your kidney???? You couldn't just go light some candles at church? Good Lord! I don't know about this. Aren't you too tiny?? Shoot. I can't believe this. I mean, who does that? You're a saint. I'm worried sick. Promise me you'll keep us in your mass emails to keep us updated on what's going on. I am completely stunned by this news. God bless you. I mean that. God bless you.**

**I'm calling Laura immediately. Love, Brandi**

And she immediately called Laura, our mutual friend, who also e-mailed me.

Subject: We must talk
Date: 6/22/2007  8:06 PM

**I heard from Brandi that you were donating your kidney to David. I can't imagine facing such a decision. I want to talk to you. I will call you this weekend. Love, Laura**

Laura, Brandi and I had worked together at Decca Records from 1995 to 1999. It was under the MCA umbrella and we'd become close friends. When Decca disbanded during the MCA/Universal merger in 1999, Brandi went to Austin, Texas with her soon-to-be husband, Monte Warden, who was also a hit songwriter. Brandi landed a gig working with Willie Nelson, my all-time favorite singer. She would call me to say things like "I'm riding with Willie in his truck," or "I'm sitting at Willie's pool." Uh huh. Could I get anymore jealous? Laura went on to work with Tim McGraw's management company, and then to Atlantic Records before heading down to Austin, Texas to be with Brandi and meet her dream man, Mark. I went on to work at other record labels. I always say that our industry is a very friendly industry. Most of what we do involves being in a friendly, party atmosphere. But it can also be a very fake, back stabbing industry where you never really know who your friends are. It's only when you are no longer working together and can't do anything for someone that you find out who your real friends are. Laura and Brandi are real friends, one of the blessings I have gotten out of the music industry.

I was asked by many people if I had kept a journal of my kidney donation process, and sadly, I had not. However, by re-reading all the e-mail communications, I realized that technology had allowed me to journal it without my realizing it. I relied heavily on those e-mails to recount my story with accuracy.

Keep in mind that every story of donation is different. I've talked to living kidney donors who never questioned their decision, whether donating to their mom, cousin or someone else. Then, there are those of us who question every minute of the decision going back and forth between "I want to do this" and "I'm scared to do this." There are some who don't get nervous until afterwards, when they're in pain and surprised that their recovery is going to take time. What I have yet to encounter however, is any donor who regretted saving another's life. While this is only *my* story, I find that all donors have similar experiences and feelings that allow us to connect and relate.

Donor Girl

# IgA Nephropathy

So the question that begs answering is: "What caused Dave's kidneys to fail?" I often get asked, "Was it something he did?" That answer is a resounding **NO!** Quite honestly, if I felt Dave's kidney failure was self-inflicted, I wouldn't have sent my kidney to live in such poor conditions. After all, my kidney was used to the excellent things I fed it, like M&M's, Mountain Dew and all things chocolate. I didn't live with smoke trailing through my insides or mass amounts of alcohol. I wouldn't send a part of me to live in an environment that would abuse it. After all, my kidney had served me well and stayed healthy despite my junk food habits. It deserved the best!

Other than the occasional beer or glass of wine, Dave had never been a drinker. He stuck to a pretty healthy diet and maintained a healthy weight. Although he had briefly smoked when he was younger, it had been decades since he'd had a cigarette, and drugs were never something Dave used. Sometimes, people with healthy habits and lifestyles get sick. There's no rhyme or reason to it; it just happens.

Despite being an otherwise healthy person, Dave did have an autoimmune condition that he was unaware of. It all started in 2004 with a panicked phone call from my sister, Kelly. I was in Nashville on a business trip, staying in the spare bedroom at my boss's house. It was 2:00 A.M., and a cell phone ringing at 2:00 A.M. is rarely a good thing. It's either a drunk dialing friend (which is never as fun for the recipient of the call as it is for the caller) or it's just plain bad news. This was plain bad news. My sister was crying rather hysterically, but I managed to understand that her husband was in the emergency room at the local hospital with extremely high potassium levels. This was the first sign we had that he had kidney problems. Potassium levels that high can cause a heart attack or stroke. Dave survived the hospital stay, but it was determined that his kidneys were weak and in the beginning stages of failure.

Over the next few years, there would be more hospital stays, more concerns of kidney failure, and the continued deteriorating health of my brother-in-law. Being an overall healthy person, Dave was able to remain very active despite his declining health.

At one point, Dave's potassium levels were so high that the doctors could not understand how he had not stroked out. The most common serious complications from high potassium are cardiac arrhythmia, cardiac arrest and changes in nerve and muscle control. They put him through a stress test and were amazed that he did so well. Despite all of his health issues, Dave still ran seven miles three times per week. This is probably what saved him. Even in the months prior to surgery when Dave had swelling in his feet from gout (a potential side effect of kidney failure) and had days when he couldn't get out of bed, on days when he could, he still walked his seven miles.

So what did Dave actually have? A biopsy would reveal he had a disease called IgA nephropathy. According to an online source, The National Kidney and Urologic Diseases Information Clearinghouse (NKUDIC), IgA nephropathy is a kidney disorder that occurs when IgA, a protein that helps the body fight infections, settles in the kidney. After many years, IgA deposits may cause the kidneys to leak blood and sometimes protein into the urine.

Many people with IgA nephropathy leak blood into the urine, but this leakage does not mean they will have long-term problems. Others leak both blood and protein into the urine. If too much protein leaks into the urine, the hands and feet can swell. After 10 to 20 years with IgA nephropathy, the kidneys may show signs of damage. About 25% of adults with IgA nephropathy develop chronic kidney failure. Chronic kidney failure is more accurate than total kidney failure, and is defined as less than 10% to 15% of normal capacity or function. Only 5% to 10% of children develop chronic kidney failure. Symptoms of kidney failure include swelling in the hands and feet, nausea, fatigue, headaches, and sleep problems. By the time these symptoms occur, total kidney failure is near. Total kidney failure means the kidney damage is permanent. People with kidney failure need dialysis or a kidney transplant.

How do people know that they have IgA nephropathy?    In the early stages, IgA nephropathy has no symptoms. This disease can be silent for years, even decades. The first sign of IgA nephropathy may be blood in the urine. The blood may appear during a cold, sore throat, or other infection. At times, blood in the urine can only be detected by a doctor or nurse using special tests. If the amount of blood increases, urine may turn pink or the color of tea or cola. The condition is not always a sign of a serious disease; for example, heavy exercise can cause blood in the urine. This is what had happened to Dave.  During a routine test, and years prior to being diagnosed with kidney disease, they found blood in Dave's urine.  Doctors chalked it up to the fact that he was a runner. We often wondered what would have happened had they diagnosed Dave earlier and treated him correctly.

How would they have treated his disease?    When it came to treatment options, there wasn't really much they could do. Treatment of kidney failure focuses on slowing the disease and preventing complications.    One complication is high blood pressure, also called hypertension. Hypertension damages the kidneys. There are several types of blood pressure medicines called angiotensin-converting enzyme (ACE) inhibitors and angiotensin receptor blockers (ARBs) protect kidney function. These medicines not only lower blood pressure, but also decrease the loss of protein into the urine. Because of this effect, they are often used

Donor Girl

in IgA nephropathy to protect the kidneys. People with IgA nephropathy may develop high cholesterol. By watching their diet and taking medicine, they can help to lower their cholesterol level. Lowering cholesterol may help slow kidney damage. Medicines such as prednisone may help treat IgA nephropathy. Prednisone belongs to a class of medicines called corticosteroids which can have harmful side effects. In research studies, fish oil supplements containing Omega 3 fatty acids also slowed kidney damage in some patients. Vitamin E may help lower protein in the urine but not in the blood. One of the newer immunosuppressive agents called mycophenolate mofetil (MMF) is also being tested in treating IgA nephropathy.

Dave had high blood pressure and was being treated for it. Unfortunately, they didn't know he also had kidney disease, so they weren't treating him with kidney- friendly medication. We don't know if the medication aided the disease or played any part in its getting worse. Although Dave had a variety of symptoms like the blood in the urine, high blood pressure and gout, it took a while for it all to be combined into a diagnosis.

It was all a moot point by the time they diagnosed Dave since there was no turning back the damage or the clock. Dave was in kidney failure. While doctors tried diet and medication to keep his kidneys functioning for as long as possible, they were nearing the end of their ability. Two options remained, and one had to start as quickly as possible. By the end of the year, Dave would either be on dialysis or he'd have to have a kidney transplant.

**Source: National Kidney and Urologic Diseases Information Clearinghouse (NIH)**

Donor Girl

# My Pre-Donor Life

I didn't just wake up at 41, a soon-to-be kidney donor. While many people don't understand why I would donate to a non-blood relative, those that know my family and know the relationship between my sister and me understand it completely. My sister and I come from a very small, tight knit family. My parents are both only children, meaning there are no first cousins, no aunts and no uncles. By 2006, all of our grandparents had passed away, leaving exactly 4 adults and 2 children in our immediate biological family.

My sister and I are soul mates. She is 22 months older than me, and from the day I was born, we have been best friends. We were blessed with parents who encouraged our friendship and highly discouraged any fighting or animosity. That's not to say we didn't have our arguments. However, we always seemed to have more in common than not. We were both in the school bands, both in the school musicals, both in church groups. When we were only 8 and 10, my parents built a cabin in the mountains of Pennsylvania and most weekends were spent there. With no other children in the area, my sister and I had no one else to play with except each other. It allowed us to stay out of trouble and to become best friends. As we grew up and our friends back home were discovering parties and drinking, Kelly and I were whisked away to our cabin in the woods where life was pure, innocent and very family oriented.

Kelly and I were raised in a lifestyle that was more like the generation prior to our own. Our father worked as a CPA for McCormick Spice Company while our mom was a stay-at-home mom. Dad was the rock of the family and a very strict disciplinarian. Mom was the heart and soul of the family; always

Donor Girl

the mom who chaperoned the school field trips; presided as den mother for the Brownies and Girl Scouts; led the band boosters for the Joppatowne High School band; and acted as Sunday School teacher. Our family had bowling night. We rode our bikes to the hot dog stand on Saturdays and watched Saturday morning cartoons with hot chocolate and Dunkin' Donuts. Our parents were only 21 and 23 when they had my sister, so they were young parents. We were lucky that they were healthy; dedicated to Kelly and me; and stayed married. If we'd been in the sitcom *Happy Days*, we'd have been the Cunninghams.

I certainly don't mean to imply that we never had any family problems. We were all human. As I'd said, my dad was a strict disciplinarian and ruled the house. When dad was happy and in a good mood, there was no one funnier and more fun to be around. When dad was stressed, he could be very tough. And when dad was tough, we were all nervous. It would be a recurring theme throughout our lives. We spent a lot of time trying to figure out what we should tell dad and what we shouldn't, a common theme with daughters and fathers. There were times we'd be so afraid to tell him something, only to find that he would wrap his arms around us and give us all this amazing support. Then there were times that his wrath would send us running to our rooms. As I've grown up, I've come to realize that this was the normal life for most of my friends. It was the end of an era when fathers' words were final and females were just starting to realize that they could be strong too. Mom and dad were both strong parents, but in very different ways.

Kelly and I were as close as two people could be and I often believe that we were meant to be twins. When we have a bad day, our first thought is to call each other. When we have a good day, our first thought is to call each other. We were raised to be close, and that's what we've always been.

Donor Girl

I'm often asked if David would have donated his kidney to me had the situation been reversed. I don't honestly know the answer. I joke that if it weren't for him having my niece and nephew, I'm not sure I'd have donated to him. How would I know if he would or could do it if I'm not sure I would do it had the situation been different? Like so many difficult, life changing decisions, I don't believe we know the answers until we are truly, not hypothetically, faced with the question.

That being said, there is nothing my sister wouldn't give to me, and equally, nothing I wouldn't give to my sister. When you donate a body organ, you don't just donate to one person. You donate to everyone who loves that person. It's bigger than two people. So while I don't know if Dave would have donated to me, I do know that Kelly would have donated to *my* husband. And knowing that was enough for me. In fairness to Dave, he had a very difficult upbringing and wasn't raised in a family environment. Different from Kelly and me who had all the love available and resources far above most, Dave had neither. Every little thing he owned was a valued possession.

My sister had already shown her willingness to be there for Randy. When Randy wanted to buy the photo business, my dad helped put up the money. But he needed collateral. I put up my stock for collateral, and my sister offered hers as well. I've never forgotten that she was willing to do that for Randy. She would have been first in line to offer to donate a kidney to my husband, so that was enough for me to offer to donate to hers.

I was a bit of an odd duck in high school. While my friends were into AC/DC and KISS, I was following Willie Nelson, The Oak Ridge Boys and Alabama. I went to see Willie Nelson in concert when I was 15. From there I went to see them all: Waylon Jennings, Kris Kristofferson, Charlie Daniels, Johnny Cash and

Donor Girl

Alabama. When I was 16, I stood in line for over two hours to meet Randy Owen, the lead singer of Alabama. Little did I know I'd end up working with him years later.

Growing up, my life was filled with family, friends, church, music and the martial arts. I took karate with my dad when I was nearly 7 years of age. Four and half years later, I obtained my black belt alongside my dad. At age 11, I became one of the youngest female black belts in Maryland at the time and would continue with karate off and on throughout my life. My dad and I appeared in magazines, including *National Geographic World Magazine* for kids. We were featured on the international TV show *Kids World*. Of course, that was the end of my 15 minutes of fame. I was a has-been at 13! I never drowned my sorrows in beer or drugs like so many other famous kids. Maybe it's because I wasn't famous.

While Kelly came into her own and began dating (always having some hot, popular guy asking her out), I was nicknamed "sexless" for my lack of certain body parts. Yes, I was a carpenter's dream; flat as a board! Kelly, on the other hand, was nicknamed "King Tit" in honor of the song "King Tut" made so popular back then by Steve Martin. So how did the genetics in this family get handed out??

Kelly left for college in 1981, while I still had two years left of high school. I was lost without her. Weekends visiting Kelly were what got me through that first year. I even considered graduating early to join her in college. However, I started dating my first real boyfriend, as opposed to my many imaginary ones: boyfriends like Leif Garrett, Shaun Cassidy and John Travolta. I decided to stay and graduate with my class, and it was a decision I never regretted.

During this time, I reunited with two of my friends that had become estranged and now were my best friends again. Between my boyfriend, Rick, and my friends, Libby and Phyllis, it turned out to be a great senior year. I was inducted into the National Honor Society and graduated 13th in my class of 210 students. Not too bad. I graduated in 1983; and Libby, Phyllis and I enjoyed senior week in Ocean City, Maryland before we all went our separate ways to college.

In the summer of 1983, I entered my first semester at Shippensburg State College, which soon became Shippensburg University. The students had wanted it to be Shippensburg University College so our acronym could be S.U.C. Such things are funny to kids 18 years old. Needless to say, the college didn't agree with our thought process.

I had two years in college to be with Kelly, and they were two more great years of friendship. We would laugh at our lack of partying as we'd attend a frat party together, share a beer, stand alone and try to talk to each other only to leave the party early and go back to our dorm room so we could spend real time together.

While I had wanted to room with Kell, she had the foresight to realize that what had happened to me in high school would happen to me in college if I didn't form my own support group. I'd be there for two years and then she'd leave again, leaving me without her or any of my own friends. I spent a lot of time in her room and we were in the same dorm, but I didn't room with her.

If we didn't request a roommate, the college gave us one. I received a letter with my roommate's name on it. She was from the Greek side of Turkey. I was very excited about having a roommate from another country. She spoke very little English which made communication difficult but she was friendly and nice. I remember hearing her talking to another professor in the hall one day. He was also from another country with heavily accented English. They could barely understand one another and I realized my roommate had taken on an amazing amount of work just to do what comes naturally for most of us. I remember her alarm clock was the old fashioned Big Ben that rang LOUDLY. And she got up early every morning to study. I can't say I appreciated the wake up alarm every morning, but I admired her determination and tenacity.

While she was a nice person, my roommate was not the typical American student and after watching my sister and her roommates, I knew I preferred to have someone more similar to myself. Hence my friendship with Jodi. Jodi was also looking for a different rooming situation due to her roommate being a smoker. So, when we ended up in Geography together, we became acquainted and decided we would request rooming together for the 2$^{nd}$ semester. Luckily, it all worked out and after Christmas break of '83, Jodi and I were roommates on the 3$^{rd}$ floor of Lackhove Hall.

The second semester was a blast. Jodi and I were great together. I was Oscar and she was Felix. She would clean up my messes and make my bed. She was the neat one, I was the messy one. But we had so much fun together it didn't matter. We had befriended a group of guys from the 2$^{nd}$ floor and hung out with them all the time. Brooke, Eric, White, Eduardo from Brazil, and others. My first year would end up forming lifelong friendships. Jodi had a car that we would all pile in to go to the mall. Eric brought along his new cassette of the Thompson Twins one time and it got stuck in Jodi's tape deck forever. All we ever listened to when in the car was the Thompson Twins, Side A. I still can't hear the song "Hold Me Now" without thinking of Jodi and Eric.

Jodi would go on to be my best friend for the next 20 years. We only roomed together for one year before she chose to move back to New York to finish school, but we formed a strong bond that wouldn't break. Even though she was no longer at Shippensburg, we spent spring breaks together. In '86 we went to Ft. Lauderdale, and in '87 we flew to visit Eduardo in Rio de Janero as he had graduated the semester before me. I'm still shocked our parents let us fly all the way to Brazil! It was a blast. I made many friends while in college, but that first year was unlike any other.

Kelly graduated from college in 1985 and began her career as an elementary school teacher. She started at a parochial school and then joined the public school system in Carroll Country Maryland. I missed her at college but was happy to see her starting a career that she worked so hard towards.

Jodi ended up transferring back to Long Island and the second floor guys moved on as well. I found a new set of friends and moved into a house with five other girls. While no one could ever replace the support group of my first year, these girls were great, and we had a lot of fun. I was involved in the karate club and college band. I thoroughly enjoyed my college years and in 1987, graduated with a B.A. in Radio/TV Communications with a minor in music.

It was shortly after college that I met my husband, Randy. I was working as a sales rep and part-time deejay at a small country radio station, WCHA, in Chambersburg, Pennsylvania. Randy worked for one of our clients, and I developed quite a crush on him. When I found out he played racquetball, I challenged him to a game. Of course, he had no idea I'd never played before! He was opening a new camera store and managed to forget our first date. I actually married a man who stood me up on our first date. He wanted to make it up to me by taking me to dinner. I came home and told my mom, "I'm going to marry that man." We finally played that game of racquetball and my secret was out: I couldn't play racquetball. I'd never played racquetball. I had never held a racquetball racquet! So after I challenged him to a game with the mantra, "Oh, I can so take you in a racquetball game," Randy realized I didn't own a racquet and had never played. He seemed to like me anyway, and within 5 months we were engaged. One year later, on March 4, 1989, we were married. It would be nearly

Donor Girl

20 years later that I would choose to donate my kidney, against Randy's wishes.

I followed my love for country music and Willie Nelson into radio and became a deejay full time. I spent roughly 5 years working at various country radio stations and in 1989, I landed a job in Carlisle, Pennsylvania at a privately owned radio station, WHYL. The owner was young (32), and it was when country music was exploding. Garth Brooks, Clint Black, Trisha Yearwood, George Strait, Tim McGraw, Faith Hill, Alan Jackson, Diamond Rio, etc. were just hitting it big. We rode the wave for the next 6 years. I ended up being the music director, program director and midday air personality, which is a fancy name for a disc jockey. I spent 6 years at WHYL with owner, Lincoln Zeve. We were a young, excited staff with more energy than knowledge. We learned by making mistakes, and sometimes, shocked ourselves by succeeding on long shots.

It was 6 wonderful years. I had the opportunity to meet and spend time with some amazing singers. I was backstage at an event when Garth Brooks got his first ever Gold Record, and I was able to pose for a picture with him. He later signed it, and I laughed as he wrote: "Thanks for Nashville." I found that funny. I had the pleasure of meeting Garth a handful of times, and he was always the kindest guy. He always remembered my name. When I'd take my mom or Randy with me, he was just as nice to them.

Garth Brooks was extremely close to singer and rodeo rider, Chris LeDoux. I had the pleasure of meeting Chris a few times and once met his dad. I mentioned wanting to interview Chris on the radio. His dad gave me his home phone number and said, "Just call him." That's the kind of guy Chris was. Garth made Chris famous in a song, "Much Too Young to Feel This Damn Old." He was a huge fan of Chris's, even though Chris was mainly known as a rodeo singer. He had a large following among the cowboys and cowgirls on the rodeo circuit but not among the mainstream.

Donor Girl

When Garth sang the line, "A worn out tape of Chris LeDoux..." in his song, it brought Chris into the mainstream. Chris would end up with a record deal on Capitol Records, where Garth was signed, and he would have many hits of his own.

Chris developed liver disease and was in need of a transplant. Who was there but Garth Brooks to offer his liver? It would turn out that Garth was not a match, but I have enormous respect for Garth that he was willing to be tested and go through what would have been a very emotional surgery. Donating your liver is different from donating a kidney. You can donate part of your liver and have it grow back to full size, while the other part will grow to full size in the recipient. With kidney donation, they take one complete kidney while leaving you the other. I understand donating a liver, however, is much more difficult on the donor than kidney donation.

As much as I enjoyed working in radio and had a great career, as I was nearing 30, I knew it was time to move on. It was very difficult to leave the staff, station and Lincoln. I had some wonderful experiences while in radio and I met some icons like George Jones, Kenny Rogers, Alabama, George Strait and finally, in 1993, I met Willie Nelson. This was the man I fell in love with at age 15 while watching *Honeysuckle Rose.*

But it was time to make better money and the only way to do that, in my case, was to move to the record side of the industry. In 1994, record companies started to call me about jobs. I was in weekly contact with record labels when the promoters called me to ask me to play their songs on WHYL. The radio and record companies work hand in hand, and we all know each other. The offers I had weren't what I wanted, but there was a label that had my interest. Decca Records Nashville opened up in 1994 as a subsidiary of MCA Nashville. I liked what they were doing and wanted to work for them. Unfortunately, I was not able to land a gig there when they first opened. But a year later after they expanded, the VP of

Donor Girl

Promotion, Shelia Shipley, called me and offered to fly me to Nashville for an interview. We were supposed to meet for dinner and then have a formal interview the next morning. My flight was canceled in Chicago, and I never made the dinner. Here I was, interviewing for the job of a lifetime which involved much travel, and my first attempt at travel ended in my canceling dinner with the person I was trying to impress! Luckily, she was very understanding. I finally landed in Nashville around 11:00 P.M. We met the next morning, and I'll never forget one of the important questions Shelia asked me: "Are you prepared to spend every weekend worrying about what would happen on the charts every Monday morning?" I said, "YES!" while thinking, "Uh, not really." But, I didn't completely understand what she meant, and the job looked exciting. The money would double my income.

I waited two weeks for Shelia to call, and when she did, I was in the bathroom at WHYL. I heard the receptionist say over the intercom, "Lee, Shelia is on line one." OH, what to do?? There was a phone in the bathroom, and I wanted this to be a private conversation anyway. So while sitting on the toilet, I answered the phone. "Lee, are you still willing to come work with Decca Records?"

Oh dear Lord, I was about to get hired for my dream job **ON THE TOILET!** "Yes," I replied.

"Then the job is yours!" We discussed salary, vacation, details, and eventually ended the conversation with me promising to give a two week notice to Lincoln.

I would start the job at Decca during CRS, Country Radio Seminar, in Nashville. Eventually, I told Shelia about the bathroom hiring and as recently as 2008, I heard the story come back to me through a third party. Some things live on in infamy. In hindsight, now that I know what I do about the music industry,

Donor Girl

getting hired on a toilet was probably the most appropriate place for it to happen!

I started with Decca in March of 1995. It was 4 years of exciting times as we broke artists like Lee Ann Womack and Gary Allan. I was able to work with excellent talent like Mark Chesnutt as well. Our sister label, MCA, had major stars Reba McEntire and George Strait. When our new act, Rhett Akins, went on the road with Reba, it was one of the most exciting tours I'd ever experienced.

I became friends with Lee Ann Womack and found her to be one of the most grounded and talented artists I'd ever met. I had the pleasure of working her first #1 hit, "The Fool," and still have the note that says, *Lee, #1! Whew. Thank you! Lee Ann.* It wasn't an easy #1, and we had to work hard for it. But we got there, and it was like climbing Mount Everest and planting our flag. Ten years later, I would be honored with an invitation to fly to Luchenback, Texas (home of Willie, Waylon and the boys) and attend Lee Ann's surprise 40th birthday party.

While at Decca, we had hits with Rhett Akins' single "That Ain't My Truck"; hits with Gary Allan like "Her Man"; and from Mark Chesnutt, "It's A Little Too Late." I will never forget riding down the road with Gary and his guitar player, Jake, when they pulled out their guitars and sang and played the whole two-hour drive. It's one of those "bottle it up" memories that make this job worth it. It's one of the highs that we live for.

Sadly, as country music was losing audience after a surge in the late 80s to mid 90s, labels were consolidating. In January of 1999, Decca had Mark Chesnutt's remake of Aerosmith's "I Don't Want to Miss a Thing" at #1, and it would stay there for 5 weeks; Lee Ann Womack was in the Top 25 and Gary Allan in the Top 40. Our album sales had just put us in the "black" where we were named one of the Top 10 Nashville labels. It wasn't enough to keep us open, and Universal announced that they'd be closing

Donor Girl

Decca and folding our artists into their parent company, MCA. I was without a job for the first time since graduating high school.

Luckily, I had 6 months remaining on my contract. The first thing I did was call Randy and tell him to pack up the boat, scuba gear, bikes, golf clubs, and suggested we head to Key Largo for a few weeks. We had a wonderful trip and the sunshine had a healing effect on my professional sickness. I came home 3 weeks later, revived and ready to move on. I'd spent my entire life studying the martial arts and ironically, my former instructor called to ask if I had any free time. Uh, yeah! So I started teaching a class for him 4 nights per week. Considering I hadn't worked out regularly in about 10 years and was now in my mid 30s, it took about a bottle of Advil to get out of bed every morning. In just 3 weeks though, I was in the best shape I'd been in years. I also took a temporary job as a data entry person, and worked nights at Waldenbooks. Randy joked that it was to pay for my habit as a bibliophile, which sounds dirty but means a person who loves to read.

I remember bringing home my $83 paycheck from Waldenbooks and being embarrassed to show it to Randy. He took it and said words I'll never forget. He said, "I'm more proud of this paycheck than any other you've ever had. This proves that you are not too proud to go out and work wherever you can for whatever you can. You should be proud too." He'll never know what that meant to me.

Randy had bought a camera store from his previous boss in 1990. We named it Pictures Plus. Randy would prove to be an excellent businessman, and Pictures Plus expanded into Pictures Plus Studio. He turned a $250,000 business into a million dollar plus business. He works harder than anyone I know and always refuses to give up. When film went digital, he saw the potential downfall for the photo processing business and started focusing on the photography end. He made that a huge success. Digital downloading was affecting both of our industries, but he saw the potential in the service end of the business. After all, parents will always want professional photos of their child's soccer team, cheerleading team, baseball team, and so on.

A few months into my unemployment, I got a phone call asking if I'd be interested in working Kenny Rogers' comeback song, "The Greatest." I was thrilled to work a Kenny Rogers song and immediately said yes. I resigned from my data entry job and started calling radio again. They were very receptive to the single and I was soon out on the road with Kenny Rogers. He was by far the biggest artist I'd ever worked with, and a true professional. He was always on time, prepared, and treated everyone with respect.

My record career would go through some more ups and downs before stabilizing. I went to work for the Warner Brothers' label, Giant Records, with amazing artists like Joe Nichols, Clay Walker and Blake Shelton. I wasn't with Giant Records long, however, when I chose to switch to the Warner Brothers' label, Atlantic. That lasted 10 months, until AOL bought them and shut us down. We'd had a huge hit with John Michael Montgomery called "The Little Girl"; some hits with Tracy Lawrence; and one with Tim Rushlow called "She Misses Him." I would not have fared any better at Giant Records since both Giant and Atlantic were closed in the Time Warner/AOL merger.

I was once again out of work and considering studying for the LSAT's to go to law school. One of my artists from Atlantic Records, Craig Morgan, convinced me to stick it out with him and in August of 2001, we joined a fledgling country label called Broken Bow Records (BBR). Together, with some other former Atlantic Records people, we met with the owner, Benny Brown, and convinced him to make some changes and really go for it. Benny agreed, and a year later we had a Top 10 hit with Craig Morgan's "Almost Home." It would be the first of numerous hits for Craig including, "That's What I Love About Sunday," "Redneck Yacht Club" and "International Harvester," just to name

Donor Girl

a few. We also had hits with Sherrie Austin, Joe Diffie, and broke through newcomer, Jason Aldean, whose hits included "Hicktown," "Why," "Amarillo Sky" and "Johnny Cash."

If I had to name my favorite time period in my record career, it would probably be the years 2004 and 2005. We had offered radio stations the opportunity to do an acoustic show with Craig Morgan and Sherrie Austin. This was pre-Eliot Spitzer and everyone seemed to think that singers doing concerts for radio listeners was a great idea.

We boarded a bus with Craig and his drummer, Mike, and guitar player/co-producer/co-writer, Phillbilly; Sherrie with her guitar player/co-songwriter, Will Rambeaux; and a solo artist on our label who played fiddle for Sherrie, Megan Mullins. Megan was 15 at the time. We toured around on a bus and sometimes in a van for weeks and had an absolute blast. Craig was having hits from his first CD; Sherrie's *Streets of Heaven* was climbing the charts; and we were just simply having fun. At one point, Philbilly was driving a full-size van with all of us piled in with legs and limbs all over each other. Megan, being a typical teenager, was asleep on me in the back of the van while everyone else was joking and laughing. I remember thinking, "Remember this moment as one of your favorites." It was a time when our label was going from not even being noticed to having the #1 song of the year with Craig Morgan's "That's What I Love About Sunday." We would go on to have another #1 with Craig's "Redneck Yacht Club" and hit it again with Jason Aldean's "Why."

We had proven we could break an act who had originated on our label with no prior introduction to the country music community: Jason Aldean. And every step up and each little or big hurdle jumped was cause for celebration. We were the team that wasn't supposed to be able to climb to the top of Mount Everest, yet we had climbed there and returned time and time again.

Donor Girl

By 2007, we were a successful Nashville record label, consistently in the Top 10 top Nashville labels. We had celebrated #1's, Gold CD's, Platinum CD's and an ACM Award. It was while I was working with BBR that I would start on my journey toward kidney donation.

# David Hornby

David Hornby was born on September 28, 1952, in the small town of Pemberton in Western Australia. He was second born to Kenneth and Emily Hornby. Allison Hornby was 14 months old when her little brother arrived. Following David, there would be 6 more brothers, all born in the span of 10 years. David's parents were thrilled to have a baby boy after the birth of a daughter. Little did they know that their son, who appeared to be healthy, was born with an autoimmune deficiency disease that would take 54 years to destroy his kidneys.

David's parents couldn't properly care for so many children, so at the young age of 7, David was sent to Castledear Boys Home by the Child Welfare Department. Alone and separated from his sister and brothers, he stayed there until 5th grade when he was then sent to Clontarf Boys Town. Dave doesn't talk much about this time in his life but one can imagine it was not a pleasant place to live. This is what a Web site had to say about Clontarf:

*In the late 1980's, allegations of abuse and cruelty were made against the Christian Brothers by former students and residents of various institutions run by the Brotherhood, including Clontarf. An organization named VOICE (Victims of Institutionalized Cruelty, Exploitation, and Supporters) was established to represent and provide counseling for those who had experienced abuse at the Christian Brothers' orphanages. The Christian Brothers accepted that there was strong evidence that many of the allegations were true, and made a public apology. A legal action brought by over 200 former students ran from 1993 in the New South Wales Supreme Court and was finalized in 1996 with an out of court settlement.*

*Source http://en.wikipedia.org/wiki/Clontarf_Aboriginal_College*

Donor Girl

We can only assume that it took an amazing amount of strength for Dave to survive this kind of upbringing. He had two choices, as does anyone in this situation. You can let something like this ruin the rest of your life, or you can become determined to succeed and stay positive in spite of the horrible upbringing. Dave chose the latter route and would not only become successful, but maintain an air of optimism that amazes me.

At the age of 16, Dave left Clontarf and set off to begin experimenting with different jobs, trying to find the one that would become a career. He became a beekeeper, farmer and bricklayer. The Australian Army called, and at 18, Dave answered. He joined the Army and became a Royal Australian Engineer. He then trained as a firefighter for the Aviation Brigade. During his teen years, Dave also became interested in running, surfing and playing amateur Aussie rules football. By eating right and taking interest in exercising and being fit, Dave decided to start bodybuilding. Bill Robertson (Mr. Bodybuilding Australia at that time) was renting rooms in his home and offered Dave a place to live. Dave lived there in his early 20s while training to become a bodybuilder. Dave had saved enough money, so he made the decision to travel and see the world. He went to Europe on holiday and while on tour thought that he could do the job of a tour driver. He trained, got his bus license in England and began to drive tours around London. He applied to the tour company, Top Deck Travel, and got the job. Tours all around Europe quickly became a part of Dave's life. One year during the off tourist season, Dave got a job as a security guard at a place called Young World on Kensington High Street. A tall, young beautiful woman came in to buy Pink Panther ornaments for Charles. As you can guess, the young woman was Princess Diana.

Dave started driving tours all over Europe and training others to tour drive as well. In 1983, Top Deck sent Dave to America to drive tours for a year. He was based in the Los Angeles area. He was then sent back to Europe. During the off season, Dave toured

Donor Girl

other countries. On one such break, he went to South Africa and traveled on the Blue Train from Johannesburg to Cape Town. Apartheid was in full force, and this adventure left a lasting impression on Dave.

Dave left Top Deck in England and started working for Contiki Tours. He had been away from home for quite a while, so he returned to Australia and continued to work for Contiki Tours. After dropping passengers off for an excursion, Dave could often be seen running his 6 mile trek along a beautiful coastline or in a city park.

It was while working in Australia that Dave and his fellow tour guide, Trevor Wilson, picked up a group of American tourists. It was July of 1990, and little did anyone know, but this tour would change the life of Dave forever. On the tour was a young woman named Kelly Adams and her mom, Drew Adams. Dave and Kelly became interested in each other, and once the tour ended 16 days later, they kept in touch over the next year through letters and phone calls.

Over the next two years, Kelly and Dave traveled to see each other and meet each other's families. In July of 1992, traveling with the same group of people that had toured to Australia, Dave asked Kelly to marry him aboard the Princess Cruise ship to Alaska.

In December of 1993, Dave came to America on a 90 day fiancé visa. Kelly and Dave had all of 90 days to have some form of normal relationship before taking the plunge. Their entire relationship had been built on visits to each other's country. It was one big vacation. Now it was time to experience the real world. Kelly had bought property; built a house; and Dave moved in. For anyone who has ever tried to enter our country legally, they know how difficult the INS can be. I joked with Dave that he should fly to Cuba, get on a boat, and float to Key West. Then he could just

Donor Girl

walk into the country. It's easier that way. He and Kelly spent years meeting with the INS in DC, taking photos, letters and eyewitness accounts to prove that they were truly in love and not just marrying to get Dave into the U.S. Finally, the INS agreed and Dave was allowed to stay. In March of 1993, pushing the 90 days to practically the last possible day, Kelly and Dave were married. Randy and I stood in as best man and matron of honor.

While Kelly was teaching school full time, Dave started out in the bus driving industry in the Baltimore area. The industry didn't have nearly as much to offer as the Australian touring industry. After a couple of years of doing one day and local runs; driving minor league baseball teams; and some longer run tours, Dave decided he now had a home and a wife and wanted a career that was more home based. Having always been interested in home improvements, Dave took a job with Lowe's and quickly moved up through the ranks. It was while he was working at Lowe's that Kelly became pregnant with Will. Figuring that Kelly had the more secure, better paying job with excellent benefits, they decided Dave would be the stay at home parent. For a person raised in a boys' home and not by his own parents, this would be a learning process for Dave, and one he took to very well. Will was born in May of 1999 and soon became the love of all our lives.

I was out of work when Decca Records had closed, so Dave and I decided to get our real estate licenses. It was the first time I really noticed the difference in Australian English and American English. Dave and I would read a sentence and interpret it completely differently. Since I was American and being taught by an American, I was the one who usually interpreted it correctly. Dave and I worked together to get him to understand the meaning of some aspects of real estate. We studied hard and passed our state and local tests. While I chose not to pursue real estate, Dave did. He had a successful career that allowed him to work from home and set his own hours.

Donor Girl

As much as Dave enjoyed real estate, his main passion continued to be home improvement. He started studying and taking classes and passed the test for his contractor's license. Dave continued to stay at home after their daughter, Mikayla Lee, was born in May of 2002. Oddly, Mikayla was named after Dave's brother, Michael, and me; the two siblings who would offer to and be tested for donation of our kidneys.

Once Dave passed his contractor's license, he needed about $8000 to get started in the business with tools, a trailer and advertising. With Kelly and Dave now having two children, money was somewhat tight. I told Dave I'd loan him the money, but he wanted to think about it. About two weeks later, he asked if the offer was still open. I said it was and loaned him the money. Dave got his trailer "wrapped" with his logo, phone number and information, and the calls started coming in. With his connections to the real estate community, he was able to get work through them.

He also signed up at Lowe's to be an installer. Dave managed to pay back, with interest, the entire $8000 in mere weeks. He was off and running with a new and successful career. The children were of pre-school and school age, and Dave was now able to kick-start his job full time.

Then, illness struck. One evening at 11:45 P.M., after a yearly blood workup, the doctor wanted Dave in the emergency room because his potassium level was 7.0, a very dangerous level. The closest family was 45 minutes away. So a dear friend, Mary Garner, came and slept on the couch so that the children did not need to be disturbed. Blood tests were run; stress tests were given; and a kidney biopsy was scheduled. The result was that Dave had IgA Nephropathy, an autoimmune disease that attacks a person's organ. The organ under attack is different for each person. Dave's body chose to attack his kidneys.

Donor Girl

Dave and Kelly now had to cope with a very serious illness and raising two small children; no easy task on either account. My parents had always been close to Will and Kayla, and thanks to them and some good friends, everyone pulled together to give Will and Kayla a "normal" childhood through this tumultuous time. Words like potassium, creatinine and bun levels became everyday vocabulary. Low potassium diets and diets low in protein to keep gout away became daily routine.

Between the two diets, there was not much to eat that would keep Dave healthy. After two years of watching the kidney numbers in blood tests fluctuate, the nephrologists finally told Dave to get on a donor list. And that's where I come in!

*Chapter written and contributed by Kelly Adams-Hornby.*

Donor Girl

# Thank God

I was raised Christian and have always had a strong faith. My parents raised my sister and me in the church, and our faith in God has always helped us through tough times. I remember as a teen going to the Episcopal Church at 8:00 A.M., then up to my friend Phyllis' church for the 10:00 A.M. service. While I liked the structure of the Episcopal Church, Phyll's church was just plain fun. We sang and danced, and the preacher, who was from Trinidad, had a booming voice and would witness to us more than preach. I was fascinated by her church. I took part in both youth groups, and it was at Phyllis' church at the age of 13 that I accepted Christ as my personal savior. I still remember the feeling of warm water passing through my body when I made that decision. It's unlike anything I can explain.

I attended a Catholic Church during college since it was the only one within walking distance. I went to my parents' Methodist Church following college graduation. For a while, when living near my sister, I went to the Church of Christ. When I moved to the home I currently live in, I joined an amazing church, Harmony United Methodist, where I belong to the praise group. I play flute, guitar and mandolin while lip synching!

My church is very involved in a Christian retreat known as the Walk to Emmaus. The year before my donation, I went on the Walk to Emmaus. It took me 8 years and about 10 sponsors to finally get there. At the last minute, my sponsors moved so my friend Magda, stepped in. Without her, I'm not sure I'd have gone. It further bonded Magda and me, and her friendship would help me through some upcoming tough times. Emmaus is a very intense retreat. We are dropped off "on the mountain" without access to a car, phone, or outside correspondence. We would stay three to a room and have a lot of togetherness time, something I'm not very

Donor Girl

good at. The week prior to going, I talked to my pastor and said, "I don't like crying and hugging." He laughed, shook his head, and said, "Oh Lee." Everyone knows that at Emmaus there are a lot of emotions.

Then I said, "Pastor Ray, I'm not worthy to go to Emmaus."

He replied, "I worry more about those who think they are."

It was an amazing 4 days, and I met many wonderful women, but especially my friend Colleen. Colleen is not only beautiful, but she truly has an "aura." You can almost see it. I was drawn to her like a moth to a flame. She and I were put next to each other during lunch one day, and I commented in her presence that the weekend would only be made better if there was a masseuse there. She replied, "I'm a masseuse," and gave me her business card. She has become my friend and masseuse and is by far the best masseuse I've ever had. She would help me through my surgery as well.

I read one of Jodi Picoult's books, *Change Of Heart*, about a man on death row wanting to donate his heart to his victim's sister. For various reasons, he was being made out to be a Christ-like figure. Jodi made the comment that, "Organ donation is not salvation, it's altruism." While this is very true (and it is most definitely NOT salvation), there are few times in my life I have felt as close to God as I did when I was going through the donation process. We aren't often asked to sacrifice our lives for another. And while my chances of survival were near 100%, there's always that chance during surgery that you won't survive; or in kidney donation, that your other kidney will become diseased or otherwise fail. Is it salvation? Absolutely not. However, I often hope my list of good deeds will outweigh my list of bad ones in the end. Sometimes I feel they run neck and neck. I'd be lying if I didn't hope this gave me a few extra points in the "good girl" column.

Donor Girl

# On the Donor List

It was September of 2006 when my sister informed our family that Dave was told he needed a kidney transplant. After years of taking medications, watching his diet, exercising and following doctor's orders, his kidney function was down to roughly 15%. Dave was put on the transplant list by the University of Maryland Medical Center. He was warned it could take 5 to7 years to find an O donor. O is the most common blood type, with roughly 37% of the population having it. However, Type O is the universal donor. This means that O people can donate to any other blood type. However, when a person who is O needs a transplant, they can only get it from another O person. And that person still has to match. This is why the donor list for O is longer. It was recommended that Dave find his own living donor. They didn't say that if he didn't, he wouldn't make it, as dialysis remained an option. However, the longer a person is on dialysis, the more it takes a toll on other body organs. If it took 7 years to find a cadaver donor and Dave was nearing or in his 60s, he might not be well enough to have a transplant. He would miss out on years of being active due to a dialysis treatment schedule which is usually 3 times a week for 3 to 5 hours at a time.

Kelly sent an e-mail on 9/28/06 to her address book of friends and family. It read like this:

*Hello Family and Friends, Many of you know that two years ago David was diagnosed with kidney disease. His kidneys have been functioning fairly well over these past two years. Recently, there was a turn of events and we were advised he be put on a kidney transplant list. We had our meeting today at the University of MD Kidney Transplant Center.*

Donor Girl

*They are predicting that David will need a kidney transplant between now and a year's time. David will need a kidney from an O positive blood type donor. Please pass this urgent message to anyone you know who may have it in their heart to want to donate an organ. O Positive blood type is rare and the list is a 5-7 year wait. Unfortunately, David's kidneys can't wait that long. Thank you for understanding our need to reach as many people as possible with this plea. Please keep us in your thoughts and prayers on our journey into the unknown. May God Bless you all. We know God is in control. Love Kelly.*

My reply: *9/28*

*Nicely written Kell. I'm going to post it on MYspace in a bulletin and ask all my friends to re-post it. It should get out to thousands of people that way. I'm also going to have our Emmaus prayer list post it. That should get out to hundreds. And I'm going to appeal to all the churches. There's a lot of good people in this world, and one of them is willing to give Dave a kidney! Keep the faith!! De Colores! Leez*

Kelly had some of her facts wrong, and like with any layperson trying to make sense of medical terms, she would sometimes get a few facts confused. For one thing, she put in her e-mail that O+ was rare. She had misunderstood the difficulty in finding an O+ donor to mean that it was a rare blood type. This started to cause elation followed by surprise and more confusion when we started having a lot of people say, "I'm O positive." With some Internet research, we discovered it was not rare, just difficult to find donors. A journey had begun, and I was dedicated to helping Kelly find a donor. I just wasn't dedicated to it being me!

# The Road to Donorship

So here we were in our 40s, I at 41 and my sister at 43, and we were facing a family crisis. My brother-in-law needed a kidney transplant. Later, I remember my surgeon asking me, "How did they ask you if you would be a donor?"

I answered, "They never did." I was never asked to be a donor. My family is simply the type that comes to the aid of one another in need.

We were all sending out prayer requests. My sister had done her Walk to Emmaus shortly after I did, and we both experienced how amazing it was. The West Virginia Emmaus community has a wonderful prayer chain that I appealed to for prayers.

This is an e-mail I sent to Kelly:

*On Oct 3, 2006, at 12:08 PM, I wrote:*

**This went out to the WV Emmaus community. Maybe someone will come forward. Love you.**

*From: Lee Adams  To: wvemmaus@yahooo.com*
*Date: October 3, 2006 11:52:11 AM EDT*
*Subject: Prayer Request*

**My brother-in-law, David Hornby, just found out he needs a kidney transplant within the year. Being O Positive, only 17% of O Positive blood donors can donate an organ. So my sister and our family have an uphill battle. I'm requesting prayers from the Emmaus community. Both my sister and I have attended Emmaus. Thank you. Lee**

Donor Girl

In a quest to find a donor, we all started talking to people and putting out feelers. My sister appealed to her school and church. I appealed to my church and even put the request on MySpace. That generated some interesting responses. I received a phone call from an Omer in Australia that wanted to contact Dave and Kelly. I thought it was cool that he was Australian and gave Kelly his number. Sadly, Omer had misunderstood the MySpace message and Kelly e-mailed the following:

*In a message dated 10/8/2006 5:48:11 P.M. Eastern Daylight Time.*

**Kellyhornby writes:**

**Done! I called Omer and he thought we just needed blood. I thanked him anyway for wanting to help a fellow Aussie. Kel**

*10/8/2006:*

**Darn, I was afraid of that. :-( Sorry. Leez**

We had friends and relatives telling us they were O+, but unless they said the words, "We'd like to be tested as a donor," Kelly didn't push it. She did have a teacher friend who really wanted to donate. She spoke to her husband about it and even though they wanted more children, he agreed she should get tested to donate to Dave. Kelly told her she'd keep her name on the list, but she was very concerned about her being the donor. Knowing she wanted more children concerned Kelly. Irony being what it is, before the woman could get tested to donate to Dave, her dad went into renal failure and she was a match for her dad. She called Kelly crying, telling her she was going to donate her kidney to her dad. Kelly encouraged her and was very thankful that she had been willing to donate to Dave.

Donor Girl

Dave contacted the family members he was able to find. His sister, Allison, was willing but not a blood match. One of his brothers said no. His brother, Michael, was willing, but communication with him would prove sporadic over the next few months. In the meantime, my immediate family requested paperwork from my sister so we could begin the testing process. She gave the forms to my parents and filled one out herself, but weeks went by and I still didn't have any forms.

I really wanted to start the process. For one thing, I doubted I'd be a match. So it was easy to say, "Test me!" But there was also my niece and nephew to think about. I wanted my niece and nephew to grow up with their dad. And I wanted him to be healthy enough to actually be a part of their lives, not just a spectator.

My niece, Kayla, was only 4, and my nephew, Will, was 7 when this started. They were way too young to be facing either their father's death or his lifetime on dialysis. I don't have children. Will and Kayla are the closest to children I'll ever have. I would do it for them. So many people have asked, "Would you regret it if they divorced?" And I always say no. No matter what happens between Kelly and Dave, he will always be the father of Will and Kayla.

So why didn't I think I'd match? First of all, my family was all A+, and Dave was O+. We were told that although O+ was a universal blood type able to donate to anyone with a positive blood type, they could only accept donations from O. This is what makes it so hard to find a cadaver donor for O. It's hard for any blood type, but especially O. We had heard there was some kind of exchange program where if you had a willing and healthy donor, but they didn't match their recipient, the hospital would pair you up with another set of people in the same position. So I went into the original paperwork assuming, at best, I could do the exchange program, feeling this would even be a stretch. Actually, they might say, "Thanks, but no thanks. But be proud that you did the

Donor Girl

right thing." That would make me smile. I'd done the right thing but still had both my kidneys. That would be the perfect case scenario.

It was early December, and I still didn't have paperwork. Will had a choral performance one evening that we were all attending. When I mentioned the forms, Kelly told me she didn't think I should fill them out. She proceeded to upset me greatly by saying things like, "You wouldn't be able to handle having scars on your body. You spend a lot of time in bikinis and low-rise jeans." She implied that my vanity would get in the way. She went on to say similar things as reasons for me not to fill out the paperwork. It was painful and mean and very upsetting. I got furious, and we barely spoke the rest of the evening. As soon as Will's portion of the show was finished, I left. I was fuming the whole way home.

Later that evening, I received an e-mail:

*In a message dated 12/10/2006 8:59:39 P.M. Eastern Standard Time, KellyHornby writes:*

**Leez,**
**I just made the toughest decision of my life. I mailed you the questionnaire. No one (with the exception of Lois and Bee) knows how close we are. You are my soul mate, my comforter, my best friend, and so much more. I watched Grandma when (her sister) Lois left this Earth and a part of her went with Lois. Should you be a match, the operation would probably go without a hitch, but if it didn't, I would want to be buried right along with you. I don't expect you to understand how it feels to ask you to do this, but it's so hard that there are no words to describe it. Your kidney is just as good as anyone else's, but I WOULDN"T WANT TO LIVE WITHOUT YOU!!! I love you very much and I'm sorry I didn't give you the papers before. I was hoping**

*for a miracle and none seem to be coming. I sent a picture of Albert with the papers. I figured I needed help asking your forgiveness. Thanks for coming today. You should have seen Will when he got your message. I don't think he believed me that you were there. Love, ME*

I replied on the 11th:

*Kell, I appreciate the e-mail and I do understand. Equally, you don't understand that as your sister, I want to help save your husband so he can raise his children with you. Your kids deserve better than two ill parents with only one kidney each. Do you realize that in order to "save" me you are leaving your children with NO parent that could donate a kidney to them? We don't know that this isn't hereditary. I may be overly pragmatic, I have my father in me, but I think you and I both agree that Will and Kayla even come before you and me. As much as I would be doing this for you and Dave, believe me, it's for Will and Kayla. Without them, I'd say "Yea, cut Kelly first. She enjoys surgery."*

*With that said, we are sisters. I love you more than anything and I've offered to help out of love for your family. Quite honestly, if something were to happen to me, it would be much less than if something were to happen to you. Mommies are irreplaceable. If the kids were grown, maybe a different story. But they are not. I'm healthier than you and I stand a better chance of surviving this and going on to live a full life. I will fill out the questionnaire and let's both pray that another option comes through than EITHER of us having to donate. Love you, Leez*

Donor Girl

Putting myself in Kelly's situation, I can absolutely understand her hesitancy. Back when Kelly first started dating Dave, Randy used to tell Dave, "You have to get the hierarchy straight. First, come the sisters; second, the parents; third, the pets. You and I will come in somewhere around number four." While I'm not sure the pets really come before our husbands, and Will and Kayla have definitely taken over first place, the sentiment was there. At times, I believe the pets do come above them. Kelly and I put each other first, often at the expense of others. For Kelly to have to put her husband's health above mine went against the grain of 41 years of precedence. For us, it was not the natural order of things. But for me, I *was* putting Kelly and the kids first by offering to donate to Dave. So our numbers were off. By my sticking to the "sisters' rule," I was forcing Kelly to break it.

On July 10, Kelly sent me a letter along with the questionnaire. I received it a few days later:

*Dearest Sister,*

*I'm sorry for things said Sunday. I don't know what I'd do without you and the thought of asking you to do something that could be risky is hard for me. Just because I have children doesn't make me anymore or less valuable for being the donor and the same vise versa. Here is the questionnaire. Do with it what you will. You don't have to tell me a thing if you don't want to. David tells me that I'm trying to control the situation. I don't think I am controlling it as much as I feel responsible for anyone who offers to give their kidney. Somewhere between me caring too much and David just wanting a (any) kidney is the person we need to be. Asking you to do this goes up there with one of the hardest decisions I've ever made. I'm sending Albert to beg forgiveness because how can you say no to him? I love you more than you will ever know. Love, Kel*

Donor Girl

Randy and I have a place in Key Largo, and once a year, we drive a car there for the winter months. Randy and I couldn't get a weekend off together to drive down, so Kelly and I went the month before. We went to a water park called "Theatre of the Sea" in Islamorada and watched the parrot show, dolphin show and sea lion show. There was a sea lion, Albert, who stuck his tongue out and made us laugh so hard that we later had the trainer make him do it so we could take a photo.

Kelly sent me the paperwork, and in the envelope along with the necessary forms was a photo of Albert with his tongue out. That made me laugh. I sent her an e-mail:

*Got the questionnaire. If I hadn't already forgiven you, Albert definitely would have made me. I laughed, and laughed. Thanks for the picture.*

*Love you! Leez*

In the end, I had to get Kelly to understand that this was not her decision to make. It was mine, and she didn't have the right to take it away from me. She understood, but at the same time, *she* needed *me* to understand the impossibly horrible predicament it put her in. I did understand, but there was one other thing I understood: she would unquestionably offer to donate to my husband if the roles were reversed. That's the kind of sisters we were.

I sat down that night in December of 2006 to fill out the paperwork. I don't have the strongest stomach in the world, but I'm also not a real wimp. Earlier in the year, I'd come upon a car accident right after it had happened and literally had to step over a dead woman to get to someone to talk to. I didn't freak out or overreact; I just acknowledged she was lying there, mangled in death, and moved on. Of course, I would later have flashbacks of seeing her. Even today, 3 years later, I still think about her. So it's

Donor Girl

not that it didn't affect me because it did. My point is just that I didn't freak out, become hysterical, faint, start crying or have any other reaction.

I recall the accident because filling out the paperwork almost did make me faint. Right there, in my living room, I almost fell off my couch in a complete faint. I don't know if the realization hit me or why it had this effect. But it did. I was woozy and light-headed, and stopped short of putting my head between my legs and breathing into a bag. I finally finished the questionnaire around midnight and put it in an envelope to send. This would be step one in a long series of steps. Somehow, I managed to stand on my own two feet and walk into the bedroom.

I sent the paperwork off, complete with my blood type as A, and waited to hear back. I figured I'd most likely pass the first step since I didn't have any medical issues. It was still a bit unnerving actually sending it out. With the first step completed comes the commitment to donate my kidney. I was now committed to giving away a working body organ. I would lay awake and try to visualize what that would actually be like. I would see the knife cutting into me and think of how I'd feel after my kidney was in another human being. This was part of the OCD/hypochondriac coming out in me. Something in my mind, heart and soul told me that it would come down to me, so the obsessing was already starting.

Donor Girl

# The Holidays

Randy and I had booked a sailboat cruise for the British Virgin Island of Tortola. We were going with an outfit called "Tradewinds Cruise Club" and would spend a week on a 45' sailboat with 6 other couples. Five couples were guests, and the sixth couple was the captain and first mate. It was the most incredible trip. I had been very nervous about being on such a small boat with that many people, but it didn't feel small at all. Our tiny cabin had a private bath and shower, and there was always somewhere to sneak off to if you needed some alone time. The first mate doubled as cook and dive master. The captain was also a dive master. Randy and I were the only scuba divers on the boat and we were able to go right off the back of the sailboat. The diving was amazing. The island of Tortola has so much to offer. It was truly 7 days of heaven. Randy and I are real water people, so this was our kind of week.

We returned with a day to spare before Christmas. We'd be home just a few days until our annual trip to Key Largo where we'd be until late January. When I returned home, I had received a kit that held blood vials and explained how I needed to get blood drawn and fill out further paperwork. I called to ask some questions and explained how I was about to go out of town for roughly a month and I didn't think I'd have time to get blood drawn before then. The hospital emphasized the dire need for me to have the blood drawn immediately. That was very unnerving, but I finally relented and agreed to have it done the day after Christmas, right before leaving for Key Largo.

On Christmas day, our family was visiting my cousins when Dave's situation came up for discussion. My parents said their paperwork had come back denied due to health reasons. My sister's and my paperwork had come back approved. It was

Donor Girl

recommended we move on to the next step and have blood drawn. The family was adamant that Kelly should not be the one to donate. We didn't know what the recovery would be like, and with Dave having major surgery and not being able to work afterward, they would need Kelly's job and her insurance. Kelly is a tenured schoolteacher and has excellent benefits. On top of that, with two young children, it wasn't a good idea for them both to be convalescing at the same time. Even though they were assured that Dave's disease wasn't hereditary, they both worried it could be, and we thought it was best for Kelly to save her kidneys in case one of the children ever needed one. Kelly chose to submit her blood work anyway.

I could tell my dad wasn't happy that I'd been moved on to the next step. He made a statement about being told that after kidney donation, a person shouldn't water ski. Dad knew that water skiing was one of Randy's and my passions, and I would be devastated if I could never water ski again. He told me he'd been told that when talking with a doctor about being tested for kidney donation. I wasn't sure if it was something he'd really been told, or if it was his way of trying to convince me not to get tested. It was quite upsetting for me, and I carried this with me all day and into the evening. Never being able to water ski would not be reason enough to stop me from donating; however, it would be a major change to my lifestyle and one I wouldn't relish. In hindsight, I realize my dad was putting me first and trying to do anything possible to convince me not to be the one. While as an adult, it was hard for me to understand at the time, I saw my dad look at me later as his "little girl" and it made much more sense.
On Christmas night, I went over the paperwork for the next day's blood test. I felt like fainting (yet again) as I realized they'd be testing me for so many diseases. Did I really want to know if I had one? I would be tested for HIV, AIDS, Hepatitis and a host of others.

Donor Girl

Considering I'd never been an IV drug user and had been sexually monogamous for over 20 years, I still went through an "OH MY GOD" moment when thinking about having the tests. It was absolutely imperative to be tested for these diseases because if I had one lurking in there, and I donated to Dave, he would most likely get the same disease.

There was a case recently where a cadaver donor was tested for HIV and Hepatitis C, and the results were negative. Three hospitals in Chicago in 2007 went forward with transplants based upon the negative tests. The false negative test could have been due to the donor acquiring the diseases in the last few weeks before death. The transmission of HIV through cadaver donation had not happened since 1994. The process of donation remains extremely safe. However, nothing is ever 100%. The recipients had to be contacted and made aware of the probable HIV transmission.

It's always sad when children die. No matter what the cause or reason, it is before their time. So the decision to donate their organs so that others might live has got to be a heart-wrenching decision. To make that decision and feel like your child's death at least had some meaning and then find out the donation had devastating consequences on the recipients, is like experiencing the death all over. Recently, a fifteen-year-old boy passed away from what his parents were told was bacterial meningitis. However, he actually had a rare form of lymphoma. His parents made the amazing decision to donate his organs, only to later find out that the recipients got cancer from the donation. Again, this is very rare and should not ever be a reason to not donate organs. The hospitals test for every possible disease to insure that this will not happen. But as in anything in life, there are errors, and this is no different. While extremely rare, it can happen. This is the reason for the numerous tests I had to undergo.

Donor Girl

Considering there can be devastating and deadly consequences involved in organ donation if all the tests are not run correctly, I understood why I had to be tested for so many diseases. While under normal circumstances, cancer wouldn't be contagious, putting a cancerous organ from one person into another would cause them to come down with the disease themselves. While I would be devastated to find out I had a disease, I would be even more devastated to find out I had passed it on to Dave. So, bring on the tests! I will pray that God has blessed me with no diseases.

There was also a question that asked if my blood type was not compatible with one of my parents, did I want them to know? Knowing my parents, I couldn't imagine that would be an issue, but I found it an interesting question. How many people take part in such an altruistic undertaking only to find out that one of their parents isn't actually their biological parent? Again, I felt queasy just reading it. But on December 26, I went up to have the blood tests performed anyway. On a wing and a prayer, I was on my way.

If I thought the paperwork was scary, having the blood drawn was horrible. I'm a complete and total needle wimp. I turn my head during hospital shows when they show needles going in; I only became blood friends with one friend because sticking my finger with a pin was awful. Libby pricked her finger like it was nothing, all the while with a smile on her face. ME? It took hours, days, weeks. Ok, not that long, but it felt like it. Is it any wonder that years later, Libby handled having cancer better than I handled donating a kidney!? Needles are not my friend.

Yet here I was with a rubber band thingy around my arm, my veins being tapped, and my blood being taken. About 10 years earlier, I had to get blood drawn. I walked in like a wimp, asking if I could lie down in case I fainted and requested a cup of orange juice to be close by. The woman sitting in the chair next to me, who appeared

Donor Girl

to be 92 years of age, calmly said, "Now don't worry honey, you'll be fine." Oh dear God; I am such a weenie.

As always, it didn't hurt, and I was on my way in minutes. The phlebotomist seemed like she did many of these and wasn't shocked by any of it. I asked, "Have you had people come in before with kidney donor workups?"

"Yes, fairly often, actually," she answered. Of course, the next time I asked that question it was "No, not really." But it was nice to hear someone say yes.

Kelly had gotten somewhat confused on the details of who could and couldn't donate to Dave. At one point, Kelly had believed A+ could donate to O+. By the time they were drawing my blood, we knew that wasn't true. However, we could still do the exchange program. Approximately one-third of all willing living donors do not match their recipients. So a program is in effect that will find another donor/recipient that don't match each other, but match the other couple. For instance, Mary is willing to donate to Bill but Mary is A+ and Bill is B-. If there's another couple where Ken is willing to donate to Jody, but Ken is B- and Jody is A+, they will match Mary with Jody and Ken with Bill and simultaneously perform the surgery. This can get even more confusing when they start doing three couples, four couples, and more. But it has been done with success.

Donor Girl

## What Will the New Year Bring?

The New Year kicked off with a little black cloud over my head as I wondered what I would find out about my tests. I would not only discover if I was a match for Dave, but I'd see if the tests revealed anything about my health. There is always a percentage of people that become HIV positive without ever knowing the source. It's a small percentage, but it exists. Hadn't I read somewhere that mosquitoes can carry HIV? As long as mosquitoes exist, there's a natural needle with blood from someone else flying around and stinging at random. I was suddenly obsessing over every mosquito bite I'd ever had; and there were plenty. Mosquitoes love me. And I don't think it's ever been proved as a transmission of HIV. But I could always be the first, right?

Right after the first of the year, I received an e-mail from a family friend, an Australian, who is also a medical doctor. My parents had met her years ago while on vacation, and she became a close family friend. When the family had visited Australia so we could spend time in Dave's home country, we visited Joanne. She had been to the states many times to visit us as well. She asked if Dave had been put on the donor list in Australia as he might be able to find a donor faster there. I asked Kelly to check it out. We were all trying any avenue we could as weeks and months were ticking away. We were already into the fourth month of a twelve month directive. I was hoping for any avenue other than the Lee avenue, so I strongly encouraged they try Australia. Don't they pay for medical care over there? And they could visit family while there. I thought it was a great option!

During this time, my dad was going through his own health issues. We had noticed at Christmas that he had lost weight and wasn't looking as healthy and robust as usual. He started a series of tests that checked for everything from cancer to Lyme disease. He was

Donor Girl

lethargic, had joint pain, fatigue, etc. Unfortunately, his symptoms matched many diseases, and nothing was coming back definitive. For every test that came back negative, we were elated, yet still confused. Dad and mom did remember dad having a bull's-eye type bite on his arm back in August. While dad tested negative for Lyme disease, his doctor decided to treat him for it anyway since there are many false negative tests for Lyme's. We at least felt like they were doing something.

Kelly's blood test results came back in early January, and while she was in good enough health to donate a kidney, she was not a match for Dave due to her blood type of A+. Kelly told the University of Maryland Medical Center representative that she might as well pull my blood test as I was also A+. The woman checked the records and informed Kelly that my blood had already been sent off to be tested. No one in the family wanted Kelly to donate, either directly to Dave or in the exchange program. I figured I was still in the running for the exchange program, although my parents were beginning to express their concern over me as the donor. Dad had made it clear that he did not want me donating. Funny, dad neither did I!

While Randy and I continued our vacation in Key Largo, we decided to go "boat camping" over the Martin Luther King holiday weekend. We had read about people taking their boats from marina to marina while camping out on the boat. We have a 23' Sea Fox with a cuddy cabin; so on a windy Friday afternoon under a "small craft advisory," we left our marina in Key Largo to head for Bahia Honda State Park. It was a three and one-half hour ride with our Border Collie, Jacke, in tow. It was a rough ride, and I found myself subconsciously singing, "A Three Hour Tour," as we dealt with wave after wave after wave. Here we were, the USS Minnow, and me without my evening gowns!

But we made landfall right before 5:00 that evening. We checked in with the dock master. He gave us what was left of the diner

Donor Girl

food, and we started our first night boat camping. We were there in time to walk up to the "bridge to nowhere," a bridge that simply ends and is an amazing place to watch a gorgeous sunset over both bayside and Oceanside. We had access to bathrooms and headed back to the boat. It didn't occur to us that we wouldn't have electricity, and after a couple of hours of reading by flashlight, we went to bed. Sadly, our first night was rather painful. The mattress in the cutty cabin was not comfortable, and I awoke praying it was morning. Randy looked over and said, "What time is it?" I looked at my cell phone to discover it was only 11:59 P.M. It was turning out to be the longest night of my life.

At 5:30 A.M., when the sun started coming up, I couldn't wait to get out of the cabin and decided to take Jacke for a walk. Randy was as ready as I to get up and moving, so we watched the sunrise from the same bridge as we had watched the sunset. After enjoying a breakfast and a morning walk, we headed down to Key West and stayed at a marina. We had decided not to go to bed until at least midnight since the previous night had been so long. We walked around Key West, had a great dinner and hit a cool island bar where we could take Jacke. We really enjoyed the Key West marina, but the winds were picking up and we were afraid to leave.

As it was, almost every boat in the marina was a yacht. In fact, our 23 foot boat was smaller than the tender boats on the yachts. It was really rather funny. One yacht in the marina belonged to the Hendricks Racing Team. Their tender boat was 35 feet.

But we had a great time and wanted to come back the following year. We left in rough weather and the theme from *Gilligan's Island* kept looping through my head again. I didn't tell Randy that, but Jacke and I were definitely concerned. Randy didn't tell me until we'd finally arrived back at Bahia Honda State Park that if one wave had broken over the bow, he'd have turned us in to somewhere safe. We could have tied off in the mangroves and weathered the storm. Keep in mind that outside the Intercoastal Waterway the water was only about 2 to 3 feet deep. We weren't exactly concerned about drowning if we could make it to shallow water. At one point, I realized we were the only boat on the Intercoastal Waterway. I told Randy that's like being the only car on I-95. It's not a good sign.

We spent another night on the boat and left the next day; it was my birthday, January 15th. I had seen a dolphin ring in the gift shop at the state park that had an Atocha coin. The Atocha was a ship that had sunk off the Keys hundreds of years before. It wasn't a real coin, but one made from the silver bars found on the ship. I thought it would be a great birthday gift to myself, but I didn't buy it.

We left late that morning back to Key Largo for the rest of the trip and were greeted by a live water park show. First we saw a sea turtle, and then we saw 18 dolphins that played with us for an hour. It was a wonderful birthday, but I was regretting not buying the dolphin ring.

We arrived back that evening, and everyone in our park was delighted to see us. They hadn't wanted us to leave during a "small craft advisory" and were thrilled we had survived and returned.

I mentioned the ring to Randy and he said, "Man, I wanted to get that for you, but didn't." It would take over an hour to get back to Bahia Honda by car, but I called and asked them to hold the ring. We decided to drive down on Friday.

Right before we were due to leave, I received a phone call from a Maryland number. I answered; it was the University of Maryland Medical Center. I was expecting the call since my sister told me that she was denied for being A+ and I would be, too. The woman on the other end of the phone said, "You may want to sit down." I

# Donor Girl

sat. "I realize you believe you're A positive, but your blood tests revealed you to be O positive. You passed all the tests and have been approved to move on to the next step if you are still willing. Are you still willing to donate your kidney to David?"

The blood drained out of my face and I felt like crying. And I don't cry. "Oh dear God! Are you kidding? I'm supposed to be turned down for being A positive. I was just trying to be nice, trying to be polite. I don't want to donate a kidney. **NO!**"

That's what I thought about saying. In reality, I barely whispered, "Yes." She gave me a number to call to set up my next appointment. Then it occurred to me: How can I be O positive? OMG, who's my daddy? My dad used to tease me when I was a kid that I was found in the "silly hole" and brought to my parents and was only allowed to stay until I started lying. I guess I told lies when I was little. That and the fact that my mother refused to allow my dad to take pictures of her when she was pregnant with me because she didn't like the ones of her pregnant with Kelly; there was no *proof* that she carried me. Add to it the fact that I look Italian instead of English/Irish/Welsh, and I had to ask again, "Who's my daddy?" When I verbalized that concern, I was assured that my dad was indeed my dad. Two A+ parents have a 25% chance of having an O+ child. I said, "When I tell my dad that, I'm going to need a pie chart so he doesn't put my mom in a headlock." She chuckled and we hung up.

I sat there with the phone in my hand and was probably white as a ghost. Randy looked at me and knew. Without me saying a word, he knew. He asked, "You're O positive?" I responded yes. We barely spoke the whole way to Bahia Honda. Randy did not want me to donate my kidney to Dave. It was difficult having my husband not want me to do something that I was afraid to do yet knew if called to, I would do it. It's not that Randy didn't want me to donate to Dave in particular; he just didn't want me to donate in general. I called my sister from the car and got her voice mail. I left her a message saying to call me, that I had heard from the hospital. When she called back she said, "I know what this is about. We heard from them, too." I asked if they had heard from Dave's brother, Michael. They had not heard back from him, and I was getting desperate for them to solidify Michael's resolve to donate.

I told Kelly, in a rather indignant tone, "I need to feel like David is making an attempt to find a donor. If I'm willing to do all this, I have to feel like he is as willing to save his own life as I am." Kelly said they would try to contact him that night. I also said, "I am willing to get tested, but not until Michael comes over and gets tested. I don't want to donate my kidney, only to find out that Michael would have been a better match and have my kidney get rejected for being less of a match." Kelly agreed. Dave and Kelly had been trying to get the hospital to send Michael a kit, but they were refusing. It turned out that they don't like to do kidney testing out of country. The blood could get contaminated on the way over and would most likely not reach the U.S. in the time required. Kelly explained to the University of Maryland Medical Center that they needed to test Michael first. Until they were willing to test Michael, they weren't allowed to test me. That gave me a little bit of comfort.

Randy and I drove to Bahia Honda and bought the ring. We stopped for dinner on the way home. I needed to try and get Randy to understand where I was coming from. Randy's best friend, Steve, had passed away from ALS when he was 35. His son was only 8. I asked Randy, "If you could have saved Steve by donating a kidney to him, would you have?"

He answered without hesitation, "Yes."

I said, "I would have had to respect that, and I need you to respect this." Like me, Randy felt a little better knowing they were first going to try and find Michael. I felt badly for Randy as many times men would say "I'd never let my wife do that." In our nearly 20 years together, Randy had never allowed or disallowed me to do anything. He's always had complete respect for me as my own person. That's why I respect and love him. It's mutual. While he didn't **want** me to do it, he'd never dream of telling me I ***couldn't*** do what I knew I had to.

Donor Girl

# Compartmentalizing

I would now start living what I considered a double life. If I didn't compartmentalize my situation, I would run the risk of having the kidney donation overtake all aspects of my life. I had a very busy and demanding career that required a lot of travel, energy and time. I couldn't let my potential surgery affect my ability to do my job. After all, when you are a Type A, hypochondriac, OCD personality, you tend to obsess over things you can't control. And have no doubt; I was no longer feeling in control of the kidney donor ride I was on. It was like being on a roller coaster blindfolded and just praying that whenever it stopped, you'd be safe.

So, I would have my personal life of tests, worries, concerns and hospitals. And I would have my professional life of travel, songs, artists and charts. I couldn't let one affect the other. While I had told my immediate bosses about the situation, I didn't discuss it with coworkers, and even the owner of my company didn't know. I chose to tell a couple of radio programmers whom I was especially close to, and they all were very supportive. Well, except for the one that called me a crazy bitch; but he did say he admired me.

In January, we were working two songs and about to launch a new act. Craig Morgan had a single called "Little Bit of Life" that was entering the charts near the Top 10. Jason Aldean had a single called "Amarillo Sky" that was in the Top 5. I didn't have any travel in January and was able to enjoy almost an entire month in Key Largo. One of the great things about my job at that time was I worked out of the house. All I really needed was a computer and a phone, and I could do my job from anywhere. Early on in my career with Broken Bow Records I had negotiated that I could work the month of January from Key Largo. I was never a fan of

Donor Girl

cold weather, and the older I got, the less I liked it. Spending time in Florida made me a much happier person. Hence, everyone around me was nicer. Or at least I perceived it that way. They annoyed me less, and I annoyed them less, thereby making everyone happier.

We had been going through a tough decision with Craig's single "Little Bit of Life." It was starting to stall in the teens, and we weren't sure we could get its chart position higher. Our southeast regional, JoJamie, called me, greatly concerned that we were considering pulling the song and moving on to the next. She felt her region was 100% behind the song and it would hurt hers and Craig's reputations if we pulled it. She said our VP disagreed with her; she didn't know where to turn. I listened to her and said I'd see what I could do. I then called our west coast regional, Layna, who felt the same way. Our southwest regional, Mark, disagreed. His radio region wasn't a big fan of the song, but he understood the other regionals' feelings and was willing to keep it going and "fight the good fight." I called our VP and shared the feelings. He fought me on it and said we couldn't get the song Top 10. I then e-mailed all the reasons we should stay on it. We continued to argue via e-mail until he finally said, "Fine, if you think you can get it there, prove it and get it there."

I went back to Layna and JoJamie and said, "Okay, we can give it a try, but it's our tushes on the line if it doesn't make it." However, for the promotions staff, being in the Top 10 yet again would give us more power to fight for the next single. We ended up fighting for it, and we got it into the Top 10. It was Craig's fourth Top 10 hit.

By February 1, I was on the road. Jason Aldean had a radio show in Virginia Beach with WGH Radio. I had reserved a limo to take Jason and his band to the venue in style. I would be dropping them off at the hotel around 9:00 P.M. and then driving for 3 hours to Fairfax, Virginia where Craig Morgan was performing with Trace

Donor Girl

Adkins the next night. They were calling for ice, and I do not like to drive on ice. Does anyone? Any sane person anyway? I opted to take the car service (although not a limo) all the way to Fairfax. I was so relieved not to have to drive in ice and snow. Naturally, since I had planned for someone else to drive, we made the entire trip on dry roads. Craig was excited the next day to have a cool SUV limo-type car to be driven around in. We visited XM Country Radio – Highway 16, and Craig went on the air with Jay Thomas. We then visited WMZQ/Washington DC's St. Jude Event where Craig signed autographs and encouraged listeners to pledge money. Later, we headed back to the venue to kill time before the show. Randy came down later that evening to attend the show and also to give me a ride back home since we lived about 70 miles NW of DC.

I would spend a majority of the next two weeks on the road. I had a one-day run in Baltimore with Jason before heading out with Craig for 3 days. Due to the routing of Craig's run, it was easier for me to ride the band bus than travel separately. I had set it up with Craig's bus driver in advance to route through Baltimore on his way from Tennessee to Atlantic City to pick me up at a hotel. They showed up early in the morning. I jumped onto the bus, and thus began a 3 day tour. It was cold, snowy and rather miserable compared to Florida. Randy and I had flown back to Florida the weekend before to spend time with my parents, who spend the month of February in the Keys. It was fun to be with mom and dad, and the weather was lovely. Not so much in the tundra of the northeast.

However, Craig's tour was fun and Trace Adkins is hilarious. He is truly one of the funniest men I've ever met and I enjoyed time talking with him. Craig had re-designed his bus and now had a bedroom/office in the back of the bus. Since he spent time sound checking and preparing for the show, he was nice enough to let me use the room. It was warm and cozy and a nice break from the cold. We had been hearing about the 100+ inches of snow they were getting in upstate NY, and we were due in Syracuse on Sunday. We were all excited about the idea of seeing that much snow. However, they had just gotten more snow that day and the tour finally decided it would be best to cancel the show. Even if we could get there, no one would be able to come see it. We finished the show in Atlantic City, went on to Reading, Pennsylvania, and then the bus headed back to Nashville, dropping me off in Falling Waters, West Virginia. I'm sure there's a country song in there somewhere about being dropped off by a band bus at a truck stop in WV. Ah the glamour! Living the high life!

Life was going on as normal. Back on the kidney side, Dave was able to contact his sister, Alison, who basically told his brother, Michael, "You will go to America and get tested." So Michael booked a plane ticket and was heading over to donate his kidney to Dave. It wasn't easy because there were some problems with Michael's getting a passport. Apparently, he wasn't always the most well- behaved little koala in Australia. But Alison was able to convince the powers- that-be that Michael *had* to get to America and donate his kidney. So Michael was on his way. What a relief for me, at least for a short period of time.

This e-mail came from Kelly to family and friends.

*In a message dated 2/3/2007 8:40:16 P.M. Eastern Standard Time, kellyhornby writes:*

**Hello Family and Friends,**

**David's brother, Michael, is coming over on Feb. 20th, to donate a kidney to Dave. Please keep us in your prayers, as we are not sure yet whether he will be a match or not. We know that they are the same blood type, but Mike will need to be tested to make sure he can live with one kidney. David's blood test numbers were**

not very good the last time he went to the doctor. Dr. Nasir said that with numbers like he had, they usually begin dialysis. However, with Michael coming over in a short time, he said that we would just go ahead with the kidney transplant. Also pray that Mike has a safe trip over. I'm not sure he's ever been on a plane before. His visa is for a 3 month stay, so maybe some of you will be able to meet him. I will continue to keep you posted on upcoming events. Thanks for keeping us in your thoughts and prayers. We need them.

*God Bless you all-Kelly, Dave, Will, & Kayla*

Donor Girl

# My Stay of Execution

I call this time my "stay of execution." Kelly kept exclaiming, "I'm so glad it won't be you." But I told her I couldn't think that way. I had to keep thinking *it would be me* and stay in that mindset. It was hard enough to get to the point where I accepted it would be me, but to start thinking it wouldn't happen and then have to get to that point again, well that was too much.

We had decided not to tell my parents about my being O+. It was bad enough that my dad had always said, "You girls had better have blood type A positive, since your mom and I are A positive. If you're not, I'm not your daddy." It would be a fun conversation telling mom and dad, "I'm O positive." Who's your daddy? Who's your daddy? I did the little dance in my mind and laughed. If you've ever watched *Scrubs* and seen the way they take their thoughts and physically create them, then you have an idea of what I was visualizing: Dad and I doing the "Who's Your Daddy" dance. Crazy thoughts come at crazy times. I knew dad wouldn't be laughing or dancing.

Dad was still going through some health issues, and now was not the time to upset my parents, especially with Michael coming over. So Kelly and I decided that no one outside of the four of us were to know that I was next in line after Michael.

Kelly kept the family updated regarding Michael's arrival:

*In a message dated 2/25/2007 2:26:08 P.M. Eastern Standard Time, kellyhornby writes:*

**Hello All.**

**First and foremost, thanks for all of the thoughts and**

Donor Girl

*prayers. David's brother, Michael, has arrived safely in the good ole' USA. They have not seen each other for 25 years, so it has been wonderful hearing them share stories and experiences of long ago. He came in on Wed. and Thurs. David and he went to the Univ. of MD hospital for blood tests and Mike's psychological exam. The next set of tests will be on March 15th. Prayers are still needed that Michael is a match. The blood test will determine if we can move to the next step. Until then, David intends on showing his brother as much of the USA as he can until the surgery. Michael is here for 3 months, but we're not sure how well they'll feel after the surgery to do traveling. Michael is a super nice guy with a sense of humor that matches David's.*

*The kids adore him and for me it's been fun seeing my husband interact with his sibling. I don't get to witness this often. Mike's never seen snow, so we've been taking many photos. Watching an adult be so enthusiastic about something we take for granted has been heart warming. David and Randy have taken him up to Eagle Rock, PA. Michael is enjoying the snow there, but hasn't braved the ski slopes yet.Again, thanks for all the thoughts and prayers as they are being felt. We truly feel blessed in every aspect of this chapter in our lives. May God Bless you all, too. Kelly, David, Will, Kayla, and Michael*

Michael also didn't know that I was the backup plan. We had decided it was best not to tell him so he would go in with a clear head to all of his testing. While waiting for the tests to be processed, Dave wanted to show Michael some of the country. Dave and Michael weren't hitting it off 100% well. For as sick as he was, Dave appeared quite healthy, which I think was a shock to Michael. He made a comment, "I didn't expect to come here and find you healthier than me, mate." Considering Michael and Dave

Donor Girl

hadn't seen each other in decades, it was surprising to all of us that Michael came over at all. Back when Dave was sent to the boys' home, Michael was sent to foster care. As Dave and Michael grew older, Dave would go out of his way to go to Michael's foster home and spend time with him. Once Dave started driving, he would pick up Michael and another brother, Collin, and take them out. Michael said he never forgot Dave's efforts to keep the family together, and when he looked at pictures of their youth, it was those memories that made him want to help Dave.

Dave did appear very healthy even though his kidneys were rapidly failing. He had remained fairly asymptomatic on the outside, and only he really knew what he was dealing with inside; the pain, the itching, the forced diet or attacks of gout if he didn't stay on that diet. No one but Dave knew what he was experiencing.

Dave made an effort to show Mike a good time and took him up to their condo at Eagle Rock near the Poconos in Pennsylvania. Randy had joined them for two days. Dave and Mike stayed a couple of extra days.

*In a message dated 2/26/2007 9:40:04 P.M. Eastern Standard Time, kellyhornby writes:*

**Talked to David. He and Mike are having fun at Eagle Rock. Mike is a great cook and has been happy making them meals. Dave says he cleans the whole kitchen when he's done. I said I think we should keep him. They played Backgammon today and Mike won. His time is still messed up as he was up at 4:00 and was just heading to bed. It's tough to come that far and be off schedule for a while. David said Mike said that if he's not a match for Dave, he'd be willing to do the exchange program. He's such a great guy. For having such a rough childhood, those two have turned our very well. Love and miss you. Kel**

Donor Girl

*On Feb 26, 2007, at 9:43 PM, I wrote:*

**Wow. Mike is amazing to offer that. I really respect him for it. I'm so glad they're getting along so well. I know Randy had fun! Love and miss you too. Leez**

I had a seminar in Nashville, the annual Country Radio Seminar, and I was there at this time and glad to hear that Dave and Mike were getting along. It was very important to me that Michael not change his mind on wanting to give Dave his kidney. The more kidneys Michael gave up, the more I got to keep!

CRS is a pretty crazy time, and there are actually nights when it's mandatory that we stay up until 1:00 A.M. or so. It's tiring, yet fun and productive. CRS is basically the meeting of thousands of radio programmers, record promoters and artists. You can hear amazing music and be a part of the excitement as it's happening. If you can imagine a group of 30 and 40 something-year-olds acting like they're in college for a week, you get an idea of our seminar.

We had a Tuesday night gathering at Keith Stegall's house. Keith is best known as the producer of Alan Jackson and George Jones. Keith was BBR's head of A&R and hosted our "listening party" for the new Jason Aldean CD. It was his sophomore project for BBR, and we were very excited about the new music. We had radio Program Directors coming in to hear Jason's CD for the first time. It was a great private event, and radio PD's had the chance to spend time with Jason and get an idea of what music would be coming in 2007. CRS gives us the opportunity to introduce our label's music to PD's from across the country in one spot. Whereas it normally takes us 8 weeks to visit every radio station, especially if an artist is traveling with us on a radio tour, CRS is a time when we can see a majority of them in one week. Sounds easier than it is, though, because *every* label in town is doing the same thing. So if there are roughly 80 to100 of our PD's in town,

# Donor Girl

and 15 of us are vying for their attention, it becomes a bit of a grab fest. We're all grabbing for the same people. As soon as we plan a concert with one of our artists, some other label brings in someone like Jon Bon Jovi to do a concert, and everyone flocks to see him. This leaves the other labels with fewer PD's in attendance.

With Jason's first CRS, in 2005, we were lucky. Clear Channel, the largest owner of radio stations, had decided to hold all-day meetings and invited labels to introduce their upcoming music. We had the opportunity to have Jason perform for the first time for radio in front of 50 major market programmers. That CRS launched his first single, "Hicktown," which became a Top 10 and led to a platinum album!

We had our big show that Thursday night of CRS. We had all of our other artists perform, including Craig Morgan, Megan Mullins and Crossin Dixon. This was always attended by a huge number of people; a night where we stayed up until about 2:00 A.M. In fact, we weren't allowed to leave much before 2:00 A.M.

By Friday night, we were all exhausted after all-day meetings and all-night parties. I always joke that as the week wears on and the circles under my eyes get worse, my shirts get lower cut. It's best to get their focus somewhere other than on my face. If CRS lasted one more day, I'd have to go topless.

By Saturday morning, we finally were able to fly home and relax for all of one day before Monday started again.

Donor Girl

# Only One Month To Go

Almost every year of our marriage, either Randy or I was at a seminar during our wedding anniversary. Randy's Photo Marketing Association convention, the PMA, is held either the week before or the week after CRS. So it was rare to celebrate our anniversary together *on* our anniversary.

This year, we'd both be home. We were planning to go to a spa in Berkeley Springs, West Virginia to pamper ourselves with massages, facials and hot tubs. I had an e-mail from Kelly:

*In a message dated 3/4/2007 8:54:00 P.M. Eastern Standard Time, kellyhornby writes:*

**HAPPY ANNIVERSARY!! Did you have fun today? It was a great day to be inside and pampered. It was so cold and windy outside.**

**David called and said he and Mike got into a fight. Mike didn't want to go to FL. David said he wasn't going to let Mike come to America and just sit and watch TV. Mike said he was expecting David to be on his deathbed and not healthier than him. I asked David if he told Mike that Dr. Nasir says the same thing every time he sees him. David is in better shape than his doctor, so his doctor is always baffled about his disease. Anyway I told David to ignore him and just keep going. Mike can sit and do nothing in warm weather. I think Mike enjoys the kids and misses them when he's not with them. But that's my personal take. He's a good guy but has very simple pleasures. Have fun trying to get him to go on the boat. Dave will go but I can't promise you that Mike will. Maybe you can talk him into going.**

*Anyway, are you still coming down tomorrow night? Don't feel you have to if you're too tired and want some time at home. I will certainly understand that. Just let me know.*

*I love you, Me*

*On Mar 4, 2007, at 10:15 PM, I wrote:*

**I don't know what to say about the fight. A part of me feels like if Mike wants to stay home and do nothing that should be respected. He's already come a long way just to get here. And I think Dave's visual health is one of the reasons Randy doesn't want me to donate. He doesn't "see" the immediate health risk.**

**I'll keep praying for them. I'm sorry it happened. I still plan to come down tomorrow night. I do have a bit of a cold though. Fair warning in case you don't want me to come down. We had a great time and the pampering was incredible. I could do it every day! Thanks. Love you too. Lee**

*In a message dated 3/5/2007 6:54:30 A.M. Eastern Standard Time, kellyhornby writes:*

**I talked to David last night and he said everything is fine. Mike beat him in two more backgammon games and I think that helped. He finally admitted to Dave that he misses the kids. Do I know my bro in law or what? I said what about me. He said Mike said that it would not be right to say that because I'm his wife. The guy has some pretty strong morals. I think they're fine now. They're siblings. What can you say? See you tonight unless I hear otherwise. Love you too. Kel**

Donor Girl

*On Mar 5 2007, I wrote:*

**It's pretty cool that he feels so close to the kids already. I guess it's different for him being around a "family" and he wants to spend every minute he can with everyone. Can't blame him.  Hopefully they'll enjoy Florida.**

**See you tonight.**

I had to go to Raleigh, North Carolina for a Jason Aldean show with WQDR.  I was also going to visit WRNS in Greensboro.  The WRNS visit was postponed, so I decided to fly out the night after the WQDR visit.  I called my friend, Erik, to see if he wanted to grab a bite to eat before I went to the airport.  We met at a sports bar type restaurant and ordered a drink and some food.  I decided to open up to him about my offer to donate my kidney.  Erik and I met each other when I was out on tour with Craig Morgan.  Craig and I were in Springfield, Massachusetts visiting WPKX and were having drinks at a bar.  Craig noticed the Special Forces insignia on Erik's shirt, introduced himself, and bought his friend and him a drink.  Due to his and Craig's Army background, they became fast friends.  I became the mediator between them.  It isn't always easy to reach Craig with his travel schedule, so I would help Erik get in touch or invite him to concerts.  In the meantime, Erik and I became very good friends, and ended up talking almost daily either through e-mail, text, IM or phone.  Erik and I can argue like siblings, but we also have a deep respect for one another.  I can say he is probably one of my closest friends.    Well, I have a deep respect for Erik.  You'd have to ask him about his respect level for me.

"So, I told you my brother-in-law needs a kidney.  Looks like I might be the match," I told Erik.

"Really?  And you're comfortable with that?" he asked.

Donor Girl

"No, not really," I said laughing. "But someone has to do it, and it might come down to me. His brother is going to get tested first and flew over from Australia. But I'm next in line"

"My sister once thought about donating to someone from her church, but it didn't work out. I wasn't in favor of it 'cause this was a stranger, and seeing as I'm her twin, I might someday need her kidney." We both laughed because that was such a typical Erik statement.

Surprisingly, Erik didn't tell me I was an idiot for thinking about donation, which is what I was expecting. We didn't say much more, but he was supportive and told me to keep him informed. I asked him to not say anything to Craig yet. I knew Craig wouldn't be in favor of it, and I didn't want to upset anyone I worked with. He agreed not to.

Erik's support over the course of this donation would mean a lot to me. We never got sappy, as neither of us goes down that road, but he was there for me. In fact, he actually sent flowers to me in the hospital; and I still laugh at the card. "Hugs and Kisses…yea right." That is so Erik. But he *did* send flowers. I always tease him, "Now I know what it takes to get flowers from you. I just have to give up body organs!" It meant a lot to me that Erik supported me because he is too blatantly honest to lie. So if he really believed I shouldn't do it, he would have told me. It gave me one more person to talk to and at that time, I needed all the supporters I could find.

For two people who rarely show affection, we actually hugged when I left for the airport. I was definitely finding myself more emotional, and I discovered that the idea of my donating an organ brought out a different reaction in my friends.

I went down to Florida the week after I was in Raleigh. Michael and Dave were there visiting our place in Key Largo. They were

Donor Girl

not getting along at all. Michael didn't want to be there, and Dave was frustrated. It had been a long drive with a stop at the Space Center on the way down. Dave thought they had a blast, but Michael said he was miserable. We would later find out that he had a much better time than he said he did. It was just hard for him to tell Dave.

After I arrived, Dave and I went out to dinner, but Michael didn't want to go. Dave and I went to Snappers for dinner and then went to the Turtle Club. They have a game called the "Ring Toss" that I'm very good at. It's made of fishing line with a ring at the end tied to a bar. You swing it to a hook on the wall with the goal being to hook it. Dave and I enjoyed playing, and I had fun showing up all the guys in the bar. There were actually men in the bar that were praising me on my amazing "Ring Toss" skills. I had the rapt attention of every drunken local man in the bar. I was the queen of a game no one had ever heard of. My parents would be proud since they had first made a ring toss game when my sister and I were kids. They could take credit for this incredible talent of mine.

Dave and I talked about Mike's behavior. I tried to explain it from Mike's point of view because I was the only one who truly understood how Mike felt. The feelings of fear and apprehension, mixed with the knowledge that you may have been chosen to save a life, are truly overwhelming in a way that only those who have been called to do it can understand. While I couldn't understand how it felt to be in Dave's shoes, he couldn't understand how it felt to be in Mike's or my shoes.

The next day, Michael was ready to go home. He and Dave left around 10:00 A.M., driving straight through for 18 hours. I went on to Key West for our friend's 50th surprise birthday party. Randy flew in to meet me. We had a fun night and enjoyed the next day on the water.

In the meantime, Michael and Dave would continue with their medical testing.

*In a message dated 3/15/2007 6:58:46 A.M. Eastern Daylight Time, kellyhornby writes:*

**David and Mike go to Univ. of MD hospital early today for another battery of tests. This is round two. Thoughts and prayers are needed today that the tests are successful. If everything goes well this time, the surgery date will be in the window frame of April 12 to the 23. Thanks for your prayers so far, as the first set of tests went well, so we're able to go onto the next step, which is today. Your prayers are being felt by all of us and we are very grateful. I'll be in touch as soon as we know the results of the tests today. God Bless you all and thanks again. Kelly, David, Will, Kayla, and Mike**

Thus far, things were going well. Michael was passing the tests and a surgery date had been set for April. Just one month away! While I was still keeping it in the back of my mind that it could come down to me, I was feeling better about things. A part of me was starting to believe that Michael would be the donor, and aside from rejection, my need to donate would no longer be at the forefront of my mind. However, I always kept the thought that it could be me. Until the surgery actually happened, it was still just a "stay of execution."

Although I hadn't told my parents or any family members that I was O+ and the backup plan, I had told my church family, though. I'm in the praise team at church, and our service has a very small congregation. We are very close; I knew I could trust them to pray for me. My congregation knows that I handle fear with humor so every week I'd ask them to pray for Dave, Michael and my kidney. I'd remind them that I was "on deck," and it was very important to

Donor Girl

have Michael come through.  I had discussed this with my kidney, and it really, *really* wanted to stay in my body.

I also discussed it with the women at Curves. There was a great group of us that went regularly and would meet there on Monday nights to work out. They were wonderfully supportive.  I've never wanted a tattoo, but I joked that if I had to give away my kidney, I'd get a tattoo where my kidney used to be.  One girl jokingly said, "Then you'll have to write 'was here' underneath." Humor is a great way to get past fear.

At the end of March, we had the first hint that there was a problem with Michael donating his kidney.  Kelly's e-mail told it best:

*In a message dated 3/25/2007 Kellyhornby writes:*

**Hello again.  Mike and David went on the 15th for the next set of tests. All tests went well except for the last one, which was blood pressure.  After sitting there all day waiting to see the doctors, Mike's blood pressure was high.  During a physical he showed no other signs of hypertension, but they're concerned none the less.  The doctors feel it might be "white coat" syndrome.  So, Dave and Mike are back to the hospital on tomorrow for a blood pressure monitor that will be attached to Mike for a 24 hour period.  Please pray that the numbers are good for the 24 hour period.  If they are, the surgery is scheduled for April 12th.  Please keep us in your thoughts and prayers on this day as well.  If you don't hear from me again before April 12th, you'll know that the surgery is "on" and I'll be in touch afterward.  Thanks for all your support and prayers.  We don't know what we would do without them.  God Bless you all.  Love,  Kelly, David, Will, Kayla, and Mike**

**PS Happy Easter and Happy Passover.**

Donor Girl

*In a message dated 3/5/2007, I wrote:*

**Wow Kell. I didn't realize he had to wear the blood pressure monitor before being given the go ahead. Bummer. Keep Dave away from him during that period. They seem to raise each other's blood pressure. haha Believe me when I say I am saying MY prayers!! Leez**

I tried not to express my fears too strongly to Kelly as I know they were all upset. When I talked to her on the phone, she said the household was very somber, and everyone was walking on eggshells. Michael wanted to be the donor, so he was very upset that he might be ruled out. Dave was ready to have a kidney and start feeling healthy again. They were trying to get him to go on dialysis. The only thing allowing him to hold off was the thought that surgery was right around the corner. And Kelly was panicked thinking her sister was going to have to start getting tested. It was a very sad night in the Hornby house. It wasn't a great night in the Adams/Kuhn household either.

It was around this time that I read an article in *People Magazine* about a guy who donated a kidney to a complete stranger. He found her on "matchingdonors.com."

I have to admit my first thought when reading the article was, "Seriously? You just decided 'What the heck, I think I'll give up a kidney to a person I've never met?'" This was a thought process that I couldn't begin to process no matter how much I respected it! I recommended Kelly sign up on this Web site. In my gut, I knew Michael was not going to make it through the blood pressure tests. I was getting very nervous and scared. It was overwhelming to know I was next in line. I envied the man who felt so comfortable just "giving up his kidney." That is true altruism! I remember reading on a donor Web site where a woman wrote: "I wish there was no such thing as living donors, that way I wouldn't have to make this decision." How true.

Donor Girl

## Back On Donor Row

April didn't bring good news with regards to Dave and Michael. My apprehension had been growing as we all waited to hear the results of Michael's 24-hour blood pressure monitor. We received the news in early April, and Kelly updated family and friends:

*In a message dated 4/3/2007 8:42:03 P.M. Eastern Daylight Time, kellyhornby writes:*

**Hello Family and Friends. Thanks so much for the thoughts and prayers you've given us in the past few months. We continue to ask for your prayers as Mike was not able to donate due to health issues that came up. God has given us a wonderful visit with Mike and we are grateful to God for that. We know that God has a plan. We just don't know what that is at the moment. Continue prayers that an O positive donor comes into our lives. Again, thanks and may God's blessings shine on you and your family. Love, Kelly, Dave, Will, Kayla, and Mike**

*On Apr 3, 2007, at 8:54 PM, I wrote:*

**You do realize God already answered that prayer. What are the chances I'd be O+?? There's a reason sis. You can't turn away from a tablet in a burning bush. ;-)**

**Love you! Leez**

*In a message dated 4/3/2007 10:27:24 P.M. Eastern Daylight Time, kellyhornby writes:*

**I know-I just don't want to mention you until we've had**

Donor Girl

*time to talk to Mom and Dad. You know how news gets around. I don't want them to worry before they need to. Love you too. Me*

*On Apr 3, 2007, I wrote:*

**And we don't tell mom and dad until I've had all the tests. No sense in worrying them until we know if I can do it. It'll just be between you, Dave, Randy and me.**

Randy was someone that I was very worried about during this time. He did not want me to donate my kidney, but he'd always been an amazingly understanding husband. He never questioned my decisions and always supported me 100%. I only wish I'd supported him half as much as he did me throughout our marriage. Even though I often feel like a nag, he still stands by me. This kidney donation was something he was struggling with, but he kept his opinions to himself, knowing I was determined. While he had told me he didn't want me to do it, he would support my decision. Randy loves me enough to know that only I could make this decision. He couldn't make it for me. And had he tried to force me not to do it, and succeeded, I would have had to live with that decision, not him.

I sent Kelly another e-mail to try and ease her worries.

**Please know that I am committed to being there for David. And Randy is now behind me. He said tonight "you don't have a choice but to do it." He understands and will be supportive. It's all going to be ok.**

**Maybe God wanted David and Michael to find each other and have this time together. And maybe my reason for being on earth is to give life to David. So let's just stay positive and pray that I am healthy enough to do this. If**

Donor Girl

*it's meant to be, then I'll be healthy enough to donate. If it's not meant to be, I won't. It's in God's hands. Love you, Leez*

What I really wanted to say to Kelly was, "Make it work with Michael! Make a miracle happen. Do something, but don't let it be me." But that's not what I said. Nobody was more devastated than Kelly that it couldn't be Michael. And it was *me*, not Kelly that had started the ball rolling toward me. Kelly wanted anyone *but* me to do it. I couldn't let her know I felt the same.

Kelly spent a lot of time wondering why Michael had come into their lives with the offer to donate a kidney only to not be able to donate. Kelly is a strong believer in God's will and God's path, and while she didn't *question* it was His will, she was struggling to figure out what His will was! As was I. We worked through it together and decided His reason was to give Dave and Michael a sense of family that they hadn't had before. God has mysterious ways, and everyone enjoyed Mike's visit, especially Will and Kayla who now knew their biological uncle.

Donor Girl

# Surfing the Web

I started doing what most of us in the technology age do when we need information; I turned to the Internet. I started searching for information on kidney donation while avoiding anything that might tell a horror story. I found some interesting information. I was worried that if Dave and I weren't a full match on all 6 points of the criteria, then his body would be more apt to reject my kidney. But I discovered that there was a better chance of him accepting a 1/6 match from a living donor than a 6/6 match from a cadaver donor.

I later asked Meg Baker, my transplant coordinator and RN, what all the criteria actually are and here's what she said:

*There are really two different criteria we look at when donors are tested. First we look at blood type compatibility, ie-ABO blood group (A, B, O, and AB). Second we look at how the donor' and recipient's blood mixes together-this is the cross match, and negative is the operative word. Cross match determines if the recipient has antibodies to donor DNA. If it's negative, the recipient doesn't have antibodies to donor DNA and will accept the transplant. If the cross match is positive, it means the recipient red cells destroy the donor red cells, and rejection would occur. Along these same lines, tissue typing is done. We all have 6 different tissue antigens: we get 3 from each parent. You can be anywhere from a 0/6 to a 6/6 match.*

*A 6/6 match is a perfect match or zero mismatch. Even unrelated donors who are a 0/6 match can donate, as long as blood type is compatible and cross match is negative. Siblings have a 50% chance of being a 3/6 match, 25% chance of being a 6/6 match, and 25% chance of being a 0/6 match.*

Donor Girl

Living kidney donation actually dates back to 1954. According to the UNOS.org Web site, the first living kidney donation was between twin brothers. The first successful living donor transplant was performed between twenty-three-year-old identical twins. Doctor Joseph E. Murray and associates at Peter Bent Brigham Hospital (now Brigham and Women's Hospital) in Boston, Massachusetts, transplanted a healthy kidney from Ronald Herrick into his twin brother, Richard, who had chronic kidney failure. Richard went on to live an active, normal life, dying eight years later from causes unrelated to the transplant. Still alive over fifty years since the transplant, Ronald is a retired math teacher from Maine.

On April 4th, Kelly contacted Dave's caseworker, Deb Evans, to let her know that Michael could not be a donor and I was next in line. You'll notice in the e-mail that Michael is referred to as "Joe." Apparently, he changed his name while in Australia. We found it best not to ask why. We had our suspicions, but found ignorance is bliss.

*Kelly Hornby  4/3/2007 8:32 PM*

**Hi Deb. By now you have probably heard that Joe was not able to donate due to blood pressure issues. My sister would like to know where we go from here with her. I told her that I was not sure but that I would contact you. Please let me know that you get this email. You don't have to tell me what is next, but please email my sister and let her know what she is to do.**

**Thanks for your cooperation and help in this matter. Sincerely, Kelly Hornby**

*From: "Deb Evans"*
*Date: April 4, 2007 10:49:00 AM EDT*

Donor Girl

*To: "Kelly Hornby"*
*Subject: Re: David Hornby*

**Please ask your sister to contact Meg Baker @ 410-328-7649. I know we have an opening next Thursday for her to come in to start the donor work up.**

I responded to both Deb and Kelly:

*4/4/07, I wrote:*

**I will contact Meg tomorrow. I am available on Thursday Just let me know what time I need to be where.**

**Also, due to the fact that I travel a lot, I want my sister to be able to get information at anytime on my behalf. If there's something I need to fill out to allow that, please let me know. Anything I hear, Kell's going to hear anyway. Thanks. Lee**

One of Dave's and Kelly's friends came forward at this point and seemed willing to be tested. I tried to see if they would test us both at the same time. After all, maybe she'd be a better match and thereby better for David. Then it occurred to me: "Why should Tammy get tested at the same time as me? I'm the relative. It should come from family before friends." Why shouldn't it be me? I assure you, I am no one special. This seemed to be something that someone nicer and sweeter than me should be doing. I remember once talking to a woman who had just met my sister, and the woman said, "You and your sister are nothing alike. She's so sweet and nice." Uh huh. She never completed the next thought, but it was implied. How do you even respond to such a thing? But in my mind, sweet and nice people should donate kidneys; not people like me who tended to piss people off when it was called for. Or even when it didn't call for it but my mood was bad enough that I just felt like it. Brandi, whom I referenced earlier, once said, "I love you 'cause you don't take any crap from anyone." For everyone that loved that quality in me, I assure you, there were those that hated it.

Kelly and I e-mailed back and forth about Tammy as a potential donor. First, Kelly forwarded me an e-mail from Tammy responding to Kelly's e-mail about Michael not being able to donate:

*In a message dated 4/4/2007 kellyhornby writes:*

**Check out Tammy's response. You are right about her being a silent but true friend. I emailed back and asked her if she was considering being a donor.**

*From: Tammy*
*Date: April 4, 2007 1:43:52 PM EDT*
*To: "Kelly Hornby"*
*Subject: Re: Fwd: David*

**That sucks! I believe I am O positive and I am very healthy! Tammy**

*On Apr 4, 2007, at 8:10 PM, I wrote:*

**Wow. Yes, she wouldn't have responded that way otherwise. While I remain willing, it might be worth it to see if she's a better match.**

I truly admire Tammy for stepping up. I wanted someone else to get tested and be proven a better match. I would have been delighted if that were to happen. Not only for my sake, but for Dave's. So Kelly pursued that option. It turns out the hospital prefers to test only one person at a time due to the cost of the testing. The hospital covers the costs of the donor's testing, and to

Donor Girl

test more than one person at a time is unnecessary spending. If the person being tested matches, then they don't need a backup.  I needed a backup. They didn't.

*In a message dated 4/4/2007 kellyhornby writes:*

**Can you believe that? She said she was O positive last time, but didn't offer, so I'm not sure what she meant. Dad said "Can you imagine Tam's kidney in Dave's body? He'll argue with himself when he gets up first thing in the morning!" I laughed, but I hope he doesn't say that to Dave.**

We got a good laugh out of this. Tammy, Dave and I are all very similar personalities.  All of us have the ability to have a good argument with each other.  Dad's comment offered some levity to a very serious situation.

I did see one glitch, however, and responded to Kelly with my concern:

*4/4/2007 I wrote:*

**Wish you hadn't told dad about Tammy. Randy will latch onto ANYONE other than me and I can't afford to argue with him anymore. Please keep all further information between the 4 of us. I know dad will mention it at Easter and Randy will wear me out over the possibility. Thanks.**

It's not that I didn't want Randy to know about Tammy, but Tammy still hadn't said she was willing to donate.  And time was running out on Dave.  He needed a kidney *yesterday!*  We already knew that I was a match and was farther ahead in the program. The only way they would test Tammy is if I said, "No, I'm not

Donor Girl

willing to donate." And as much as I sometimes felt like I couldn't go through with it, I wasn't willing to back out. Had Tammy come forward before I did, it would have been fine. But I came forward first, and I had to keep going.

Of course, there was also a big part of me that wanted to donate my kidney. It was such an amazing honor and opportunity to do something this big. There's no real way to describe the mixed emotions that I was feeling. Now that I was this far into the process, I didn't want to back out. I wanted to be able to say, "I donated a kidney to save a life!" I didn't want to do it but I *did* want to do it. It was a dichotomy within me that was like a raging war.

# **Testing**

Kelly and I seemed to find it easier to communicate via e-mail. This was for two main reasons; the first being her children. Little children have big ears, and Will already understood way too much of what was going on. Second, this was very emotional for Kelly and me. It was hard to talk about it. When I e-mailed her, my true emotions could be hidden behind comforting, positive words. The truth was I was scared out of my mind. Petrified. I had never had surgery before, and I did not want to have it now. I was caught up on a treadmill taking me toward kidney donation. While I'd been mentally preparing for months, it was now hitting home that I was next in line. It had come down to me. Believe me when I say I wasn't feeling worthy of this amazing opportunity bestowed upon me.

Kelly had done everything she could to protect me from being a potential donor, yet there were moments when I felt anger and resentment toward her for moving me forward in the process and contacting the hospital. My anger toward her was ridiculous because no one wanted me to **NOT** donate more than Kelly. I had fought with her to get the information so I could be considered. I think I wanted to want to donate, and I wanted to go through all the motions. But I wanted to be told I couldn't donate. So I would've done all the right things but could still keep my kidney. That was my plan. God's plan was different. God is still laughing.

Little did I realize it when reading the simple e-mail from Deb Evans about contacting Meg Baker that Meg would become my lifeline. Meg is an RN and would be my transplant coordinator throughout the months of testing, right up until I was released from the hospital after surgery. She would walk me through every step of the process and answer my endless questions. Meg would reassure me and be there for me at all times. I'm not sure Meg

Donor Girl

realizes what a gift she is, but one donor called her the Angel of Mercy, and I agree. Meg turned out to be about my age, very beautiful, and someone I would later call a friend.

I called the number given and spoke with Meg about possible dates to be tested. My travel schedule with work was crazy at this time of year, and they mainly do their testing on Thursdays. I was limited by when I could go in. The testing would last from 7:30 A.M. to 4:30 P.M. and include a variety of tests along with a psychological exam. We made the appointment for April 19, and I immediately called my masseuse and scheduled a massage for the 20th. She's the one I met on my church retreat, and she always had a way of seeing everything through these beautiful eyes of faith. When I was not feeling the faith as strongly as I needed to, I could trust that being with her would increase my faith once again. She is so in touch with God. I feel closer to Him just being near her.

I still had to pass a mountain of medical tests, but I didn't think I'd have any problems. I was 42, had never smoked, rarely drank and worked out regularly. At 5'3", I averaged anywhere from 105 to 110 lbs. My blood pressure had always been low, my cholesterol good and my overall vitals healthy. I'd never had children, so nothing had upset the inner workings of my body. While I enjoyed my Mountain Dew and chocolate, I was a relatively healthy eater. Ok, I don't like anything green except string beans; and if it's really loaded with cheese, broccoli. Green M&M's don't count. I like them. But, aside from that, I was a fairly healthy eater. So I did not foresee being denied for health issues.

Meg and I would spend the two weeks from April 5th until the day of my hospital testing, conversing; mainly because I had a ton of questions. Meg was always there to answer my questions and put up with my Type A/OCD personality. I don't know if every donor takes the role of finding out everything possible prior to surgery, but I didn't want to leave anything to guesswork. The e-mails went like this:

Donor Girl

From MBaker to Lee Adams:  4/5/07

**Hi Lee,   As per our conversation, please have your primary care provider fax recent Pap smear and mammogram to my attention:  410-328-0532 I will wait to hear if you are available for donor evaluation on 4/18/07, then will have my assistant, Priscilla Eaddy arrange your itinerary that day.**

**Have a good evening.  Meg Baker RN, BSN Transplant Coordinator**

From LAdams to MBaker:  4/11/2007 10:57 AM

**I have not heard from Priscilla.  I am down to tomorrow and Monday as the only days I can have blood drawn.  If I don't hear from her before then, I will have to re-schedule for the 19th.  Just an FYI.  Lee Adams**

From MBaker to LAdams:  4/11/07

**Hi Lee, I got this email as you were speaking to Priscilla.  Sounds like things are on track, let me know if you need anything further.  Meg Baker RN, BSN**

From LAdams to MBaker:  4/11/07

**Just reading the list of things I'm being tested for almost made me faint.  haha I just hope I test fit enough to be able to donate. Thanks.  I'll try to go tomorrow morning. Lee**

This blood draw was different from the other in that they had to take so many vials of blood. They told me it would take about 3 minutes to get it all.  **THREE MINUTES??**  These people were vampires! I thought, "Will there be any blood left in me?" I could

Donor Girl

donate to a small nation in 3 minutes. When I asked how many vials of blood they'd be taking I was told about 25. Oh My God! Can people survive something like that??

Having been a radio disc jockey, I know how long 3 minutes is. I can use the bathroom, put on a cup of tea, toast a Pop Tart and *still* get back before the next song. Most blood draws take what, 30 seconds? I actually choked up, which I had been doing more of lately. I asked one of the vampires, "May I listen to my iPod?" I was told I could, and I put in Kenny Chesney's "Blue Rocking Chair." God bless Kenny! He got me through the 3 minutes.

In an email to Meg Baker…4/12/2007 12:01 PM

**I had the blood drawn and urine test today. I assume that unless I hear otherwise, I will come into Univ. Of MD Hospital for all day testing next Thursday. Thanks. Lee**

From MBaker to LAdams: 4/12/2007 12:42:39 P.M.

**Hi Lee, I am out of the office on Monday, but will review labs Tuesday for sure. No news is good news, and if anything needs to be repeated, we will do it when you're here on Thursday. Meg Baker RN, BSN**

From LAdams to MBaker: 4/12/2007 4:25 PM

**Does everyone feel a little nervous about hearing the results or am I different? Lee**

From MBaker to LAdams: 4/17/07

**Lee, Your preliminary labs look fine. Try not to be nervous, I know easier said than done. This is a long process, and it is the rare person that sails thru initial evaluation without needing something repeated. It's my**

Donor Girl

**job to worry, so don't stress until I tell you to :) Looking forward to meeting you on Thursday. Meg Baker**

From LAdams to MBaker: 4/17/07

**Thanks. Glad to know nothing "glaring" came through on the preliminary's. I just think back to my grandfather saying "You're never sick until you let them start testing you." haha**

**My husband's sense of humor came through. He looked at my schedule and said "Babe, your first appointment is the psych evaluation. You'll be home by noon." Gotta love the sense of humor that gets you through! See you Thursday. Lee**

I received a phone call from Meg. Although my tests had all come back fine, she was slightly concerned about my low creatinine levels.

*Creatinine is a chemical product that is generated from <u>muscle metabolism</u>. Creatinine is transported through the bloodstream to the kidneys. The kidneys filter out most of the creatinine and dispose of it in the <u>urine</u>.*

*The kidneys maintain the blood creatinine in a normal range. Creatinine has been found to be a fairly reliable indicator of <u>kidney</u> function. As the kidneys become impaired the creatinine level in the blood will rise. Abnormally high levels of creatinine thus warn of possible malfunction or failure of the kidneys, sometimes even before a patient reports any symptoms. It is for this reason that standard blood and urine tests routinely check the amount of creatinine in the blood.*

*Normal levels of creatinine in the blood are approximately 0.6 to 1.2 milligrams (mg) per deciliter (dl) in adult males and 0.5 to 1.1 milligrams per deciliter in adult females. (In the metric system, a milligram is a unit of weight equal to one-thousandth of a gram, and a deciliter is a unit of volume equal to one-tenth of a liter.) Creatinine levels that reach 2.0 or more in babies and10.0 or more in adults may indicate the need for a dialysis machine to remove wastes from the blood.*

Source:
**http://www.medicinenet.com/creatinine_blood_test/article.htm**

My creatinine levels were right around the .8 mark or a little lower. Meg was worried that it was too low to donate since the minimum amount they require is a .8, and out of my two tests, both were shy of .8. She told me not to worry, that the surgeon would look over everything. She just wanted me to be aware of it. I remember getting the message, before I called her back to get details, and thinking about the fact that this could possibly keep me from donating. What a mixture of emotions I had. One part of me thought, "This is my out! I won't have to lose a kidney." Yet I was surprised by the feeling of disappointment I felt. I was shocked to realize that I would be very upset if I was told I couldn't do this. I had already wrapped my mind around the fact that I might be chosen to save a life. It was something so much bigger than me or anything I'd ever done, and the opportunity was about to be taken away from me. I suddenly felt the need to immediately prove that I could donate, that this was normal for me and it was not going to stop me from saving Dave's life.

For months now, I'd been a potential kidney donor. I suddenly felt I had this reason for *being*, for existing; maybe not a calling, but a purpose. As much as I didn't want to do it, I didn't want to *not* do it. What a dilemma I was in!

I called my family doctor to get my past records from blood and urine work. I found out that my creatinine levels from my October of 2004 test were at .08. This was my normal. In fact, I went

# Donor Girl

online to learn more about it and discovered that as small as I am, it could be normal for mine to be even lower. I immediately e-mailed Meg to let her know what my past numbers had been. I've often wondered if this could be my "out" if I wanted one. If it was a test of sorts to see if I'd jump on it and say, "Well, then I think I should be taken out of this as I don't want my health to be at risk." Did I pass the test? They kept moving me forward, so whatever issues there may have been with my creatinine levels, they didn't stop the process.

Donor Girl

# The Children

It was around this time that seven-year-old Will started having problems. Will is a very smart young boy with roughly a 140 IQ. He understood why Mike was here and that the surgery was to save his dad. Kayla was only 4 and didn't understand as much. Will was older and remembered his dad being healthy. Dave had been slowly losing the ability to play like he used to and was often tired and in pain. He had gout attacks and would be unable to get out of bed for days. He was getting regular cold sores as his body was less able to fight infections. And his doctor was recommending he go on dialysis, which Dave was fighting. Will understood that Michael was not able to donate to Dave, which to Will meant Dave would die. This was extremely disturbing to me. I wanted to tell him I was there to help, but knew he wouldn't be able to keep it from my parents, Nana and Poppy. We still decided not to tell them. When, and if I was told I could donate, we would talk to them then. So my parents and the children remained in the dark.

After Michael learned that he couldn't donate, he decided to go back to Australia. Although he could have stayed for a few more weeks, he was ready to go. Michael had never spent time with Dave, Kelly and the kids before, and everyone grew very attached quickly. Kelly continued to agonize over why this had happened; that Michael would be able and willing to come all the way from halfway across the world to get tested yet not be a match. It had all seemed to come together with Michael being willing to donate, flying over from Australia, going through all the testing, being a 3 out of 6 match, and on and on. Yet here we were with him going back to Australia with both his kidneys. But as we talked and prayed, we came to the conclusion that Dave needed to reconnect with his brother. The kids needed to meet and spend time with their uncle, and that possibly God's plan was just to bring Dave and Michael and the family together. God has his own plan, and we sometimes put our wishes into the circumstances and say, "Yes, that's what God wants." But God sometimes turns around and says, "No, that's not what I want. This is what I want." I guess we could have found no purpose in the visit, but Michael affected us all in some way. He's a very Christian man and has a strong faith and belief system. He's quirky, which made him even more appealing to the kids. And most important, he was willing to do the ultimate to save his brother. It was a wonderful time we all had to spend with Michael, and no one felt it was a wasted trip or wasted 6 weeks of time.

I, for one, realized Michael's purpose more than anyone. It helped me to know that there was someone else who knew exactly what I was experiencing. Even if I talked to other donors, Michael was the only one being tested for the same person as I was. He was the only one that felt the need to help the daddy of Will and Kayla, and the husband of Kelly. He was the only other person going through this with me. Even though we really only spent the one night talking about it, the time spent with him meant a lot to me.

When it was first announced that Michael couldn't donate, I met with him at Kelly and Dave's house. He spent time explaining everything he'd experienced up to that point. We went downstairs alone, sat and talked about all the tests they'd run on me, the people I'd meet at the hospital and some things I could expect. There were some questions that he chose not to answer, feeling I'd be better served by experiencing it on my own. We talked about our fears. He had seemed to handle everything rather effortlessly and isn't one to share emotions. I asked him if he was scared during the process, and in his Australian accent he said, "Aw ye-a. It scared the hell out of me. But I'd have done it. I'd have gone through with it." I expressed to him how moved I was that he was willing to donate to Dave. I was the only person who could truly understand the emotions and feelings that Michael had experienced. We shared a bond through this that no one else could understand.

Donor Girl

I noticed that my nephew was watching us and wondering why Uncle Mike and Aunt Lee, who barely knew each other, were quietly going off to talk. When he tried to join us, we had to explain that we needed to talk alone. Later, Will got very quiet and wanted to go to bed early, around 8:00 P.M. This was not the typical behavior of this seven-year-old. I pulled him onto my lap and asked him what was wrong. He explained that everything was changing, and it was making him sad. When I pressed him to explain, he told me his dad had remodeled his bedroom and it was different. Knowing how much he loved his new room, I knew that wasn't the problem, but Will was unable to verbalize what he was thinking. I assured him everything would be ok and explained that change can be for the better.

One thing Michael made sure to express about his initial visit to the hospital was how wonderful the staff was. He assured me their entire mission was to make me feel as comfortable as possible. He said he'd walked out of the meetings feeling like he was a very important person and had been treated like royalty. He was especially a big fan of the social worker, Nina. She's the one that makes sure the donors are psychologically sound to go through with surgery. I think he had a bit of a crush on Nina, but he was very clear that it would be inappropriate since she was married. But he blushed when he said it. As we went through a folder full of information, I saw a pin that had a red heart in a special design. It's the symbol for organ donors. I asked Michael if he'd like to keep it and he said no. I reminded him that he had been willing to donate and had flown all the way from Australia to get tested. The point wasn't that he couldn't medically do it, but that he was willing to do it. In my eyes, he deserved to have and wear the pin. However, he didn't seem to feel the same way. "I would have done it, Lee. I was scared, but I'd have done it," he said as we finished our conversation. I know Michael. I know.

Some of what Michael told me that day reassured me in ways I can't put into writing. My main reason for not wanting to write it

Donor Girl

is there are things that only potential donors should know about donation. It's not something that should be shared with the general public. I realize that sounds very secretive, like we have a secret handshake or something, but those that have been through the process will understand.

Michael and I joined the rest of the family and enjoyed the evening. As I was leaving, Michael said, "I'm glad it wasn't me that could do it." Right as he said it, he got this horrified look on his face. "Oh my gosh! That's not what I meant to say. I wanted to say, 'I'm sad I couldn't do it.' I really didn't mean to say 'glad.'" While I don't agree with everything Freud believed, I do believe in the proverbial "Freudian slip." While I think Michael truly wished he could have donated and that it wouldn't be left up to me, deep down there was a part of him that was also glad he couldn't do it. He apologized so many times I lost count, but I kept telling him not to worry.

I said, "I won't lie; I wish it **HAD** been you and it wasn't me." I wasn't offended by his slip of the tongue. More than anything, I understood 100% why he would be glad. I'm not sure Michael has yet forgiven himself for saying that to me.

Michael had given me a folder of information, and I would later get a similar folder of my own. It had all kinds of information regarding living kidney donorship. It answered the question, "Why living donor versus waiting for a cadaver donor?" First, it's a 4 to 5 year wait (or longer), and in that time, people needing kidneys will either be weakened by years of dialysis or will die waiting for a kidney. A live kidney is better in quality due to the minimal amount of time the organ is out of a living body. Living kidneys offer better initial function. They tend to kick in faster and start making urine immediately. There's an increased long-term graft survival, meaning kidneys from living donors last longer than those from cadaver donors.

Donor Girl

In the folder there was a list of basic information regarding what a donor's health has to be and also what it cannot be. A donor must **NOT** have: high blood pressure (although this was not absolute); cancer; diabetes; kidney disease; heart disease. A donor **MUST** be: blood group compatible; healthy; willing; cleared by multi-disciplinary review committee.

Initial blood results needed include blood type compatibility (optimal); negative cross match (optimal); degree of antigen match (0 match is acceptable). I was already tested for HIV, Hep B and C, kidney function, liver function, past childhood virus exposures, West Nile virus, urine function, EKG and chest X-ray. Additional tests included my Pap smear, mammogram, PSA, exercise stress test, two-hour glucose tolerance test and pulmonary function test.

I would also have to have a CT angiogram to determine the specific anatomy of my kidneys and urinary tract so doctors could then make a decision on which kidney they would take; the left versus right. The CT angiogram would show the surgeon how many blood vessels were going into and out of the kidneys; the number of ureters going into the bladder; and any masses or lesions in the kidneys and abdominal cavity.

Michael wanted to see the country's capital before leaving, and the family headed down to DC before he went home. The day Michael flew home, I felt a strange sense of loss. I guess as long as he was in the USA, there was a part of me thinking, "Something could change and Michael could still donate." But when he and his kidneys boarded the plane back to Australia, I knew I was alone. It was now only my two kidneys that could possibly help Dave.

Donor Girl

# My Support Group

During this time, I had to find people to lean on for my support system. I had always counted so much on my parents, yet I wasn't able to turn to them at this time. By limiting who I shared the information with, I was limiting my support group. However, my church knew from day one what was happening, and I couldn't have done it without them.

My church, Harmony United Methodist Church, is my haven. I joined the church shortly after moving to the area in 2000. I joined the 11:00 A.M. Contemporary Service, and it wasn't long before they were asking for volunteers to play in the praise group. I am not the best musician in the world, but I do play a few instruments. That seemed to be enough for them. The late service had a very small congregation and we all personally knew each other. In the fall of 2006, one of our praise group members, Magda, was diagnosed with Myasthenia Gravis. She had to undergo a rough surgery. Magda and I had become instant friends when she joined the church. We both later admitted to looking at the other one and thinking, "I think I could become friends with her." Although much taller than my 5'3" self, Magda and I had similar hair color and coloring, and we were sometimes asked if we were sisters.

The church family rallied around Magda. At Christmas, when she wasn't well enough to make it to the service, we went to her house and Christmas caroled in her front yard. Shortly afterward, another member of the praise group, Debbie, had to undergo a hysterectomy. That was 2 out of 3 of us. I started threatening to quit the praise group as I kept thinking, "I'm next." It was a joke, but I started to wonder if I really would be the next one to undergo surgery.

Donor Girl

The first time I announced to the congregation what was going on I tried to use humor. I had asked everyone to pray for Dave and explained how Michael was being tested. I joked, "I need everyone to pray very hard that Michael can donate, 'cause it turns out that I'm also a match and, therefore, the backup plan. I had a long talk with my kidneys last night and they explained that they were very happy right where they were and didn't really want to be separated." The congregation gave a nervous chuckle as they realized I was trying to make light of a serious situation I was facing.

After church, one of the women in my praise group, Anne, said, "You'll never be able to donate. You are way too small." When I informed her that I'd already passed the original tests and the doctors felt I could donate, she was very surprised. She'd be one of many people to tell me they thought I was too small. I had already been asked to not lose any more weight prior to being tested for surgery. They needed me to stay around 110 lbs. I would later find out that Anne was very involved in the organ donor issue herself. Her young daughter had died during a motorcycle accident, and Anne had made the amazing yet very difficult decision to donate her daughter's organs. Her daughter's death saved others' lives. I have an enormous amount of respect for Anne.

Another church and Emmaus friend, Donna, was undergoing treatment for cancer for the third time. She is unlucky in that her cancer keeps recurring. She is fortunate in that her body reacts very well to chemo and treatment. I kept telling myself, "If Donna can go through what she's going through then I sure as heck can do this." She doesn't know how much strength she gave me just by being a role model.

I was trying to shield Randy from as much of the testing process as I could. I had decided not to put him through an 8 hour testing process, but I had no one to go with me. Kelly had taken so much

Donor Girl

time off work for Dave's testing that she couldn't take any more. I didn't have any close friends in the area, and I hadn't told my parents or Randy's mom. So I asked Magda if she was feeling up to it. My pastor overheard me and offered to take me. We decided if Magda couldn't do it, Ray would be my backup plan. Pastor Ray is probably the best pastor I've ever known, and I felt so lucky to have a pastor willing to make a 3 hour round-trip drive just to support me.

Magda felt well enough to go with me, so at 5:30 A.M. on April 19, we left Falling Waters for the University of Maryland Hospital. Magda did not have a very good surgical experience, and it was taking her a long time to bounce back from such a major surgery. She was very concerned about me donating, and worried my experience would be similar to hers. She expressed being upset with my sister for wanting me to donate to Dave. I was shocked as it never occurred to me someone would feel that way. She said she'd never let her sister donate to her husband. I explained that Kelly was adamant about me not donating and had done everything possible to stop me. However, just as I told Kelly, I told Magda that the decision wasn't Kelly's, it was mine. I couldn't justify not saving Dave simply because my sister didn't want me to. Magda felt much better knowing that Kelly had tried to stop me from doing this. I've met people since my experience that had an enormous amount of family pressure to donate to a family member. While the psychological exam is designed to find out if the potential donor experiences this kind of pressure to donate, if the person is still adamant about wanting to donate; it won't necessarily rule them out. I was lucky that no one was putting any pressure on me other than myself.

Donor Girl

# My Hospital Staff

We arrived at the hospital, and Magda was a blessing. She had all my paperwork. She made sure I knew what building to go to and I arrived at my appointments on time. We had quite a laugh when I was told I was supposed to get a "red plate." I checked in and was given a red card, sort of like a credit card. It had my information on it as to who I was and what I was doing. After getting all my information, I asked for my "plate." Magda looked at me, and she and the admissions woman pointed to my card. Magda laughed and said, "Did you really think you were getting an actual plate?"

"Yes, I did." It was probably the only laugh we had that day, but we found it funny.

Unfortunately, I did not experience the warmth and comfortable feeling that Michael did. In time, I would experience it, but on my first day, warm and fuzzy would not be my description.

My first meeting was at 9:00 A.M. with the staff social worker, Nina Shroder, MSW. When I went into her office, the woman there wasn't Nina. It turned out that Nina had to attend a family funeral, and they had given me another social worker. The problem was this was a social worker for **recipients**, not donors. She was simply not prepared to talk to me and counsel me about being a donor. She had a list of questions and asked them in a very perfunctory manner. She started by saying, "I really don't know what I'm doing..." as she lifted the pages and skimmed the questions. I instantly felt uncomfortable. I went into the day feeling extremely uneasy, but had decided to try and do my best.

Yet here I was in an awkward situation from minute one. As I answered her questions, I noticed that she was writing down a word or two, even though I was answering in multiple sentences. I finally asked, "Shouldn't you be recording this if Nina is going to assess my answers to decide if I am able to mentally survive the surgery?"

She responded by saying, "No, this is fine." Being a Type A personality, if someone isn't taking control of a situation, I will. So I felt like I was taking control of the situation. The counselor asked, "Is the recipient on dialysis?"

I answered, "No."

She switched to the next page. "And how long has the recipient been on dialysis?"

I responded, "He's not on dialysis."

She went back and read what she'd written and realized her mistake. At that point, I knew she wasn't really listening or paying attention, and I basically stopped talking. Again, I didn't blame her. She was doing the best she could after being thrown into a situation she wasn't prepared for.

When the interview was over, I went back out to where Magda was waiting for me. She asked how it went and I told her we'd talk outside. I had to go get a radiology chest X-ray at 11:00 A.M. in another building. Once we were out of the building, I told her about my experience and she said how sorry she was. I left the counseling session feeling very unnerved. I went into the X-ray room, signed in and did as told. The X-ray was uneventful; it was time to move on.

At 12:00 P.M., I was to meet with my surgeon. God is smart and He knows me well. He knew how to give me a comfort level. The surgeon assigned to me turned out to be the type of doctor who immediately puts his patient at ease. Dr. Cooper looks you straight in the eyes when he talks and makes you feel like you are the most

Donor Girl

important part of his day. Many doctors I met with later, while being efficient, made me feel like a number, not a person. I was given the surgeon with the best bedside manner. For a hypochondriac, that's important. As I would later learn, it's *extremely* important. Had he not answered all my questions patiently; understood my personality so well; or had he in any way been cold and uncaring, I may have said, "Thanks, but no thanks."

As a donor, I wasn't there to have someone save *my* life. I was a part of a process to save another person's life. In my mind, I was my surgeon's tool to a certain extent. He and Dave's surgeon couldn't save Dave's life without me! That put me on their team. Had I been assigned a surgeon who saw himself as my "savior" versus someone on his team, I probably would have been irritated. In fact, at one time, I informed a rather "holier than thou" doctor that no one at the medical center had cured me. I didn't come in sick, but was more or less made sick temporarily *by them* in order that they could save someone's life. It's a very different relationship between doctor and patient when you are part of the cure. I wasn't going to take any flak from some conceited doctor. But my surgeon was different. He has an immense amount of respect for living donors and never made me feel anything less than a hero; a title I was still very uncomfortable with.

Dr. Cooper's bio instilled confidence as well. His official title is Associate Professor of Surgery and Director of Clinical Research in the Division of Transplantation. His medical degree came from the Georgetown University School of Medicine. Very nice! Georgetown is well known to those of us from the area. He did his residency at the Medical College of Wisconsin which, quite honestly, meant nothing to me. I was neither impressed nor unimpressed. However, he did his fellowship at Johns Hopkins Hospital in multi-organ transplant. Now *that* meant something to me and impressed me. Being a Baltimore girl, I grew up hearing about Johns Hopkins, and it's known worldwide as one of the best. Dr. Cooper's bio read like this:

Donor Girl

Matthew Cooper is a fellowship-trained, multi-organ transplant surgeon who comes to the University of Maryland as an associate professor of surgery after five years at Johns Hopkins Hospital. In his new role, Dr. Cooper assumes clinical responsibilities in kidney, pancreas, and liver transplantation while becoming Director of Clinical Research for the University of Maryland Division of Transplantation.

Dr. Cooper received his medical degree at the Georgetown University School of Medicine. He completed his general surgery training at the Medical College of Wisconsin followed by a multi-organ abdominal transplant fellowship at the Johns Hopkins Hospital. Upon completion, Dr. Cooper joined the Hopkins transplant faculty in 2002 and was appointed surgical director of Kidney Transplantation and Clinical Research in 2003. While at Hopkins, Dr. Cooper was instrumental in the success of the division's Incompatible Kidney Transplant Program and the world's first triple live donor kidney exchange in July 2003.

Dr. Cooper is especially committed to increasing the supply of transplantable organs through raising awareness and acceptance of live organ donation. While well respected for his technical skills, he is equally well known for his humanitarian commitment to patient care and his strong relationships with fellow caregivers and referring community physicians.

It was a very impressive resume, and after reading it, I felt in capable hands.

Dr. Matthew Cooper walked into the room and asked for Lilli Adams. I stood up, and we went to an exam room. Immediately, I felt comfortable and at ease. We sat in two chairs that faced each other. He started by saying, "I am your surgeon. I won't be the recipient's surgeon and will have nothing specifically to do with

## Donor Girl

his case. My only concern will be you, and I need you to feel comfortable with that."

I answered, "I want your only concern to be me. I want it to be all about me. I'm very comfortable with that."

He laughed. He read over my paperwork that told the basics on my lifestyle. I was a nonsmoker, drank very rarely, worked out regularly, had never had a surgery or major injury, had never done illegal drugs, etc. He said, "You have one of the most boring medical histories I've ever seen."

I responded by asking, "So, you find me boring?"

"No, not at all. But medically you are boring, and that's my favorite kind of donor." In subsequent articles that I found about some of his surgeries, I noticed that he often would say, "The surgery was very boring. My favorite kind." For once, it was good to be boring.

He continued by asking, "What kind of sports and activities are you involved in."

I started to list them. "I water ski."

"Not a problem."

"I scuba dive."

"Not a problem."

"I bike."

"Not a problem."

"I'm a martial artist." I literally saw him wince.

Donor Girl

"That could be a problem. You should be very careful with contact sports after surgery." I was expecting that answer, so I assured him I would be careful.

"Do you mind if I examine you?"

I figured that's what I was there for, so I answered, "Not at all." I lay down on the examination table and Dr. Cooper showed me where the incisions would be.

"The surgery will be laparoscopic and you will have three one-inch incisions here, here, and here." He pointed out 3 areas including right above my navel, on my left side, and about 3 inches above my navel. He then showed me where I'd have a 3 inch scar right above my pelvic bone, similar to a C-section scar. That was where they'd bring my kidney out.

Dr. Cooper was very explicit about the fact that in rare circumstances, surgery can go from laparoscopic to open surgery. He assured me it's rare, but does sometimes happen. This would cause a much larger scar and wouldn't be as easy of a recovery. It's more likely to happen in patients who have had prior surgery where scar tissue doesn't allow for safe laparoscopic removal. He also let me know that while the University of Maryland Medical Center had never had a death in over 1,200 kidney donations, as with any surgery, it is always possible. I would be meeting with an anesthesiologist, so I let Dr. Cooper know that my mom and sister don't handle surgery well due to anesthesia.

My short time with Dr. Cooper was what gave me the confidence to come back and actually go through with surgery. I credit him for instilling confidence in me that he was very capable of performing this surgery, and in his capable hands, I would be fine. I can truly say that were it not for his calm reassurance, on a day where nothing else had gone right, I'm not sure I could have gone through with it. And that would have been horrible for Dave, Kelly, the kids and myself.

I then had a 1:00 P.M. meeting which was an educational session/financial discussion. The donor's evaluation and hospital costs are completely covered by the hospital. We are not supposed to pay for any blood tests, prescriptions, hospital stay, etc. As I was often told, donors are at the top of the hospital food chain. Meg also attended this meeting. It was a pleasure to meet her in person.

I learned some things during this session about the function of the kidneys. People are typically born with two kidneys, but 1 in 400 is born with only one. One in roughly 200 is living with only one. So I'm actually in good company. The kidneys filter blood of waste products from food, exercise and medications. They produce a hormone to create red blood cells: erythropoietin, giving oxygen to our body. They modify Vitamin D to an active form for strong bones and maintain bone balance: calcium and phosphorus. They also maintain acid-base balance and fluid balance. I was mainly focusing on the fact that 1 in 200 people only have 1 kidney and seem to do quite fine.

There are multiple reasons why someone would have a single functioning kidney, but renal agenesis, or being born without 2 kidneys, is not common.

1. Agenesis-born without a kidney on one side
2. Aplasia-born with a rudimentary kidney on one side that essentially has no normal function
3. Fused or "horseshoe" kidney
4. Secondary atrophy or destruction-due to a variety of causes (ie-chronic infection)

Incidence varies according to source, which is where the generic "1 in 400" number came from that was quoted in UMMC literature

Donor Girl

During this talk, Magda was able to come in with me. There was another couple where the wife was donating to her husband. They both knew exactly what they were getting into with a transplant. This would be his second transplant, and there were some issues with her matching him. They would have to go through some treatments to see if they could get them to match. She had been through a couple of C-sections and seemed much less concerned about surgery than I was. It was her husband she was donating to, and he was right by her side. My situation was a little different.

My next stop was at 2:00 P.M. with Lucy, the Nephrology CRNP, for a physical and EKG. Lucy was going to give me my physical. She was a wild one; red-haired and "out there." What I liked about Lucy was she was thorough and didn't hold back anything. What bothered me about Lucy was, well, she didn't hold back about anything. I had to give a urine sample. (Can any woman accomplish this wretched task without peeing on her hand? Please! Get a better system!) Then a medical assistant took my blood pressure. Keeping in mind that Michael had been flagged for high blood pressure, I had been told that there's such a thing as "white coat syndrome." This means that a person gets nervous when at a doctor's office or in a hospital and their blood pressure rises, even if they normally have low or normal blood pressure. The medical staff had thought that was Michael's problem until they sent him home with a 24-hour monitor.

For some reason, the medical assistant decided to tell me a story she had heard about a surgery that had complications. Why she did this, I have no idea. She went into details about how things had gone wrong. I told her I didn't think she should be telling me the story. It was quite horrific to hear, knowing I would soon be going through surgery myself. When I said again that I didn't think I should be hearing this she told me the guy lived and those types of complications don't happen in most surgeries. However, the image she left wasn't going away anytime soon.

Donor Girl

Once she left the room, Lucy came back in. I decided not to tell Lucy what the assistant had said. I think I was still in shock she'd said it at all. I really liked Lucy. She talked a mile a minute, and I'm hard pressed to remember a lot of what she said, but I got a kick out of her. She wanted to reiterate the statistics and make sure I understood that there are a small percentage of surgeries that couldn't be done laparoscopically and might go into open surgery while being operated on. I told her Dr. Cooper had explained that. Lucy went on to say, "I mean, you might only have a one in a million chance of being struck by lightning, but if it happens to you, it really sucks. Right?" I naturally agreed. After all, that certainly would suck.

Lucy then had me get up on the examining table. She did a basic stethoscope listen, had me breathe in and out, etc. She checked my reflexes and did all the basics you'd have done in a doctor's office while getting a physical. Then she said she needed to do a breast exam. She asked me to open the hospital gown she had had me change into earlier. She asked if I had met Dr. Cooper, and I said yes. She went on to exclaim about what a great surgeon he is. It was obvious she held him in high esteem which once again, made me feel even better.

After the breast exam, she closed my gown and said, "Go ahead and put your clothes back on. I'll be back in a few." And she was gone. I took off my gown and put back on my street clothes. My day was almost over and I could go home. I was looking forward to that moment.

I had one more test to take. It was a CT scan that would take pictures of my kidneys and show if I actually had two healthy working kidneys. Most people are born with two, some with one. Some people are born with three. I was dreading this test and had been upset that I didn't have it until the end of the day. It seemed like it was looming over me all day long. It involved a needle; I don't like needles at all. So I had to think about needles all day.

## Donor Girl

I'd also heard the dye they put in makes you feel as if you're wetting yourself. Now there's a feeling I was looking forward to.

Lucy came back in, and we sat down to go over my paperwork that I had filled out that night way back in December. It was the same questionnaire that practically made me faint. What a long way I'd come since then. Who would have thought?

"You have an allergy to sulfa, correct?" Lucy asked.

"Yes ma'am."

"Anything else?"

"I sometimes break out in hives after eating shrimp." Lucy practically convulsed.

**"WHAT?** Why isn't that listed anywhere? Nothing in my paperwork states that. Do you realize your next test uses iodine?" Lucy was clearly upset, which upset me.

"No, I didn't. I don't have a proven allergy to shellfish or iodine, so it didn't occur to me to include it," I said, trying to explain my thought process from back in December. A lot had happened since December and the memory was distant.

Lucy immediately got on the phone and called Meg. There was a slightly accusatory tone in her voice as she complained to Meg that this information was not in my paperwork. She handed me the phone.

"Why didn't you put down a shellfish allergy?" Meg asked, not accusatory but clearly upset.

"I don't know that I have one. I only know of one allergy, and it's to sulfa. So it didn't occur to me."

Donor Girl

"Well, I should have still been informed of any potential allergy."
I felt like I was being slightly berated and didn't understand why.
Like my day wasn't bad enough.

"Well, what's the worst thing that can happen if I take the test?
Let's just do it," I said, trying to make everything better. Ever the
fixer, I wanted to fix it.

"You could die!" Lucy said in a very succinct tone.

Oh dear God! Can this day get any worse? So that's why Lucy
and Meg were so upset over my little error. Where's that
wonderful day that Michael promised me where I'd be treated like
a queen and everyone would bow down to the donor? No one was
bowing down. The only one close to falling to their knees was me!

"We'll just have to reschedule. Let me talk to Lucy," Meg said. I
felt like I had disappointed everyone. Once Meg and Lucy hung
up, Lucy explained that I'd have to come back another day after a
round of Benadryl and a steroid. This would keep me from having
a reaction to the dye. It turned out to be my fortune that this test
was scheduled last. Had it been first and Lucy not met with me, I
could have gone through with the test and had a horrible reaction.

I was quite distraught. I felt like I had let everyone down by not
being able to go through all of the tests. It was like I had somehow
failed. On top of that was the knowledge that I still had to come
back and get tested again. This day was bad enough. The thought
of coming back was horrific. I was ready for answers. Would I be
the donor or wouldn't I? I'm not good with the not knowing part.
I'm the type who would rather know news, even if it's bad, than be
left in limbo. I went into the waiting room and told Magda we
were finished for the day. On the way home, I told her all about
my horrible talk with the nurse and the possibility that had I done
the iodine test earlier, I could have died. Granted, it was a remote

Donor Girl

possibility; but nonetheless, it felt very real and was still, even if remotely, a possibility.

Magda was a source of great strength. She had actually brought some prayer books thinking that we could read them during our wait times. I just wasn't in the mood. She was very understanding and didn't press. Magda had been through so much herself, and there were times when she wasn't up to certain meditations and prayers. Once, while she was going through a rough time of it, one of our church members had asked if she would come in for a group healing. We aren't the kind of church that goes wild with that type of prayer, but we would all gather around her and pray because we all believe in prayer. My gut feeling was that Magda would not be comfortable with it, but I said I'd talk to her. As I thought, she was not comfortable with it. She hadn't come to terms with her illness to a point of being ready for something so monumental. However, she gave us permission to hold it for her. And when she wasn't able to make it to Sunday service before Christmas, and the praise team went to her house to Christmas carol for her, had we asked, she probably would have politely said no. But we didn't ask, and she was very appreciative. So I knew she'd understand that I wasn't able to handle prayer books that day. Prayer, yes. Prayer books, no. My concentration wasn't where it needed to be and I was feeling very self-involved at that moment. Prayer books don't usually applaud self-involvement. I needed to be applauded that day.

Magda reminded me again about how difficult her recovery from surgery had been. I believe that deep down, she didn't want me to go through with it because of her experience. While the last thing I wanted to hear, especially that day, was a negative surgery experience, I did appreciate her concern. It would have been difficult for her if something had happened to me post surgery and she hadn't informed me of her bad experience.

Donor Girl

When I arrived home after my hospital day, I was probably as low as I'd ever get during the entire experience. The counseling session; the medical assistant; the iodine-death scare; had all combined to make me feel scared, alone and doubting my decision. All along, my prayer had been that if this was God's will I would be the match. But now I needed to reach out to God in another way. One of my favorite passages in the Bible is Psalm 46:10: "Be still, and know that I am God." I needed to spend some time being still and hearing God talk to me and having Him heal me and help me find peace. I needed to be still. I'd been on this fast-moving treadmill and was running and running -- running scared, running hopeful, running with a purpose, running to save a life -- but always running. I was tired, worn out and needed to **BE STILL.**
When I first knew I had to reschedule the CT scan of my kidneys, I had tried to find the few days I was home and make one of them work. However, I figured there was no need to rush. I couldn't possibly schedule surgery until July, so other than the desire to know, there was no reason I couldn't wait.

I e-mailed Meg at the University of Maryland Medical Center and gave her my upcoming schedule.

From LAdams to MBaker: 4/19/2007 5:31 PM

**It was a pleasure meeting you today. You shocked me by saying you were over 40. I had you pegged in mid 30's at best. I apologize again for not having mentioned the possible issue with shrimp. I've never been told I'm allergic to shrimp or iodine and it never occurs to me unless someone specifically mentions it. On rare occasion, I will have a reaction but I can't even say if that's what I'm allergic to. But Lucy was very specific that it could kill me if I am and I did that test, which made me err on the side of caution. The following dates are one's I'm available to come back in:**

Donor Girl

Monday April 23rd
Tuesday May 1st - if it's in the afternoon, I fly back to
BWI that day
Friday May 11th - same as above

If none of those work, I do have some other days I can
do later in May. Thanks. Lee

4/19/07 From MBaker to LAdams:

You completely made my day-I'll be 45 very soon, must
be the vegan diet! Anyway, please don't worry about the
CT-I just felt badly that you were hungry all day for
nothing. I will have Priscilla reschedule tomorrow and
get back to you. Meg Baker RN, BSN

4/19/2007 7:38 PM From LAdams to MBaker:

When I come back in for the last test, is there any
chance I can meet with Nina? It was a little unsettling
to meet with someone who admittedly had never met
with a potential donor before. Although she was very
nice and did her best, it was a rather sterile Q&A that I
don't feel helped me have an understanding of the
possible emotional effects of live kidney donation. I
think that would be very helpful. Thanks. Lee

4/19/07 From MBaker to LAdams:

We can absolutely make that happen, not a problem.
Meg Baker RN, BSN

4/19/07 From LAdams to MBaker:

Donor Girl

Thanks. I think it would help. I'm feeling a little overwhelmed after today and that wasn't the best start. It kind of set a strange mood for the rest of the day. Michael raved about Nina so I feel like it might help me to talk to her. Glad I made your day. You do not look 45 at all! Lee

4/20/07 From LAdams to MBaker:

Did I mention that I really liked Dr. Cooper? I wish I'd had more time to talk with him. He was very comforting and reassuring. Definitely instills confidence.

Here is my schedule for the next few weeks. Just so you think I'm not crazy, this is how each day of my week starting tomorrow plays out. I will be home for a 3 day stretch starting on May 16. I leave again on May 22nd and will be out until June 6th.

Sorry my schedule is so inconvenient.

April 21-22 - Showcase in Baltimore MD
April 23rd - home
April 24 - 27 - Upstate New York and New England
April 28 - May 1 - Florida
May 2nd - May 4th - Central and Eastern PA
May 7 - Pittsburgh
May 8-9 - Ohio
May 10 - Kentucky
May 11th - fly home
May 13-15 - Las Vegas
May 16-18 – Home

Lee

Donor Girl

I requested waiting until I was back in town for longer than a day at a time, and Meg was fine with that. She understood that I needed some time.

My sister was devastated. She hated that I had such a bad experience at the hospital. She especially wanted me to tell someone about the story the medical assistant had told me but I was too overwhelmed to say anything at that point.

I remember coming home from the hospital that day and just sitting on the couch and wondering, "How can I do this?" I prayed and thought and prayed some more. I was in a state of shock and wasn't sure who to turn to. I couldn't really tell Randy what I was going through since he wasn't in favor of my choice, and it was so important for me not to upset him. He was not giving me a hard time about doing this or being negative. He was being quietly supportive, and I didn't want to upset him any further. I still hadn't told my parents that I was being tested, so I couldn't turn to them. I had to keep things limited with regards to my sister. It was her husband I was donating to, and it was upsetting enough for her.

I was encouraged to get on a Web site that had all kinds of information on kidney donation. I found a site that had true stories of donors. It had everything from positive success stories to stories that weren't so positive and were somewhat upsetting. But reading them all was important. I couldn't bury my head in the sand and only read the happy stories. It was important to be informed on all levels. Can you say Type A??

The Web site:
http://www.livingdonorsonline.org/experiences/experiences.htm
became an important source of communication for me. At the end

Donor Girl

of the stories, there are some donors willing to let you contact them via e-mail. I was in touch with roughly half a dozen donors who answered my questions and understood my situation. I remember reading one woman's story where she said, "I wish there was no such thing as kidney donation 'cause then I wouldn't have to consider doing it." I completely understood this person. That's exactly how I felt. I wanted to do this for Dave; I just wished there wasn't even the option to do it. Every so often, I'd read something that caused me concern and I'd contact Meg, Nina or Dr. Cooper about it. One such story led me to ask Meg the following:

4/24 From Lee Adams to Meg Baker:

**I've been on the recommended website trying to learn as much as possible and I received the following e-mail from a man who donated his kidney a couple of years ago. I'm copying it below. Was wondering if you could answer:**
**1) How often does this kind of surgery trigger something like fibromyalgia...and is it even true that it does?**
**2) Since my sister has such bad reactions to codeine and morphine, should I get tested for an allergy?**

**See story below:**

**Hi Lee,**
**I am 45 w/male. I feel that in my case It wasn't the act of donation but that the trauma of major surgery is known to trigger neuropathy. (fibromyalgia) I am allergic to morphine and when I was on the pump it made me terribly sick and hindered my recovery even more. An allergic reaction to narcotics can be deadly. I didn't realize how bad it can make you sick until years later I tried the fentanyl patch and the same thing happened**

again. I take neurontin and ultram for pain and provigil for energy and ambien for sleep. I would still do it all over again and I encourage you to go for it. I can't get anyone to listen but I feel so strongly that you should be tested for a morphine allergy before surgery. If people got a free buzz to find out, so what. I will always return your questions so don't be afraid to ask me or anyone out there who has donated, we are always glad to help.

4/26 From MBaker to LAdams:

Lee,
I spoke with Dr. Cooper regarding your concerns.....he has never heard of surgery triggering fibromyalgia. As far as allergies to codeine, morphine etc.....side effects such as nausea/vomiting are not really allergies, but agreeably are unpleasant. These things are easily managed in the post-op period should they occur, but patients aren't "pre-tested" so to speak. Some donors require morphine in the first 12-24 hours post-surgery, many do not, and do well with oral Percocet.

Again, all narcotics have the potential to cause nausea, especially if taken on an empty stomach, but all of this can be easily dealt with. Meg Baker RN, BSN

4/26 from LAdams to MBaker:

Thanks Meg. I am reading up on the websites like you recommended and when I have questions, I hope it's ok that I ask them. And thanks for helping my husband earlier in the week. He was at a loss when they asked for a blood sample. Poor guy...he isn't in favor of my doing this but he's trying so hard to be supportive. I really appreciate you helping him. Lee

Donor Girl

I was never made to feel like my questions were too stupid or ridiculous. I was always treated with respect. Meg was especially helpful to Randy. He had received a call about one of my blood samples and had no idea what they were asking about. The clinic gave him Meg's number, and he called her. She was very helpful and explained what he needed to do to get me where I needed to be and what information I needed to have. I hated him to be involved in any way as the entire process was very upsetting for him, and I appreciated Meg's help even more because of that. When he later saw Meg and realized she was "hot," he liked her even more!

I finally decided to tell Meg about the incident with the assistant. My sister convinced me that it was important other people about to go through surgery don't hear the same horror story. So I emailed Meg and told her what was said. As always, she was very supportive.

4/23/2007 11:16:29 A.M.

**Lee,**

**I am very glad that you did share this conversation with me, and please know that it will be addressed at the supervisory level. Clearly the conversation was unprofessional, inappropriate and insensitive. As previously discussed, when we reschedule your CT angio, I will schedule an appointment with Nina our donor social worker. I think it also would be a good idea if we set aside time for you to meet with Dr. Cooper again as well.**

**Again, I am very glad you shared this with me. My job is to be your advocate throughout this process, and I want you to feel completely comfortable every step of the way. Meg Baker RN, BSN**

Donor Girl

## May 2007

Meg had my window of opportunity to come back and see Nina, Dr. Cooper and get the CT angiogram. I received the following e-mail on May 4:

In a message dated 5/4/2007 Meg Baker writes:

**Hi Lee,**

**I have arranged your testing as follows for 5/18/07:**

**8:30am   CT angiogram   (I will  call in your pre-medication orders earlier that week, you will start first dose at 7:30 pm on 5/17/07.)**

**You   should   arrive   at   8:00am   to   get   "red plate."**

**11:00am   Nina Schroder Living Donor Social Worker (Transplant Office, 29 S. Greene St, Ste  200)**

**1:00pm  Dr. Cooper (Transplant Office, 29 S. Greene St, Ste 200)**

**Have a good  weekend.**

I was proud of myself that I now knew what a red plate was!

My next appointment was set up for May 18.  I would have almost 3 weeks to get on with my life and pretend that nothing was going on in my life that would result in scars and missing body parts.

Donor Girl

Again, the tough part of this whole process was that I really couldn't confide in many people. Even though Randy and Kelly knew about it, they both didn't really want me to do it. So if I'd expressed any reluctance, they would have attached to that and tried to talk me out of it. I couldn't tell my parents. I didn't really want to talk about it at work too much, although my bosses needed to know. I later found out that Nina was very concerned about my lack of family support. That can be cause to recommend rejecting a potential donor. I was fortunate in that I had people to turn to: my best friends, Jodi and Sandi, my church congregation and oddly enough, the women at Curves. When I worked out at Curves, I would talk to the women about my surgery. They were wonderful. They shared surgery experiences from gall bladder to C-sections, all of which would cause similar scars and hopefully, similar recoveries. As well, there were high school friends like Jim Ormord, my lifelong pseudo brother, who called one day during all the testing. When I told him what was going on, he was overwhelmed by what I was doing. He expressed such a heartfelt respect for me that I was then overwhelmed. He wanted to visit me in the hospital which I managed to talk him out of, but he continued to call and check on me. My high school friends Phyllis and Libby would also turn out to be a part of my support group.

It's odd who you find yourself confiding in sometimes. I had talked to one of my PD's and close friend, John Shomby, from WGH in Virginia Beach. He was a true friend through this ordeal and an excellent sounding board. Shortly before surgery I was visiting my programmers in Boston at WKLB. Mike and Ginny were extremely supportive and sent me a small "zen" box filled with a beach scene to help me stay calm. I had chosen to tell Jason Aldean's booking agent, Kevin Neal. He's someone I was close to and could talk with. He kept my confidence and would often call or e-mail to ask how I was doing. His support and friendship were invaluable. Add in my friend, Erik, and my cousin, Tommy, and these were the people that let me talk nonstop about my potential

Donor Girl

surgery. I'm sure it got to the point of nausea, but they remained patient.

I had recently met a woman, Laurie Smith, who had been through an illness and remembered how her husband was somewhat left out while she got all the attention. Yet he suffered in his own way. She made a gift bag for my sister that included movies and chocolates and reminded her that she had to make special time for herself as well. When I gave it to Kelly, she cried.

And although I was trying hard to spare Randy's feelings, he was there for me when I needed him to be. He always offered a hug or a word of encouragement. He still didn't want me to do it, but he was supporting my decision. In fact, Randy took the time to get a blood test himself thinking maybe he could donate instead of me. He thought his blood type was B- but also discovered he was O+. Unfortunately, the doctor also diagnosed him with high blood pressure and put him on medication. As we learned with Michael, this would make Randy most likely unable to donate to Dave without putting himself at some risk. I did appreciate and respect his willingness to get tested to spare me. That's love!

I had recently reconnected with some of my former college friends. God has such an amazing way of putting the people you need in your life there at just the right time. Freshman year at Shippensburg University in Lackhove Hall was one of the best times of my life. I met Jodi that year and we became roommates. We hung out with a group of guys from the floor below us and two became especially good friends. Brook Bergey was just plain cool. There's no other way to describe him. Brook and I were never romantic but were just very close. He told me recently he hasn't had a good massage since I gave him one in freshman year! Brook left Shippensburg after our freshman year and moved out to Las Vegas. I went to visit him while he was there. When Brook returned from Vegas, we sporadically kept in touch. Another friend of ours, Eric Steinman, remained close. It was after I had

Donor Girl

graduated from college that I found out from Eric that Brook was in a car accident and was in the hospital paralyzed from the waist down. I went to see him in the hospital, but Brook was pretty out of it. Months later, I invited both Eric and Brook to my wedding. Eric was able to make it; Brook was not. Over the next 20 years, my communication with Brook and Eric would be sporadic at best, but we always stayed in touch in one way or another. In 2007, I was not only in touch with them, but I had decided to visit them. I'd seen Brook within the last 8 years, but hadn't seen Eric since 1987. It was fun visiting both of them. Brook and his wife, Laurie, are very strong Christians. Just by chance they knew a couple that had gone through a kidney transplant. The female needed a kidney and her boyfriend (now husband) was willing to donate but wasn't a match. He was willing to do the exchange program though, and they found another couple that they were cross matched with. Not only were Brook and Laurie willing to put us all in touch, but they gave me a very important piece of information that I had not been told. I double checked that information with Meg and found out it was indeed true.

5/6/2007 12:28 AM:   To MBaker from LAdams:

**Meg,**
**Sorry I'm such a  pain, but as I hear things, I ask them so I don't forget.**

**1)  Can I bank my own blood prior to surgery?**
**2)  I heard that if a kidney donor ever needs a kidney transplant in the future, they  automatically are at the top of the  transplant list. Is this  true?  If so, very cool!**

In a message dated 5/7/2007   MBaker writes;

**Lee,**
**Banking your own blood is not an issue; risk of needing**

a transfusion is minimal so it isn't done for this type of surgery. Also, you did hear correctly that if a donor should experience renal failure in the future, he/she would be at the top of the list.
Meg  Baker RN, BSN Transplant Coordinator

5/7/2007 8:43 AM I wrote:  From LAdams:

Sorry for all the questions.  I warned you I was Type A! haha  I'll be asking things as they wheel me into surgery.

That's great to hear on the donor list.  It makes sense, I just never thought about it.  I have some friends who were both donor/recipient, had it done at Hopkins, they did the exchange program and all 4 are doing great. Very inspiring.  Thanks Meg.  Lee

5/7  From MBaker:

Any time, and I totally understand Type A tendencies. I'm one myself!  Meg

So, while it seems like back door security, there was a slight comfort in knowing if my remaining kidney were to fail, I'd go straight to the head of the class. I traveled extensively during the next three weeks.

Due to my potential allergy, I had to take a round of drugs before doing the CT scan.  They were as follows:

5/17/07   7:30 P.M.           Prednisone 50mg
5/17/07   11:30 P.M.         Prednisone 50mg
5/18/07:  7:30 A.M.          Prednisone 50 mg and Benadryl 25mg
5/18/07: 6 hours after scan  Prednisone 50mg and Benadryl 25mg

## Donor Girl

When I was ready to return to the hospital for my scan, after taking the steroids and Benadryl, I needed someone to go with me. I probably could have driven myself, but with taking Benadryl, it can make me drowsy. So driving wasn't a great idea.

My sister was insistent on taking the day off and being with me. She had felt badly that she couldn't go with me before, especially with how horrible it was. I was still dreading this procedure since it involved a needle and dye. My sister is the one person in my life that I can feel 100% comfortable in front of. Siblings just have that ability to be as mean or as nice as the situation warrants and still have unconditional love.

So Kelly and I headed off first thing that morning. We talked on the drive down, as sisters will, about everything under the sun. Before I knew it, we were there. I checked in and got my red plate, and this time knew it was a red card. I know it's called a plate, but it's a card! My first appointment was the CT scan. The CT scan was necessary to determine if I actually had two kidneys, and if I did, were they in good enough shape to support two people. This was the final test that could possibly give me my out. If either of my kidneys were in any way not right, there would be no donation.

I had an IV put in so they could administer the dye through my body. They told me it would feel like I was peeing myself. Lovely. Next, I would be put into a cylinder where I would feel rather claustrophobic, but I wouldn't have to go in beyond my neck. Having my head left out was definitely easier than had I gone all the way in. I had to hold my breath until a little recorded voice told me to release it. I did this a few times, and before I knew it, the test was over. This test would determine whether I would donate to Dave or not. This was the final deciding factor. If there were any issues with my kidneys -- such as I only had one, or the arteries weren't attached correctly, or I had a U-shaped kidney -- then I was ruled out.

Donor Girl

When the technician came out, he wasn't able to give me any official information. But he said, "Wow, you have two great kidneys. They were so perfect, they were in there waving."

So much for my "out." I responded, "Was one of them holding a sign saying, 'Take him, not me?'"

He laughed out loud and said, "No one has ever asked that before. That's funny."

I was left wondering why I thought my kidneys were male? "Take **HIM**?" Why not, "**HER**?" What was with that?

Kelly and I headed out to have some lunch. I wasn't able to eat before the test, so we went to the little deli. I was quite hungry by then.

At 11:00 A.M., I went up to meet with Nina, and she was everything Michael had said she'd be. She was adorably cute, with curly hair and a beautiful smile. She immediately put me at ease, and having already read my answers from the previous counselor's notes, she was able to get straight to the issues. We talked about everything from my family, my parents, and my husband to my career. It's an awkward situation because you want to be honest, but you don't want to say anything that will cause them to say you can't donate. She asked if I completely understood the risks. I laughed and told her I was a "worst case scenario person." I told her, "Three things can go wrong. I could die. Surgery could go from laparoscopic to open surgery. And third, the kidney could get rejected. I've already figured that one of those will happen. If I can handle the worst case, I can handle the best case. So something bad will happen. And I've accepted that. Is this a bad thing?" I was wondering if that type of attitude had just disqualified me!

## Donor Girl

"Not at all," Nina answered. "I'm more comfortable with you recognizing the dangers and accepting them. I worry about the people who tell me they can't even think about what could go wrong. It overwhelms them. They worry me." She said she sometimes has people who put their hands over their ears not wanting to hear any potential things that could go wrong.

Meg had wanted me to visit with her between my 11:00 A.M. meeting with Nina and my 1:00 P.M. meeting with Dr. Cooper, but Nina and I talked for so long that I barely made my 1:00 appointment on time. Michael had been so very right about Nina. She was wonderful. She made me feel that my decision would be right no matter what it was. She wanted me to know that there would be no shame in saying, "I can't do this." It's an amazingly difficult decision to make and the outcome is unknown. It is true that all the statistics point to living a long, healthy life with one kidney; however, until something does or doesn't go wrong, I won't really know. If on my deathbed, my kidney is still working and hasn't caused me any problems, then all is well. However, if my remaining kidney were to ever become diseased or nonfunctioning, I have no backup plan. God provided us with a backup plan when He created us with two kidneys. I was making the decision to give up my backup plan.

Nina wanted to know how I saw myself in the family hierarchy. Was I the black sheep? The peacekeeper? The problem solver? I definitely saw myself as the problem solver. Not to say I haven't caused a fair amount of problems in the family environment myself. Haven't we all? But I do try to fix things that are wrong. I'm pragmatic in nature and am known for my strength. I don't like to show emotion in public and prefer to never be seen crying. I've actually been asked to read eulogies at funerals since I'm the one who's least likely to cry. So, pragmatic problem solver would probably be my description.

Donor Girl

Nina and I also discussed my faith and how that would play into my decision. I told her that my sister had called me to ask if I saw the kidney donation as "my calling?" I did not. My response was: "If it was a calling, I think I'd feel the need to donate to anyone. A calling isn't something you are needed to do but is something you are led to do. I didn't wake up one day, like some people do, and want to donate a kidney to anyone who was sick. But I did strongly believe that if this is God's will, I will be the one that is chosen to donate. And I will follow God's will." My prayer every night was: "If this is what you want me to do God then I will be the one healthy enough to do it." I knew I'd follow God's will. Kelly said she shared that with Dave and he cried.

I left my appointment with Nina with her phone number and e-mail address in hand. She promised if I needed her at any time, I was to contact her and she'd be there for me. This would prove to be true.

I made it back to where my sister was waiting and barely sat down before Dr. Cooper showed up. Dr. Cooper and I went into the exam room. He once again explained the surgery and told me that in rare circumstances, surgery does have to go to open surgery versus laparoscopic. But he reiterated that it rarely happened with someone like me. I didn't have any scar tissue from past surgeries; I wasn't overweight; I had no risk factors. He assured me that the nurse had been spoken to, and due to her lack of understanding that what she had done was wrong, she was moved away from working with donor patients.

He asked if I had any questions. I had no questions, but I did have one request. I think it was the first request like this he'd ever had. "I brought a Sharpie marker with me and would like you to draw on me where my scars will be," I said with a straight face.

"Well, that's the first time I've ever had this request!" We walked over to the exam table, and I lifted my shirt above my navel and lowered my jeans below my pubic bone. I remember from my last

Donor Girl

exam that this was where the incisions would be. But I felt like I needed a visual for when I got home. I thought markings would help me further wrap my mind around what was going to happen. Invisible lines shown with his finger would not translate when I was looking in the mirror and trying on low-rise jeans and bathing suits.

"I really don't want to draw on you in permanent marker, so why don't I just show you where they'll be?" he asked.

"Well, unless you and your hands are coming home with me to try on clothes that really won't be effective. And I assure you it's not permanent marker. I see breasts get signed by Sharpies all the time, and it does wash off."

He looked at me and said, "What in the world do you do for a living?" I laughed and told him I was a record promoter and that women were always requesting their breasts get signed during Meet and Greets.

So, against his wishes, he drew on me with the Sharpie. The meeting was short, but it reinforced the fact that I trusted him as a surgeon and liked him as a person. Dr. Cooper gave me his card with an office number and e-mail address, and he assured me that I could contact him any time and he'd respond. Kelly and I decided to stop on our way out and get a smoothie. I figured that's a healthy treat. We had left something in the upstairs office, so we had to go back up and find it. We ran into Dr. Cooper in the hall, and he asked, "Is that healthy?" when he saw me sipping my smoothie. In fairness, it looks a lot like a milkshake.

"It's fruit!" I said laughing. This had been a much better visit than the first one. This *was* the warm and fuzzy that Michael had told me about.

Donor Girl

I followed up my appointment with e-mails to my "team." I started with one to Nina.

**05/18/07 8:49 PM: To NSchroder from LAdams:**

**Nina, Thank you for spending so much time with me today. I came away feeling so much better than after my last visit. I didn't even need a zanax when I got home! You are an absolute delight and it's no wonder Michael thought so highly of you. He assured me you would make me feel very comfortable, and he was correct.**

**I would be happy to talk with you about my industry anytime. The funny thing is, I almost went back to school for a psychology degree. What you do I find amazing. So I guess the grass IS always greener! You have a profound effect on people's lives. That is so rewarding. Again, thank you. Dr. Cooper drew his lines and I tried on my bathing suits. One was border line but the other one, you couldn't see the scar at all. So I guess this 42 year old can wear bikinis for a little while longer! haha Hope you have a blessed weekend.**

**Lee Adams**

And to Dr. Cooper...05/18/07 8:55 PM I wrote:

**Thank you for taking the extra time with me today and talking in further detail about the surgery and risks. I told everyone that you said I was"one of the healthiest people you've seen." Of course, I followed it with "THAT my friends will get you one less kidney!" I thought being called healthy was better than boring, so I went with it. ;-)**

Donor Girl

**I tried on my bikinis when I got home and having the lines drawn was a big help. One was right on the border and the other you couldn't see it at all! So I guess I don't have to give them up quite yet! Is it just me, or does this make me sound extremely shallow?? I've been in the music biz too long.**

**Again, thank you very much for the time. You, Meg and Nina are a wonderful support team and have made me feel much more comfortable. Have a wonderful weekend. Lee Adams**

I'd read somewhere that a very high percentage of patients cannot reach their doctors via e-mail. It was up to nearly 80%. However, as he promised, Dr. Cooper responded almost immediately. And this particular e-mail didn't necessarily warrant a request. Yet he sent a quick follow-up anyway.

5/19 From Dr. Cooper to LAdams:

**The pleasure was mine! Enjoy your weekend as well.**

**Matthew Cooper, MD**

I remember having only one real serious conversation with Dave about the donation. I had called the house to talk to Kelly, but she wasn't home. Dave answered. Dave and I tend to have awkward conversation with one another, so it's difficult to remember how it even started. Dave knew I had just been to the hospital for final testing, and it looked like I passed everything.

"I know those tests were difficult, and I'm really sorry you had to go through them," Dave said.

"They weren't really that bad, and I like the team I'm working with. They are very helpful. I really like my doctor," I said.

Donor Girl

"Lee, I don't really know what to say. Thank you isn't enough, but I don't know how to express something like this. It isn't easy knowing you need someone's kidney."

"I don't think either of us do, Dave. It just is what it is. Are you scared?"

"Very," Dave said. "You?"

"Same. You know Dave, there's no way I can know what you are going through, and there's no way you can know what I'm going through. But we're in it together."

"Just know that it really means a lot that you are willing to do this."

"I do."

That was about the only time Dave and I really discussed it. At various times we'd talk about being scared, and as the weeks got closer, we'd count them down. But that was our most in-depth conversation.

I was getting ready for a trip to Hawaii, and my nerves were frayed. It's tough to leave the record promotion business for a week at any time of year. It's a 24/7 industry, and radio stations are tracked 24 hours per day, 7 days per week. Our music charts are based on radio airplay. There are roughly 125 country radio stations across the U.S. chosen as "reporting stations." There are two major charts in the industry, and every song that is heard on a "countdown" or given #1, Top 5 or Top 10 status comes from these charts. In a nutshell, the songs being played the most, by the most reporting stations, are the highest on the chart. So every day, every hour, and even every 15 minutes, we can watch our songs move up or down the charts. We were just about to release a new song from a new act, Crossin Dixon.

Donor Girl

When I had booked the Hawaii cruise a year earlier, there was no way of knowing that we'd be releasing a new song the same week I'd be leaving for vacation. There was also no way of knowing I'd be in the middle of testing to be a kidney donor. I was about to leave for a dream vacation at a very stressful time in my life. The trip was being sponsored by KIIM in Tucson, and our artist, Craig Morgan, was the performing country act.

So not only was I under stress, but I felt I had to put my best face forward since I had people that I work with on the cruise. While it was a wonderful vacation, looking back, I can see how stressed I was and how I really didn't enjoy it as much as I would have otherwise. Work stress, surgery stress... was all on my mind, but I did try to step back and realize I was on a "trip of a lifetime" and should take a deep breath and enjoy it.

When I first left the hospital on the 19th, I had told Meg I didn't want to know if it was a "go" for surgery. I wanted to wait until I returned from Hawaii. But the truth is, I'm too Type A to *not* know the answer. So, I ended up asking her anyway. The last test I had to pass was the CT angiogram. From what the guy had said about my kidneys being "perfect," I assumed it was a go. But I didn't know for sure until I heard it from Meg.

On May 22, four days before I left for vacation, I e-mailed Meg.

5/22/2007 1:56 PM I wrote: To MBaker from LAdams:

**Any reports from my CT Scan? Thanks. Lee Adams**

In a message dated 5/22/2007 MBaker writes:

**Your CT scan was perfectly lovely, textbook anatomy, which doesn't happen all that often! Not engraved in stone, but per your request, I have penciled in dates for Pre-Admission testing 7/5/07 and Surgery 7/11/07.**

**Details/confirmation to follow, but does that sound ok with your schedule? Meg Baker RN, BSNT**

5/22: From LAdams to MBaker:

**Sounds good to me. It's on the calendar. I'm going to frame that e-mail...that I have a textbook anatomy. Lee**

So there it was in writing. I stared at the e-mail and tried to digest the information. I was donating a kidney. Someone would take a knife to my abdomen, cut it open and take out a body organ. Wow! Had I completely lost my mind? NO! Just a kidney. Lord, help me. Literally, Lord, help me!

I now had a tentative date for my final pre-admission testing and a July 11 surgery date. I had chosen the dates for a couple of reasons, some of them very selfish, some not. First, summer is my favorite season. I live on the Potomac River, and my husband and I are water people. We boat, water ski, and spend every possible moment enjoying warm weather. I didn't want to miss an entire season.

However, I believed that it's easier to heal in warm weather than cold weather, so I wanted to allow myself 6 to 8 weeks of warm weather to heal. Also, my sister is a teacher and has summers off. So I figured if we had surgery in mid-July, it would give her 6 weeks to take care of Dave without having to worry about working. Also, my work schedule had a three-week break where I didn't have to travel or ask anyone to fill in for me. The promoters travel so much in their own territory that I didn't have the heart to ask anyone to cover for me.

Other than informing my bosses, I had kept the surgery fairly quiet, not wanting to tell the rest of the staff until absolutely necessary. Also, in our industry, we have what are called "Hot Faxes." They come out every Tuesday, after we see the final

Donor Girl

music charts on Monday night. Not only do they give a report card of what the Top 50 to 60 songs are doing on the charts and on radio, but they are also filled with the latest news and gossip from the country music industry. If someone is out due to any kind of illness or accident, it usually shows up in the Hot Fax. I'm a rather private person, and I was absolutely determined **NOT** to have my kidney donation in the Hot Fax. Only one of my artists knew about it, and that was Craig. I had a show the day before leaving for vacation with BBR's female act, Megan Mullins, and I decided to tell her.

Megan is like a daughter/best friend to me. I've worked with her since she was 15, and she is one of the dearest and most talented girls I've ever met. She has a scorching high IQ; graduated from high school at 15; and has been performing since she was 3. At less than 2 years of age, she saw her brother learning the violin and wanted to learn, too. The teacher quickly realized that at 18 months of age, Megan understood the technique, and she started teaching her. Megan and her brother, Marcus, started performing bluegrass with their dad at the ages of 3 and 5, respectively.

I'm often asked if I'm either Megan's sister or mother. At 21 years her senior, I could easily be her mom. We resemble each other in our hair type, hair color and petite figures. We often joke about the time she was playing violin for BBR's female act, Sherrie Austin, and a woman came up behind Megan and kept saying, "Lee! Lee! Lee!" Finally, Megan turned around and the woman said, "Oh, I'm sorry. I thought you were Lee."

Megan calls me by my given name, Lilli, and walked up to me and said, "Lilli, I've got great news. You apparently have the tush of a seventeen-year-old." She told me the story of the woman thinking she was me from behind.

I said, "Either that, Megan, or you have the tush of a thirty-eight-year old." We laughed.

Donor Girl

"I like my idea better, Lilli."

I replied, "So do I!"

I sat down with Megan and her guitar player, JB, and told them about my upcoming surgery. JB is a very kind, considerate guy whom I've known since he played in Chad Brock's band a couple of years before. He always seems to have this amazingly caring nature about him. Recently, his twenty-year-old son had passed away, so JB was going through a lot of personal emotions. When I told him and Megan that I was going to be a kidney donor, I was rather surprised to hear JB say, "I don't think you should do this, Lee. It sounds dangerous for you." Megan didn't say much, but she hugged me and told me she would pray for me. I explained that I felt I needed to do this for my sister, niece and nephew and, so far, I was the only one healthy enough to do it. I could tell they respected me, but they were wary. With JB's recent loss, it wasn't really all that surprising to have him react as he did.

It hadn't been but a few days before when we were out on our boat with a friend who had just had gall bladder surgery. When I told him about my upcoming surgery, I was surprised to hear him say, "Wow, Lee, I would think twice about doing that." I explained all the reasons I was doing it and all the thought and prayer I'd put into it. But he remained adamant that I shouldn't do it. It kind of left me a bit unnerved, and I was surprised that he would put a negative opinion out there like that. But I let it go. A few weeks later, I received the following email:

In a message dated 7/3/2007 DKeeseman writes:

**Lee**

**Not sure I would get to see you before next week but I want to wish you the best of luck. I have given our conversation a lot of thought over these last few weeks**

and I want you to know I think this is one of the most unselfish things anyone can possibly do! The more I thought about this the more I realized the meaning of family and what it means to you. Even, if for some reason this would not happen just the thought and offer is as large as it gets! My hat is off to you and once again best of luck and a speedy recovery.

I replied:

What a sweet note. Thank you. It's not all unselfish. I expect some amazing Christmas gifts from here on out. haha Nothing means more to me than family and especially Will and Kayla. They need a healthy dad and for some reason, God seems to have chosen me as the one to help with that. I trust in Him and I trust the doctors. We have our last blood tests today and if nothing gets "flagged" then it's a go for next Wed.

Many thanks again for your thoughts and good wishes.

I had told one of my dearest friends since kindergarten, Phyllis, about it a few weeks before. She's an RN, and has always been there to answer questions for my sister and me whenever there was an illness in the family. My sister had a miscarriage prior to getting pregnant with her son. When she became pregnant with Will, she started spotting. Kelly told me, "There's nothing I can do about it but pray." I called Phyllis, and she told me there were medications Kelly could take and to have her call her OB/GYN immediately. I called Kell, and she called Dr. Sidh, who put her on the medication. Eight months later, Will was born. I don't know if the medication made a difference or not, but Phyllis possibly gave us lifesaving information for Will as a fetus. Phyllis knew Dave needed a donation, but she didn't know I was going to be the donor. When I told her, I didn't hear a response. I was on a cell phone and thought I'd lost service. "Phyllis? Are you there?"

Donor Girl

I heard a meek voice say, "Yes."

I asked, "What's wrong?"

She answered, "I'm crying."

I laughed as I hadn't expected that response. "Why are you crying?"

"Because it's the most selfless thing I've ever heard of," she answered. Phyllis is like a counselor in her way of thinking and expressing things. As a teen, I would leave my Episcopalian Church service in the morning and drive up to her non-denominational Christian Church for a rousing sermon. Her pastor, Brother Collins, was from Trinidad and had a booming voice with a strong accent. When he gave testimony, you listened. She also had the coolest youth group, and we couldn't wait for Sunday nights to attend. Phyllis did as much for my Christianity as anyone, save for my parents.

I told Phyllis about how some people weren't being very supportive of my decision. She answered, "They're not being supportive because they're concerned for you out of love. You have to respect that they love you that much. They don't know David, but they know and love you."

Wow! I hadn't thought of it that way. I kept those words with me so when people didn't support my decision, I realized it was out of concern for me and respected it. Phyllis had needed brain surgery a few years before and definitely understood my fear of surgery. Being in the medical profession, she understood her own situation better than most. Sometimes ignorance is bliss. It was calming to talk to someone who'd had her own surgical experience, not to mention who could assure me that kidney donation is regarded as safe for the donor. Phyllis would end up being a huge help to me in the hospital.

Donor Girl

# Hawaiian Vacation

The day after Megan's show, Randy and I left for California. We flew into L.A. and stayed with another one of my lifelong friends, Libby, the only person I ever became blood sisters with. We would only be there for one night before flying from L.A. to Hawaii.

Libby had cancer when we were both 37. Her husband, Dave, called and started the conversation with, "Everything will eventually be ok." That's never a good way to start a conversation. Then he continued to tell me that Libby had been having issues with her throat closing and thought it was due to allergies. She finally went to the doctor and discovered she had a fast growing malignant tumor in her throat that if left for another two weeks, might have killed her. She was diagnosed with non-Hodgkins lymphoma and put on an excruciating regimen of radiation and chemotherapy. Libby handled this better than most people handle a cold.

She laughed about losing her hair and said it made showering in the morning much easier. "Two minutes and I'm done! Nothing to comb through or mess with." When she talked about her wig, she said, "I'd rather not wear it. I sit in my office and have it on the desk beside me. I only put it on because it makes other people uncomfortable to see my bald head." This included her children. So she would begrudgingly wear the wig. And she said this while laughing. She was warned that chemo might cause her to go into early menopause. "Great," she replied, "I don't plan to have any more children, and I'm tired of messing with a period." Her doctor tried to explain that early menopause isn't a good thing, but Libby didn't see it that way. She saw the positive angles. This is probably a big part of the reason that Libby is alive and well today.

Donor Girl

When I told Libby and her husband, Dave, about my decision to donate, Libby responded with a positive response full of wonder at the idea. She immediately got a huge smile on her face and said, "Lee, that's wonderful." For someone who always sees the glass half full, Lib felt this was an honor and something to be embraced with a smile. While it's always an honor to save a life, I didn't quite feel the way Libby seemed to think I should. She would have embraced this whole thing and gone into surgery with a big beautiful smile on her face saying, "I have two if anyone else needs one while I'm here!"

I was still hoping another answer would come through. Of course, I didn't want to face the fact that the only other answer would be someone dies who matches Dave 6 out of 6. I didn't want someone to die!

We spent a wonderful night with Lib and her family. They had recently moved to California and were just north of L.A. Their house was very nice with a beautiful pool and gorgeous view. Dave is a musician and has taken on the role of primary caretaker of their two children, Anna and David. Libby is a CPA and has moved her way up through the industry to be a controller. Dave and the kids had taken up surfing and loved it. Libby was still working to resolve some physical issues following her cancer treatment, but was hoping to take the sport up soon. We only had the one night before we had to fly out to Honolulu.

The first day in Honolulu was great. We had decided to go in a day before the cruise left to enjoy some land time on our own. We were to meet up with our friend, Erik, the same one from Raleigh who was one of the first people to know about my potential surgery. I remained surprised by how supportive he was. Erik can be a bit sarcastic and jokes that it's "always about him." I didn't expect him to be so open-minded to me doing something so altruistic.

Donor Girl

I was also surprised to realize Waikiki Beach looked a lot like Fort Lauderdale. It was a slightly disturbing realization. We met up with Erik at the hotel, and we all walked to the market along the beach, and then had a nice dinner on the deck of the hotel overlooking Waikiki Beach.

The next day, we met for breakfast and decided to take surfing lessons before leaving for the cruise. Now *that* I've never done in Fort Lauderdale! We had a quick lesson on the beach before heading into the water. We were all able to stand on the board by the second try, and while the waves weren't big, it was exciting. And we were able to say we surfed on Waikiki Beach. The instructor kept asking, "How much do you all work out that you caught on to this so quickly?" I don't know if he was vying for a bigger tip or was being honest, but it made us feel good.

I later saw the photo and asked Randy, "Where's the wave?" I swear when I was on it, it felt like there was a 20' wave back there. The picture shows a ripple that is barely bigger than the boat wake I ski behind! Nonetheless, I surfed in Hawaii and have the photos to prove it!

Later that day, we met up with Craig Morgan and his family on the ship. It was to be a big trip for his family with four of his children, one of their friends, and his daughter's boyfriend and parents. We were all excited about diving in Maui. Craig's oldest children and wife had just become certified, and we had a trip planned for Molokini Crater the next day.

When we arrived at the dive site, we were shocked to see the bottom so clearly and so close. "How far down to the bottom?" We asked the dive master. It looked *so* close.

"About seventy-five feet," he replied. Holy cow! It literally looked to be about 15 feet down; the water was so clear. We had a wonderful dive, encountering sea turtles, sharks, and an enormous amount of fish and coral. It was a wonderful day in Maui, and we were all refreshed and thrilled. We would do two dives that day before heading back to the ship.

The worst part about trying to vacation at this time was the stress I was experiencing. Between the pending surgery and the upcoming single release, it was difficult to relax. You never truly relax as a record promoter, even when on vacation. And with the upcoming surgery, there was a certain cloud hanging over my time in Hawaii. However, I also found that telling people about it helped. I'd tried to keep it a secret for so long, but now that it was close, I told people. Their response was always one of awe and respect. Everyone asked a million questions and then questioned their own ability to do it. It's always nice to hear good things about yourself. When people -- both those you know and complete strangers -- say, "Wow, you are amazing for doing that," you feel yourself stand a little taller; walk a little straighter; smile a little bigger. Maybe I could do this!

With the five-hour time change from the East Coast, I was getting up at 4 or 5 in the morning and logging onto my computer. I had cell service most of the time and was able to call my radio stations to try and get them to add the Crossin Dixon single, "Guitar Slinger." I was working for about 3 to 4 hours almost every morning. Then we'd get off the boat and do something exhilarating.

Hawaii was amazing. We took a helicopter ride over an active volcano in Hilo; enjoyed a luau; went scuba diving in Maui and Kona; kayaked to a waterfall in Kauia; and completed a zip line and ropes course through the Hawaiian jungle. We scaled 60 feet up a climbing wall; did a ropes course 45 feet in the air and jumped off a 40" platform, trusting that the ropes would hold us.

When I was in Kona, I saw a ring similar to one I'd seen the year before in Carmel, California. At the time, I'd thought, "I cannot justify spending that much money on a ring." So I didn't buy it. When I saw a similar ring in Kona, it was even more expensive. But I had made a decision the month prior to surgery that I wasn't going to deny myself anything. If I wanted a Mountain Dew, I'd have one. Chocolate, absolutely. McDonalds fries? I'm in! So when I saw the ring, I thought, "I'm giving up a kidney and not getting a dime for it. I deserve this ring." And I bought it. I refer to it as my kidney ring and have never regretted treating myself. It's a gorgeous tanzanite/diamond/fire opal ring that is very unique. Unique is good, right?

For Craig, this was a working vacation. He was the performing artist on the KIIM Radio Country Cruise. So a couple of nights during the week, Craig would perform for KIIM's listeners. On the last night, he invited his daughter's boyfriend up to sing with him. His daughter, Alex, was horrified. "But he doesn't sing!" she said of her boyfriend. They then invited Alex up to help. When she got onstage, it was planned that her boyfriend would propose to her. As he got down on one knee, she said, "But my dad's right there." Slowly, Alex put it together that it was pre-planned, and Craig and his wife, Karen, had given their blessing. It was a wonderful moment to be a part of.

As with most great vacations, the time went way too fast, and before we knew it, we were flying back to Baltimore. Back to Baltimore and back to surgery. It was now the end of May, and I was down to 6 weeks.

Two weeks after our return, Randy went out of town, and I was alone. I was up late and felt distressed, so I decided to e-mail Nina. By chance, she was on her computer late, and having her e-mail me back and "talk" me through my distress was another of God's blessings.

I had been asked to participate in a study that would compare sisters, one who had been a kidney donor and one who hadn't. I really wanted to do it, but it required a lot of pre-surgery testing, and I just didn't feel I could go through one more medical test. I finally made the decision not to do it and e-mailed Nina.

06/19/07 10:27 PM I wrote to NSchroder:

**Nina, Just to follow up, I don't think I'll be doing the study. I was very into doing it until they called and told me I'd have to go through an entire day of testing BEFORE surgery! Not only do I not want to ask for anymore time off work, but I cannot put myself through anything between now and July 11th. With it being just 3 weeks away, I'm already feeling enough anxiety without adding a day of needles and blood draws. I was actually appalled that they asked! I told them I'd sign any paperwork releasing all of my tests that have already been done, but they insisted they needed separate tests that would include IV's, etc. It just was too overwhelming. I feel like all my energy has to be put towards the surgery and I can't be focused on anything else. I feel badly as I'd like to help them learn as much as they can. But right now, I'm putting myself first. Just wanted to let you know. Thanks. Lee**

Much to my surprise and appreciation, I immediately got a response:

In a message dated 6/19/2007 nschroder writes:

**Dear Lee,**

**Absolutely, no worries about this. You most certainly need to do what is best for you and it sounds like you need to eliminate anything that may cause you**

additional worry.  Are you doing ok?   Do you need to talk? Please let me know and we will set something up.

**Sincerely,  Nina**

Getting her e-mail was like getting a lifesaver thrown to a drowning person.  I reached for it, grabbed it, hung on and didn't want to let go.

**06/19/07 11:06 PM:  To NSchroder...**

You are working too late! I'm doing ok. I'm just starting to have some anxiety as it's down to 3 weeks from tomorrow.  It might be regular female cycle stuff too. Mine have been off kilter lately so my emotions are a bit more erratic.  I re-read some e-mails from other donors and was relieved to see that many of them mentioned feeling scared prior to surgery. I guess by nature of the fact that we are healthy enough to donate, we also have very little experience with being sick and with hospitals, surgeries, etc.  So it's more of an unknown.  I'm just ready to be where they are! On the back side counseling someone else about the wonders of donating and how 3 months after surgery I didn't even notice it was gone! I'm ready to be there.

There's a Winston Churchill saying "If you're going through hell, keep on going.  The devil may not know that you were there."  I'm not saying I'm going through hell, but I do believe that if we're in a difficult place, it helps  to focus on 3 months down the road.  It seems like every quarter, things change.  If you were up last quarter things will be rough this quarter.  And vice versa so I'm focusing on September!   haha Well, as I read this e-mail, maybe I did need to talk.  Or at least write!  Dr. Cooper assured me I can take my zanax right up until the night before. I haven't been using them, but at least I know they are there if I need one. I'm guessing the night before I might pop one. ;-) Thanks for asking and checking in. I will certainly call if I feel I need to. Have a great night's sleep! Lee

In a message dated 6/19/2007 nschroder writes;

Lee,

I definitely think it's normal to have some anxiety about surgery. You are right about what you said regarding your inexperience with ...if you were experienced, you'd certainly have less anxiety about it, but you probably wouldn't make a great donor!

Uncertainty is one of the worse human conditions. No one likes that feeling, especially those of us who are organized planners who make a significant effort to bring order and certainty to our lives as much as possible. Uncertainty in and of itself creates some anxiety and this is appropriate. It's great that you've contacted donors who have been through this process and have related to what they have to say. I can say that the vast majority of donors I have worked with have said that worst part is the waiting and anticipation and pretty much all of them feel relieved the next day. And I've heard some feedback similar to what you heard about forgetting that the donation even happened 3 months later.

Having said that, how often are you worrying about this? Is it on your mind all of the time? Are you having panic attacks? Has it significantly affected your daily functioning in any way (sleep, appetite, concentration, interest in other things, job performance, relationships, etc.). If it has, we should talk about this soon. If it's intermittant and not causing impairment, then this is within the normal realm. Regardless, I am definitely available to talk. Nina

06/19/07 I wrote:

Thanks again for the offer to talk. I can't say a day goes by that it doesn't cross my mind, but no, it has not impaired my abilities to function. I'm doing fine at work and spent a wonderful weekend on the river; water skiing and cliff jumping with friends and Randy. I'm not feeling any panic attacks, and I'm quite familiar with them from past experience. I'm just realizing that the date is drawing near and it's scary. If I get to where I'm too anxious, I will definitely call you and talk it through.

It doesn't help that I really don't like being in the house alone (I know...I'm 42...grow up!) and that's causing a discomfort anyway. Overall, I truly feel very good about the donation and just am ready to be on the other side of it. It's a long process. I probably should have requested an earlier date, but I really wanted to get some water skiing in this summer! haha I do have my priorities after all.

Thanks again. You, Dr. Cooper and Meg are a wonderful team and I never feel more than an e-mail or a phone call away from comfort. Get some sleep...I'm about to do the same! Lee

Being alone and scared and up late had compounded to make it a difficult night. And making the decision to not be a part of the study wasn't easy. But once again, a member of my "team" had been there for me. At all hours and all times, they were there. Nina walked me through my fears and counseled me. I slept well.

Donor Girl

# You Find Out Who Your Friends Are


I had called Jodi upon my return to update her on my trip. Our conversation left me laughing. She said, "I'm so ready to get away for a few days. I can't wait for *our little vacation!*"

Hmmm..."Jodi, you do realize that *our little vacation* consists of me having my body cut open and a working organ removed, right?"

"Oh yes, but that's a minor inconvenience to what should be a fun few days."

"Really...that's how you see it?"

"No, not really. But for me, it's still a vacation, and I really need it!"

"Maybe you don't quite realize what I'm going through here," I said.

"True, but I'm a working mom with a husband and kids. You don't understand what that is like!"

I laughed. "Ok, you have me there." We both got quite a chuckle out of that. I had to agree she probably needed these few days away, even under the circumstances.

You really do find out who your friends are in situations like this. Jodi was willing to drop everything to come down and stay with me. Sandi also dropped everything to be there for Kell's children and me. Laura Flagler called and said, "I'm getting a babysitter and coming up there." Numerous others were there for me, putting my fears, needs and concerns ahead of theirs. But not everyone truly was there for me when I needed them most.

Throughout all the testing, my bosses had been very understanding and supportive. When I needed time off, they didn't hesitate to give it to me. They told me I could take as long as I needed to recover. However, unbeknownst to me, there were some things going on at the office behind my back that I was unaware of. I would later find out that for months, information about one of my radio stations was being withheld from me, in spite of my attempts to get answers.

It was June 6 when the truth was finally revealed to me. For months, I'd been asking, "Do you have any idea why this music director isn't returning my calls and e-mails?" The answer was always "No, stop being paranoid." It turned out that there was something going on, but for whatever reason, I was not being told. I was later told it was because no one wanted to upset me while I was going through my testing. However, telling me 4 weeks before surgery after months of lying didn't turn out to be great timing either. My GM got involved and agreed that I had been treated incorrectly and was owed an apology. It never came and I was now in a working situation that I no longer felt comfortable in. IF the truth hadn't been revealed until *after* surgery, I could have "bought" the excuse of not wanting to upset me prior. However, I was in a much better emotional state 4 months before surgery versus 4 weeks. The fact that the truth came out that close to my surgery date made me question the fact that they were holding back for my sake. Obviously, there was something more going on and I struggled to find out what it was. I'm a big believer in not flying off the handle and just "quitting" due to a bad situation. I always try to give everything 3 months to sort itself out. I told my bosses that I was having serious reservations about continuing to work for the company and that I would take a few months to think about it and regroup and see where I stood. They agreed to let me take that time as that would be the end of my contract anyway.

Donor Girl

I was due to fly into Nashville for Jason Aldean's platinum record party the day after this information was revealed, but I didn't even want to be in the same room as some of my co-workers. I was supposed to fly in, stay the night, and fly out the next day. Instead, I chose to fly in just in time for the party and fly out immediately afterward. It remains a blur but I'm glad I went as platinum parties don't come along every day and Jason deserves my full support.

I was now not only facing the most difficult personal decision of my life, but was now questioning whether I could continue working for a company where people would lie to me. The timing was horrendous and put me in an even more stressful situation. Luckily, things would end up happening at the company that made the answer easy for me without me having to make any hard decisions. Once again, God was working in my life, as He always does.

Six weeks later, completely unrelated to my situation, there would be a change in personnel at my label and I would be offered the VP of Promotions job. So not only did I not have to leave my beloved label where I'd served faithfully for 6 years, but I would be promoted! It all worked out for the best, but the unnecessary stress I was put under during one of the most difficult times of my life remains a wound that still hurts.

The four weeks before surgery would go by in a blur. We have an annual party at our river house around the 4th of July in memory of my cousin. We had planned it for June 30th, which would be just 11 days before surgery. My cousin had wanted to push it back to July 14th, and I finally had to tell his wife why that wasn't possible. She kept my secret. No one else knew, and the party was a huge success.

On July 2, I had to fly to Hartford, Connecticut to meet with Craig Morgan and Crossin Dixon for a St. Jude show with WWYZ. I

Donor Girl

stopped on the way to the airport to get a mammogram and pap
smear just to make sure there were no pre surgery issues.

It is always a pleasure having your breasts slammed like a
sandwich between two metal plates as the woman tries to take your
size B's and turn them into D's to get them in there. And let's not
forget the metal salad tongs used in a Pap smear. Oh boy!
Although my last test had been within the year, I wanted to make
double sure I was ok. I also wanted to get a sonogram of my
ovaries because I suspected I had a cyst. It turned out I did, but it
was small, and my OB/GYN assured me it was not a problem.
God forbid some form of something had shown up. Chemotherapy
and cancer drugs are very hard on the kidneys. It would be
horrible to wait until right after surgery to find out I still needed
both kidneys!

My OB/GYN is from India and was very supportive of my
decision to donate. She told me that God would take care of me. I
could never tell before if she liked me, but that day, I felt her
admiration. Again, I walked a little taller. Her husband is Dave's
urologist, and she is Kelly's doctor, so she had known all along
that Dave was in kidney failure.

I flew out to Hartford that night. On July 3, I had the show with
Craig and Crossin Dixon. Craig was still not a fan of my donating,
kind of like Randy. But he was being supportive. Like my dad,
they were worried about me and that meant a lot.

One of the reasons we decided not to tell my parents about my
surgery was that my mom was due to have a hysterectomy on July
3. She had been having issues with bleeding for the last two years,
and they thought they'd solved it the year before. When the
bleeding came back, her doctor told her a hysterectomy was best.
We knew that if we told my mom about Dave's and my surgeries,
she would postpone hers. While all tests for malignancy had come
back negative, the doctor said she wouldn't know for sure until she

did the surgery and could test and see everything. Mom has the same OB/GYN as Kelly and me. When I'd been there the day before, I had to ask her not to mention my upcoming surgery since mom didn't know about it.

I felt badly about not being there when my mom had surgery, but the show in Hartford was acoustic, so we didn't have any tour managers there. My job as the promoter is usually to be the liaison between the artist and the radio station. However, when we do radio shows and there aren't any tour managers on site, the promoter handles many more responsibilities. We not only work with radio, we also deal with any fan club members, sound techs, promoters and anything regarding the show that might come up. I also handled getting the artists food, hotel rooms, transportation and everything it takes for them to exist in a strange city for two days.

The show went well, and afterward, Crossin Dixon drove themselves back to the hotel at the Hartford airport. I drove Craig and his musicians to Fort Dix, New Jersey where they had a show the next day. We left around 10:00 P.M. from Hartford and arrived in New Jersey around 2:00 A.M. Craig asked me to have breakfast with him in the morning and I agreed. I had wanted to leave New Jersey fairly early so I could go and visit mom on my day off. But any day on the road is a day working. It would be about a four-hour drive home.

Craig and I met around 8:30 for breakfast, and by 9:15, I was on the way to the Carroll County Hospital in Westminster, Maryland.

My mom was doing well but was quite sore. I forced her to sit up in a chair and take a short walk down the hall. Little did I know how difficult that was. I would soon know. When I think of how much I tried to make mom do one day after surgery, I call and apologize: "I didn't know!" Now I know! I was glad to have that time with her and see that she had come through fine.

# Pre-Testing

On July 5, Dave and I had our pre-testing at the University of Maryland Medical Center. I drove separately and met Kelly and Dave there. We were due to arrive at 8:00 A.M., but Dave and Kelly were running late, so I signed in without them. They were just going to do the basics: urine test, blood work, temperature and blood pressure. We'd have the results before we left that day. Meg had asked me to stay until 1:00 and join Dave for his meeting with his surgeon. Dave's surgeon was the Chairman of the Department of Surgery at the University of Maryland School of Medicine and Chief of Surgery at the UM Medical Center. Dr. Cooper told me he was the best vascular surgeon in the state.

Earlier that morning, I had contacted Dr. Cooper via e-mail. I had been e-mailing back and forth with a man who had donated his kidney to his sister. He had told me that Dr. Cooper was supposed to be his surgeon, but due to other cadaver surgeries that day, Dr. Cooper had recommended another surgeon. I was concerned that if Dr. Cooper wasn't able to do my surgery on the 11th, I wouldn't have the strength to go through with it. I needed consistency at this point, and my team is what kept me going. On July 10, I e-mailed Dr. Cooper.

**7/5/2007 6:00 AM  From LAdams to Dr. Cooper:**

**I received this e-mail from a former donor I've been conversing with:** *My surgeon was supposed to be Matt Cooper. They had 2 cadaver cases arrive in-between the first go and our case, so it was about 6pm before we got started. Dr. Cooper excused himself from the case because he was dead tired on his feet. So I have a lot of respect for him. It was a Dr. Adrian Park who pinch-hit for Dr. Cooper in my case.*

Donor Girl

**First, I thought you'd like to see the respect he had for you. I thought that was cool. Second, I wanted to point out that on July 11th, ALL cadaver cases go to another doctor. You stay well rested for me!! :-) Ok, I realize this may not be the way it works but I wanted to make my request. I meet with the recipient surgeon today. This thing is starting to feel very real. I'm running out of xanax. My new commercial: "Xanax, it's not just for fear of flying anymore." HaHa Lee Adams**

It was known among my team that I took Xanax for my fear of flying and had asked permission to use it when feeling extremely anxious about surgery. I was told I could use it up until the night before, but not the morning of surgery. I rarely used Xanax, and a 30 pill bottle would last me most of the year since I only took it to fly. I had to admit I'd been going through a bit more in recent days. However, they were so small as to not have much effect. Dr. Cooper replied:

In a message dated 7/5/2007 Mcooper writes:

**You'll be the only one that gets my attention that day!**

7/5/2007 I wrote to Mcooper:

**:-) Thank you. Lee**

It turns out that the day of the other man's surgery, Dr. Cooper was the on-call surgeon. They'd had two cadaver donors come in, and Dr. Cooper wanted to make sure that this donor had a fresh surgeon. On the day of my surgery, Dr. Cooper was not on call, and I was his only surgery.

Dave, Kelly and I met with Dr. Bartlett at 1:00 P.M. They had the results of both Dave's and my tests from earlier that day. I passed with flying colors, but Dave did not fare as well. His creatinine levels were too high; Dr. Bartlett told him he wouldn't operate on him if he didn't have at least two rounds of dialysis, and then only if the numbers were in safe surgery range.

Dave's caseworker, Deb, came in to talk to us about what to expect the day of surgery. She described the room I would have to recuperate in.

"Lee, your room will be a private suite. It's the donor suite. You'll have a private bathroom, Internet computer, flat screen TV and a stocked refrigerator."

"Will I have a suite?" Dave asked.

"No, you'll be in a regular room in the kidney wing, with a roommate," Deb replied.

"Why don't I get a suite?" asked Dave.

I stepped in. " 'Cause I can skip town and go to Bora Bora. I don't **HAVE** to have surgery. You do. They have to do everything possible to get me to walk through that door next Wednesday."

"Oh," was all Dave said.

Dr. Bartlett's personality worked great with Dave's. Dr. Bartlett has always had an interest in Australia, so he and Dave talked about that. They really seemed to gel on many levels. Dr. Bartlett believed it was important to know who his patients were and know them as people. He discussed a study that said patients don't show any better signs of recovery when their doctors get to know them versus when they don't. But he was quick to say they don't do any worse if the doctors do get to know them. So why wouldn't you be friendly and make them feel comfortable? Both Kelly and Dave really liked that statement.

Donor Girl

While we were in with Dr. Bartlett, Dr. Cooper walked by and saw us. He backed up long enough to wave and smile. Kelly told me she had run into him earlier. "He said he's just trying to keep you grounded, Lee," Kelly said laughing.

"What the hell does that mean?" I asked. "I'm very well grounded, thank you." But in truth, I wasn't. I was scared. I was anxious, but I was resolved to go through with it. Dr. Cooper had worked very hard over the last few months to keep me grounded. Whenever I e-mailed him a question, he answered immediately.

"I'm sure he didn't mean anything by it. He just knows you're nervous." And that I was. This was our final day of testing. Sometimes, your blood will simply stop mixing with the other person's for unknown reasons, or something will have caused your levels to change. However, I was still cleared to donate, and as long as Dave's dialysis did the trick, surgery would happen on July 11th.

Dave, Kelly and I walked up to the Baltimore market and got crab cakes. We called mom to see how she was feeling, trying to disguise that we were together. I picked up a small peace lily and took it to her on my way home. She was doing better and was about to be released. She said, "You're so lucky, Lee. You have no idea what it's like to have surgery. I hope you don't ever have to." Ugh! Little did she know that mine was less than a week away.

Dave's dialysis was scheduled for Monday and Tuesday, July 9 and 10. I had to be on the road July 7 in Pittsburgh with Craig Morgan and July 9 in Fort Wayne, Indiana with Jason Aldean. When I flew home on July 10, my sister and I would go straight up to my parents' house. It was then we'd tell them about the surgery.

Craig already knew about my pending surgery, but Jason didn't. I wanted to tell him so when I missed one of his concerts, he would

Donor Girl

know why. I was on his tour bus and just stated, "I'm going to have surgery on Wednesday, and I wanted you to know I'll be out of commission for travel for a few weeks." Jason has what we call "the Jason face." Jason was blessed with beautiful full lips that women would die for. The Jason face happens when he purses his lips together and squints his eyes in an inquisitive manner.

He made the Jason face. "Surgery for what?"

"I'm donating a kidney," I said, like it was an everyday occurrence.

"You're what?"

"I'm donating a kidney to a family member."

The Jason face showed up again. "When?"

"Tomorrow." Jason shook his head and gave me a hug, and then his band guys did the same. Jason and his band are a great group of guys, and I'd known his band members since my days at Atlantic Records. There was much discussion as to who would do it, who wouldn't, who thought I was crazy, and so on. It's amazing how much I heard the words, "You're crazy," through all this. But all in all, they were very supportive and wished me well.

I flew home on Tuesday, July 10, in the morning. I remember standing in the airport looking at all the places that Southwest Airlines flew that would take me far away from Baltimore and the University of Maryland Hospital. I had visions of my cousin, Tommy, in Raleigh having to call Randy and say, "I've got her. She's here. I'll get her on the next plane home." But I didn't fly to Raleigh or Bora Bora. I boarded the plane to Baltimore.

As I was standing in the A line waiting to board, the people around me started discussing the University of Maryland Medical Center. I said, "I'll be there tomorrow." One guy asked why, and I told him. You'd have thought I just said I had discovered a cure for cancer. Their reaction was so unreal. They told me how amazing it was that I was going to do this.

"You're doing this when?" one guy asked.

"Tomorrow," I replied.

"Wow, are you nervous?" he asked.

"You have no idea," I said. They continued to rave about how amazing it was that I was donating a kidney. All I was feeling was fear, so it was refreshing and validating to hear them say so many positive things. Again, I stood a little taller.

I had read one person's account of their road to kidney donation. They said, "It's like you're on a ladder. And there are people ahead of you on the ladder and you feel like you have a buffer between you and kidney donation. Then one by one, they are ruled out and you move up the ladder. Next thing you know, you're on the top rung and they're asking, 'Are you still willing to donate?' And you have to say either yes or no."

I was now on the top rung and my answer was still "Yes," usually followed by the thought, "How in the world did I end up here." But **"YES"** was the answer. I had gotten to the point where I felt that this was what I was on earth to do: Save a life. As much as I didn't want to have surgery, no one was going to take this honor away from me; well, unless someone died that was a better match. It wasn't that I wanted someone to die, but if they had to, dear God let them match Dave!

I landed in Baltimore first thing in the morning and headed home. I was going to pack and get ready to leave for the hospital before going to my parents' house. Because I lived over 75 miles away from the hospital, they would provide me with an apartment the

Donor Girl

night before the surgery. It was a two-room apartment with a pull-out couch. Normally, I would be gracious and offer to let Kelly and Dave have the bedroom, and Randy and I would take the couch. Because Dave was the recipient and lived within 45 miles of the hospital, he wasn't offered a room. But he and Kelly still had nearly an hour-long drive into Baltimore, and we were due at the hospital at 5:30 A.M. I did offer to let them stay with us free of charge (since we weren't paying), but I didn't offer the bed. I treated Randy and me to the comfortable bed. Donors get suites and beds. Recipients get couches and regular rooms, I thought with a laugh.

On my way home from the airport, I called one of the former female donors that I had been put in touch with. Coincidently, she worked for McCormick Spice Co. where my dad had worked for over 30 years. I hadn't told her yet who I was as I assumed she'd know my dad. He was the VP of Business and Finance, and most people knew him or knew of him. She picked up the phone and talked to me for a few minutes. She said something that I held on to.

"Lee, it was a nonevent. I've had no repercussions and don't feel a bit different. It's just a nonevent."

I told her I hadn't told my parents yet and would be telling them later that day. Then I asked, "Do you know a man named Bill Adams? He worked for McCormick."

"I do," she said, "but he's retired now. Why?"

"He's my dad."

"Oh my gosh! Leeeee Adddddams!" She said my name slowly as if it all finally made sense. "That's right. Wow, Bill Adams is who you have to go tell about your kidney donation today?"

"Yep."

"Darn. I'd be more afraid of that than the actual surgery," she said. I laughed. "I am!"

"Good luck and I'll be praying for you." We hung up, but I held onto her word that it would be a "nonevent."

I got home around 11:00 A.M. and opened up my computer. I had been reading some more donor stories and discovered a few where the incision was not low and horizontal as Dr. Cooper and I had discussed. It was actually vertical from the navel down. I didn't want that. I was sure Dr. Cooper was tired of hearing from me, but I had to double check one more time. I sent an e-mail.

7/10/2007 11:16 AM  To MCooper from LAdams:

**A number of people have mentioned recently that their cuts were vertical from the naval down. I know you drew on me, but the drawing has since washed away. (I told you it wasn't permanent!) Anyway, I just want to check ONE MORE TIME that it will be horizontal below the bikini line. I even laid out in a low bikini so you could follow the tan line. haha  Ok, that wasn't really a joke...I really did that. But I do want it horizontal if at all possible. I know what you're thinking..."Take a xanax and remain grounded." Lee Adams**

In a message dated 7/10/2007 MCooper writes:

**Midline vertical incisions are done by surgeons that utilize a laparoscopic 'assisted' donor nephrectomy procedure in which the surgeon uses a lower midline incision, places a special gel-port and then puts his hand through while also insufflating the abdomen and doing part with the lap instruments. My technique is**

totally laparoscopic so the incision is there just to take the kidney out which allows it to be a low transverse incision that has to be only far enough above the pubic bone to avoid the urinary bladder which sits just below the pubis.

Truth is no matter where the incision is located you'll still be a hero so if the incision allows you to talk about/show that to the world, you deserve it! But I'll make sure to give you that option.

Try and get some rest tonight and I'll see you in the morning.

**Matthew Cooper, MD**
**Associate Professor of Surgery**
**Director, Clinical Research**

7/10/2007 11:28 AM I wrote:

**Terrible to be so vain huh? Thanks for explaining. I completely trust you to take good care of me. See you tomorrow. Lee**

Donor Girl

# The Parent Talk

Kelly and I decided to head up to my parents around 3:00 P.M. We called and made it sound like we were going to visit my mom who was still recuperating from her hysterectomy. My parents live on a mountain, so Kell and I met at the bottom of it, parked her car, and drove mine up to their house. We had both been praying that it would go smoothly when we told them. Neither was in good health, and my mom's heart condition really concerned me. As we drove toward their driveway, Kelly said, "Let's stop and pray one more time."

"No!" I replied. "We are praying how God tells us not to pray. He says not to pray out of worry and fear but to trust Him and know that 'He is'. We are over praying, and we're going to make Him mad. If there's one man I don't want to piss off right now, it's God!"

"Fine," Kelly said, "let's go."

We pulled into my parents' driveway and saw a strange car. "Great, this is just what we need: company. Geez," Kelly said in disgust.

"Let's just go get this done," I said. "And let me do the talking. You'll start crying and get all upset and that will upset them."

"Fine, you do the talking," Kelly agreed.

Kelly and I walked in the door to find my mom sitting in her recliner. We saw a man sitting on the couch facing away from us. When the man turned around, we realized it was my parents' pastor.

Donor Girl

"See, God took care of us. I told you He would," I said.

We sat down and acted like this was a social visit. And we waited, and waited, and waited for dad. Dad is a tinkerer. I refer to him as "Peter Piss Around." Truthfully, Peter is probably the perfect nickname for my dad. Peter is the name Jesus gave to Simon. Why? It means "rock." My dad is the rock of our family.

Although I call him Peter in jest for his ability to "piss around" and waste time, Peter is truly the right nickname for my dad.

Dad was supposed to join us, but he was out and about the yard doing stuff. Who knows what stuff, but apparently important stuff. I was rather eager to get it over with since I needed to go home and shower before leaving for Baltimore. They had given Dave and me a certain kind of sponge and soap to shower with both the night before and the morning of surgery.

Finally, after about 30 minutes, I asked, "Mom, where's dad? Isn't he going to say hi?"

"You know your father. He's out in the apartment doing something," Mom said. My parents have an apartment over their garage that both my sister and Randy and I had lived in during our adult lives at some point.

"Peter Putz Around," I called him, laughing at the look of horror on Kelly's face when she thought I was going to say, "Piss Around" in front of the pastor. Like it's a word he's never heard.

"I'm going to get him."

I headed out to the apartment. When I went in, he was hanging out at the computer.

"Daddy? Are you going to come say hi?" I asked.

# Donor Girl

"Sure honey, I'll be right there," he replied. I went back to the house and sat waiting in the living room. Dad joined us a few minutes later, and I started right in since time was now becoming a premium. I still had to get home, shower with my special soap and sponge, pack up and get to the room in Baltimore. Kelly still had to get home and get the kids ready for their parents' absence, and then she and Dave would also drive to Baltimore.

"This isn't exactly a social visit," I said very seriously. "We have another reason for being here."

"Oh no, what's wrong? You're scaring me. Something's wrong. Are you pregnant?" My mom asked. (My mom knows that a pregnancy was not on this 42 year olds list of things-to-do.) 'Cause if you are, don't panic. We can help."

"No mom, I'm not pregnant."

The pastor stood up at that point and said, "I should probably leave."

Kelly and I both yelled, "NO!" I said, "I'd like you to stay." He sat back down. Kelly and I would have tackled him and tied him to a chair if we had to. Luckily, we didn't. I continued.

"Apparently, two A positive parents have a twenty-five percent chance of having an O positive child. It turns out that I'm O positive. I've spent the last few months getting tested as a donor for David and I'm a match. So I'm going to donate my kidney."

There was complete silence out of my parents. In fact, it was like the proverbial passing of gas in church. I was waiting for a similar type explosion when the pastor spoke up.

Donor Girl

"I feel like I'm in the presence of a saint. God bless you. This is such an amazing example of selfless Christian love." Thank God for that man.

It was hard for my dad to follow that up by saying, "What a stupid idea. I forbid it!"

My mom spoke up and asked, "How long do I have to stress over this?" She almost sighed loudly upon saying it.

"Not long. Surgery is set for five-thirty tomorrow morning."

"What???!! Tomorrow?? Oh my God!" Mom shrieked. I immediately started worrying about mom's heart. Could she handle something this traumatic? Not only was her son-in-law having a transplant, but her baby girl was the one donating the organ.

"But mom, you are still recuperating from surgery, and I do NOT expect you to be there. There's nothing you can do but sit and worry. They told me I'd be 'out of it' until the next day and wouldn't know who was there."

My dad had really wanted to be the one to donate but had been turned down due to his health. He was quiet for a few minutes, and then asked, "Are we absolutely certain they won't let me donate?"

"Yes Daddy. If they wouldn't let Michael donate, they won't let you donate. I'm the one that has to do it."

"Well, I'm not going to lie to you. I love you more than I love David. My first concern is for my daughter, and I don't really want you to do this," my dad said.

Donor Girl

"Honestly, dad, I love me more than I love David. But I love those kids more than I love myself. And they deserve a healthy dad. I was lucky enough to grow up with a dad who could play with me and throw a ball to me, and I want to give that to Will and Kayla."

My dad started to choke up. As a joke, he made a noise that he used to make when trying to wake me up as a teenager. It was very annoying. "You want Will and Kayla to experience that?" He asked, trying to joke through the tightened throat.

"I didn't say it was all great; just that they deserve it," I said. We laughed.

"Well, I'm very proud of you, Leez," my mom said, using my childhood nickname.

Everyone stood up for a group hug. My dad is an elder at the church, which allows him to give Communion. The pastor asked if we'd like to pray, and dad wanted him to administer Communion.

We sat and talked for a few minutes with no one really knowing quite what to say. Finally, mom asked, "Well who is going to watch the kids?"

Kelly spoke up. "Sandi is here. She came in on Monday and will be staying for nine days."

Dad asked, "Can she afford to do that?"

"Lee and I are paying her lost wages, and we took care of her flight here." Kelly said.

"Well, at least let me pay her. That I can do," dad said. We had a feeling he would offer, but we never would have asked him. We'd gladly let him pay, though.

Donor Girl

The whole time we were there, my parents' little dog, Abby, was running around playing and barking. We couldn't catch her to put her in the crate. Dad came back in with juice, bread and 5 oddly mismatched cartoon glasses from childhood. I remain curious as to why he chose those, but I'm not sure his mind was 100% on the task. For me, it was oddly comforting to see those childhood Archie and Jughead glasses.

As soon as the pastor began praying, Abby laid down and put her little head between her paws. She didn't move or make a sound until after Communion ended; another miracle that day. The pastor kept calling me Kelly, which caused many interruptions while my dad tried to get him to call me Lee. It actually became rather humorous, but the pastor said he was truly overwhelmed to be a part of this family moment. We encouraged my parents not to come down the next day since it was a far drive and mom was still recuperating. Naturally, they insisted on coming down. We hugged, exchanged words of love, and everyone but me cried. Kelly and I were enormously relieved that God would give us a pastor to help us through such a difficult moment. It actually became an amazing act of love and Christianity, and I felt like God was sending me a message that everything would be ok.

Kelly and I drove back in our separate cars, elated with the way things had gone. We hugged and said we'd see each other later that night. Kelly now had to go talk to her kids, and I had to pack and get ready.

I came home to an e-mail from Nina. We had e-mailed briefly before I left for my parents. We exchanged a few e-mails before I shut down the computer to prepare for my trip to Baltimore.

In a message dated 7/10/2007 NSchroder writes:

**Hi Lee,**

Donor Girl

Just wanted to check in with you to see how things were going and to let you know that I am sending good thoughts your way. I am sorry that we weren't able to meet when you were here last week for PAT. I spoke with Meg and she said that everything went well and that you are feeling ready. You will be in good hands, Lee.

We'll both check in with you on Thursday. In the meantime, know that I am thinking of you.

All the best, Nina
Clinical Social Worker Living Donor Kidney Program

07/10/07  11:13 AM I wrote to NSchroder:

Thanks Nina. I have noticed my "fear of flying xanax" is rapidly going. I have a new slogan "xanax, not just for fear of flying anymore."  ;-)

I'm as well as I can be. Haven't booked a ticket to Bora Bora yet but have thought about it. I plan to be there tomorrow morning though. I told Randy he might have to do a fireman's carry to get me in, but to make sure I get in.

Talking to my parents about it this afternoon. I'm more afraid of my dad than I am surgery. Thanks again. See you soon. Lee

In a message dated 7/10/2007 NSchroder writes:

He's  your dad... he's going to be concerned. That's a parent's job - they worry. I hope your mom's surgery went ok.

let me know how that goes with that conversation. Hang in there. And if you need to talk at any point today or tonight, please call me. Feel free to call my cell if I am not at my desk. I should be here a little bit later this evening working on some things.

Otherwise, sending lots of good thoughts and a virtual hug to you! Nina

07/10/07 6:17 PM I wrote:

God actually works in so many amazing ways. My sister and I have been so stressed over talking to my parents and as we pulled up to their driveway, she wanted to say another prayer. I told her "God tells us not to pray that way. That we are to trust Him to know what we need and to not worry. We are over praying. God will take care of us." We pulled into their driveway and there was a strange car there. My sister said "Oh great, who is that? They have company. Just what we need." Well, the company turned out to be their Pastor. So God truly worked for us. The pastor was overwhelmed by the whole family situation and brought an amazing amount of peace to it. The first thing he said was "God bless you for making the right decision." My dad was definitely mixed in his emotions, but was very supportive. He was most sorry he couldn't be the one to do it. There were tears (mainly my sister's...haha), laughter, concern, and praying. The pastor anointed me with oil and we had communion. It turned out to be a very moving and amazing experience. My mom said "well how long will I have to worry about this?"

I said "Not long, surgery is tomorrow." I thought she would faint but she held it together. They both expressed how proud they were of me. I reminded them that my sister has been the favorite daughter for the last 8 years 'cause she had kids. Being a Type A personality, I had to find a way to beat that. It took 8 years, but I'm now the favorite daughter. haha That brought laughter.

Many thanks for your counsel along the way. I believe waiting was the right decision and peace will come to them sooner this way. See you soon. Lee

In a message dated 7/10/2007 NSchroder writes:

I am delighted to hear this! What an amazing story. Truly, your prayers were answered... I am learning that when you let go of things and try to trust that God will move things along in the right direction, the anxiety lifts a bit and is replaced with a sense of peace. This is exactly what you needed. I am happy to know that you are pleased with your decision to wait to tell them. I know you were anxious about telling them earlier so it's great that you listened to your instincts.

Very funny story about you wracking up points for favorite daughter...Your humor is wonderful and really serves you (and others) well.

The wait is just about over and a wonderful sense of calm will be upon you in less than 24 hours when you wake up and know that it's complete. Now you just need to think... Bora Bora... See you soon! Nina

7/10/07 I wrote to NSchroder:

I think I may feel more relieved that my parents know than I will after surgery! That was really weighing on

Donor Girl

**me. Thanks for everything. I'm very ready for it to be Thursday!!**

**My dad said "I still can't believe you passed the psych eval." haha Lee**

It was occurring to me that while everyone wasn't at all surprised I passed the physical tests, they were all shocked I passed the psych. evaluation. Exactly what did this mean? I'm the most normal person I know.

Another big concern of telling my parents had been Kelly's kids. This was the main reason we had chosen not to tell them before mom's surgery. Mom would have insisted on pushing her surgery back so she could watch Will and Kayla. With Dave in the hospital and Kelly needing to be with him, who would watch the kids?

And as I said before, Sandi volunteered to drop everything. She's been a lifelong friend of our family and more like a *member* of our family. She lived next door to us when we lived in Joppatowne. We met when Sandi and I were 2 and Kelly was 4. Sandi moved to Maine before first grade. Looking back, it's amazing that we managed to keep in touch for 40 years. Her parents weren't particularly close friends with mine, but they helped Sandi and me write letters. Since my dad's grandparents lived in Bangor, Maine, we took yearly trips to visit them. Mom and dad always drove the extra hour west to visit Sandi in Lewiston. It would always be awkward in the beginning as we were growing up and, at best, exchanging letters and a visit once a year. But by the time my parents were ready to continue the 12 hour journey home, Sandi, Kelly and I were reluctant to part ways.

Sandi's life took a much different path than mine. She got married at 16, pregnant at 17 and had her first child shortly before turning 18. By 21, she had 3 children; by 24, she was divorced. Sandi was

Donor Girl

adopted and didn't know anything about her birth parents. She wasn't close to her adoptive parents and will say that she always felt like she "didn't belong with them." I think Sandi felt most comfortable with our family and we were happy to "adopt" her as one of our own. While it isn't legal or official, she has always been like a sister to Kelly and me and like a daughter to my parents.

When Sandi's kids were entering their teens, they went to live with their dad and step-mother, and Sandi, having reached a difficult time in her life, moved down to live with Randy and me. She was a tremendous help to us because she took care of my grandmother at various times. When my mom had her heart attack, Sandi chipped in and would spend a few days a week with my grandmother. We would fly to Maine every 4-6 weeks to spend as much time as possible with her children. When Randy and I moved to West Virginia, Sandi stayed in the Maryland area near my sister, so we still saw each other often. In early 2007, Sandi felt the need to move to be near her children and left for Maine. While we miss her terribly, she is where she needs to be. She *IS* a party of our family.

Sandi and Dave had always had their differences. I think they were raised in such similar circumstances that they just couldn't seem to communicate to each other. It was almost like they reminded each other of some bad times and didn't want to acknowledge it. Kelly and I were both stressing over what to do with Will and Kayla while Dave and I were convalescing. I called Kelly one day with a thought, and I had no idea what her reaction would be.

"Kell, what if we offer to pay Sandi two weeks' wages and ask her to come down and watch the kids?" I asked this question fully expecting her to say, "No, it's not what Dave would want." Sandi worked at a restaurant and was paid as most waitresses; half

Donor Girl

minimum wage plus tips. We could find out what she usually made in a week and pay her to help with the kids.

Surprisingly, Kelly said, "I was actually thinking the same thing."

Dave wasn't happy about it at first as he felt they should be able to handle everything themselves, but Kelly firmly told him, "I can't do it all, and we have no one else to turn to." Dave then realized that the children needed someone there with them 24/7. Sandi was our obvious choice. Despite his and Sandi's relationship, the children loved her, and she was excellent with them. That he admitted.

Will and Kayla call Sandi, "Aunt Sandi," and just as Kelly and I think of her as family, so do they. They were sad when she moved back to Maine and would be thrilled she was coming to stay with them. She's a natural with children and the perfect person to help them get through this difficult time.

We contacted Sandi, not 100% sure of what her reaction would be. When we explained what we needed, she didn't even hesitate before saying, "Yes, I'll be there. Just let me check with my boss that she'll hold my job." We would pay Sandi's transportation costs and also her lost wages. It would be unfair to ask her to lose wages, although Sandi felt she owed us this for all we'd done for her in the past. In fact, she felt honored and blessed that we thought of her.

I booked Sandi's flight to arrive a couple of days before surgery. She flew in on July 9th. Kelly picked her up and they went straight to Kelly's house. I wouldn't get to see her until after surgery.

The night before surgery, Randy met me at our house. We packed some light bags, and I took my shower with the special sponge brush and soap I had been given by the Medical Center. We all have bacteria on our skin and the soap minimizes the amount and

Donor Girl

hopefully makes a post-operative infection less likely. Once I had done that, we headed down to Baltimore.

Kelly and Dave would arrive later because they wanted to talk to the kids first. They had told them the night before that Daddy had a kidney donor. They asked the kids if they had any questions. Will did. "Who's the donor?"

"We can't tell you that yet, Will. Any other questions?"

"No, Mom. That was my only one, and you didn't answer it," Will persisted.

Before leaving for the hospital, they sat down with the kids and discussed Dave's surgery with them. Dave and Kelly finally told them that I was the donor.

"Mom, why can't Poppy do it?" Will asked, inquiring about my dad.

"Because he's not healthy enough, Will," Kelly answered.

"Why can't Nana do it?" Will asked.

"Because she's not healthy enough either, Will."

"Okay, Mom," Will said, resigned.

Kayla, at barely 5 years old didn't have any questions.

Donor Girl

# **Surgery**

The quote: "The problem with a living sacrifice is it keeps wanting to crawl off the altar!" meant more to me this day than it ever had before. The concept of a living organ donor is a difficult one. The fact that we are *alive* while making this decision creates problems that cadaver donors don't have. For instance, a cadaver doesn't walk into the hospital knowing what they are about to do. Granted, given the choice, I'd rather still be alive; let's make no mistake there. However, the desire to "crawl off the alter" was strong.

Up until surgery day, if you had asked whether I had ever **really** felt pain, I'd have said, "I'm a record promoter! I get beat up every single day as I try to convince radio programmers to play my label's songs. Believe me when I say, 'I KNOW PAIN!'" Well, I assure you, I didn't know pain.

After 9 months of stress, worry, testing, praying and visualizing my surgery; it was time to have my kidney taken out. In fairness, I don't believe Dr. Cooper planned to gut me like a deer. He was going to make my incisions as small as possible. But my visual and his reality are two different things. I was visualizing something much uglier than what it was.

I don't care how many times I tried to prepare, tried to visualize, tried to imagine; there was no way to fully prepare myself for the rather odd idea that one of my body organs was going to be put inside my brother-in-law to make him well. It's kind of a wiggy thought actually. As one person said, "That's really gross in a cool kind of way."

I kept thinking about what Joanne, our Australian doctor friend had said. "Lee, the Western world of medicine would not do this if it was not considered completely safe." Ok, that was a good point.

Donor Girl

Throughout this process, she had also been a great supporter and advocate. With her being a doctor, it helped even more.

In essence, we are just the sum of our parts. And like a car, we can take a battery out of one and put it into another and *voila*: the other car starts. If we can do it with car parts why not with people parts? The point is we have working parts that can work in another person. It's just a concept that's odd when it's *your* parts going into someone else.

Getting to the apartment in Baltimore that night was a fiasco. We didn't get there until after 10:00 P.M. Luckily someone answered the office phone late at night. The apartment is on a side road that is really more of an alley in the middle of Baltimore city. And you have to have a code to get into the gated garage, which we did not have in advance. As we circled the same street for the fourth time, Randy and I weren't exactly getting along. Our nerves were frayed and our anxiety was high. Kelly and Dave were quite a while behind us, so we were going to have to stay up until they arrived because they wouldn't be able to get in the garage without our help. Parking was crazy on our designated level, but we finally found a spot.

The apartment building was very nice, and the apartment itself was very neat. We pulled out the couch and made it up for Kelly and Dave. I took a Xanax, and Randy agreed to stay up and wait for them while I tried to get some sleep. We had set our alarm for 4:00 A.M. since we had to be at the hospital by 5:30. At best, I would get 4 to 5 hours of sleep; and that was only if I took Xanax. Otherwise, I knew I wouldn't sleep. Luckily, the Xanax took effect and I did indeed sleep.

Kelly and Dave finally arrived. Randy got them settled, and before we knew it, alarms were going off. It was time to wake up! Dave and I showered with our special scrub sponges and soaps. We weren't allowed to wear any kind of deodorants, perfumes,

Donor Girl

makeup or anything else. Needless to say, you walk into surgery already not looking your best. You wonder why people who look fairly healthy immediately look sick upon entering a hospital. It's a ploy. It's so there's no confusion about who the patient is and who the doctor or nurse is. They'd hate to accidently stick a needle in a staff member, so they put the patient in a gown with no back 'cause what sane hospital staffer would walk around with their butt hanging out? Then they don't let you wear any makeup while the nurses all look beautiful. No mistaking there. You aren't a nurse looking like you look, so YOU must be the one that gets stuck with the needles.

So, I took my shower with my special soap and sponge and met the rest of the crew in the living room. Will and Kayla had made us cards that we read. Kelly had Dave and I pose for pre-surgery photos. Dave still had the port in his neck from his two days of dialysis. My mom had called Kelly the night before and told her to read *The Upper Room* for Tuesday, July 10, 2007. She asked her to cut it out and take it to me. I had brought my Bible with every intent of reading it prior to surgery, but once I read *The Upper Room* passage, I decided God had spoken very clearly to me. Here's what it said:

**Title: Just Do It!**

**Isaiah 6:8 -** *Then I heard the Lord say, "Whom shall I send? Who will be our messenger?" I answered, "I will go! Send me!"*

When Moses encountered the burning bush, God assigned him to lead the Hebrews out of slavery. But Moses was not eager to do it. For years after Moses fled Egypt, he had made a life for himself in the Sinai. He had a wife and children and was in charge of his father-in-law's flocks. Moses didn't want to leave all this for a difficult task with an uncertain conclusion. Surely God could see that Moses was not the right one for the job. But God could not be dissuaded, and Moses finally trudged off to Egypt.

Like Moses, we are sometimes confronted with unwelcome opportunities to deny ourselves and do God's will. Such situations are rarely convenient, and we may try to convince God that we are the wrong person for the job. But God specializes in doing the miraculous through weak, broken people.

Maybe that's the point: Our faith is strengthened and our Creator is glorified when God does the impossible for us or through us. We can trust that God will go with us, will empower us, and will see us through even the worst of situations. May God help us to replace "O Lord please send someone else" with "I will go! Send me!"

Prayer: Eternal God, nothing is impossible with you. Amen.

Thought for the day: Stop arguing with God and just do it.

Written by: Lynda R. Nedrow (Nevada)
Prayer Focus: Those facing impossible situations.

Source: The Upper Room. Used by Permission of the Upper Room. ©July/August 2007.

This spoke to me so loudly. I was definitely feeling weak and broken. Not only was I wondering, "How in the heck did I get to this point?" I was also struggling in my professional life. I felt very weak and very broken. But God had quite obviously chosen this path for me, and now that I was close to the finish line, there was no quitting. "I will go God, send me!"

Donor Girl

There was still some part of me thinking something might stop this. That the treadmill would stop moving and we'd all get off. But the treadmill kept going, I kept walking and we all piled into Randy's SUV and drove the mile to the hospital.

I hadn't been allowed to eat or drink anything after midnight; I'm not sure I could have anyway. Our instructions were to arrive at 6:00 A.M. and check in at same day surgery. At 7:00 A.M., I'd be taken into the pre-op room to meet with the anesthesiologist.

The family would then be taken to the waiting room. Anesthesia, surgery and recovery should take about 6 hours. Six hours wasn't even close to enough time for me to recover. Apparently, surgery is not my friend.

Things moved fairly quickly once we were there. After we checked in, they rushed us through to pre-op. The staff put Dave and me in the same room and started IV lines and took our stats. The nurse and I had a debate about my underwear. I don't like to be without underwear. It's been a marriage-long debate between Randy and me. I simply like to wear panties. I had to change into a hospital gown, and the nurse asked for my underwear.

"No, I'd like to keep them on"

"You can't keep them on. I need to put them with your clothes," she said.

"I'll just keep them on a little while longer," I insisted.

"I can't do that. If I forget to come back and get them, I'll get in trouble," she insisted.

"I really want to keep them on. I'll remind you."

Donor Girl

"You will be under sedation and not able to remind me. I need them now. I'm sorry."

"But I'm like a three-year-old. If you take my panties and the cold air hits my woowoo, I might pee."

"I'm sorry, but I still need the panties. You won't pee I promise." As an afterthought, there were probably a ton of embarrassing things that happened while I was in surgery. Did I pass gas? Did I pee? Did I do anything else? Do I care? Was I well groomed? I forgot I'd be naked and wasn't sure I had shaved in all the appropriate places. I bet surgery in the 70s was easy. Hair was appreciated back then! No shaving. No Brazilian wax. It was a very hairy era.

Reluctantly, I gave up my panties. Truth was, I'd never peed due to not having underwear on, but I always thought I was going to. I always thought I was weird until my sister admitted the same thing one day. Either it's a fairly normal thought or Kell and I are both weird. I remember Phyllis once saying, "Have you ever peed the bed?"

I responded, "No."

She said, "Then don't you think you're being silly?" And I think *I'm* pragmatic!

I really liked the nurse that took my panties. I didn't like that she took my panties, but I did like her. She saw that I had a book which led us to talk about reading which led to our mutual love of Janet Evanovich's series with Stephanie Plum. We laughed about the characters and discussed which actors and actresses would work best if a movie were ever made. I had every intention of continuing the discussion post surgery. Silly me! Conversation would not be possible after surgery, at least not for me. Dave would converse quite easily. Dave and I were joking about being in

Donor Girl

the same room and wanted to make sure everyone got it right. My kidney was going into him; not the other way around.

Dr. Cooper stopped in briefly to check on me, make sure I'd signed papers and say hi just as he promised he would. He met Randy for the first time as well. The visit was brief, and the best description I can come up with is he was "in the zone." There was no joking, no warm and fuzzy; he was straight ahead focused on the task at hand. While it wasn't how I was used to seeing him, I realized that he had one thought on his mind and that was the upcoming surgery. He was the consummate professional at his job, and I thoroughly appreciated that he knew when to keep me calm through joking and when to be focused on my surgery.

My sister kept taking photos. I joked that she was memorializing the worst day of my life. I admit up front that I'm vain, so this wasn't how I wanted to look for photos. When they put the blue cap on Dave, she took a photo. Knowing how wretched I would look in the cap, I insisted they not put it on until the last moment. By then, Kelly couldn't take a photo. The anesthesiologist came in to put something in my IV to "calm me."

"Calm me" was an understatement. I pretty much don't remember anything after that. Apparently, they put on my little blue cap and started to wheel me into surgery. I stopped the guy who was pushing my bed and insisted they wait while Kelly took a picture. I still don't remember doing that.

## What is Laparoscopic Surgery?

Surgeons at the University of Maryland Medical Center use a minimally-invasive procedure called laparoscopic nephrectomy to remove a kidney from a donor. The minimally-invasive technique is performed with tiny incisions. Kidney donors are able to leave the hospital within two days,

Donor Girl

on average, and return to their normal activities within a couple of weeks. During the donor's operation the surgeon makes only a small incision below the navel -- about one-and a half to two inches -- as well as (three or) four small holes which he uses to insert instruments, including a laparoscope. The laparoscope contains a miniature camera, and surgeons watch what they are doing on a video monitor. In addition to less pain for the donor, no sutures or staples, and a faster recovery, the success rate of living donor kidneys, no matter what the donor-recipient relationship, is significantly greater than for cadaver kidneys.
Source:

**http://www.orlive.com/umm/1407/content/description.cfm**

Two years later, they would be doing this surgery through the navel with only one incision. The procedure just keeps getting better and more advantageous for the donor. However, as Dr. Cooper had explained to me, I would have three small incisions for the instruments and camera, and one longer 2-3 inch incision below the navel for the actual removal of the kidney. It goes without saying that I do not remember any of the surgical procedure.

The next thing I remember was a woman saying, "Grab a bucket, she's vomiting." I wondered who was throwing up and why was I hearing about it. Where was I? I distinctly remember hearing another woman say, "If we do not raise her body temperature, she is not going to survive this surgery." I remember thinking, "Wow, someone isn't doing too well. They could even die!" Then I felt a horrible clenching in my stomach and a retching in my throat and realized she was talking about me throwing up. Then I heard them telling someone to keep the hot blankets wrapped around me to bring my body temperature back up. My thoughts continued: "Oh no! That means I'm the one that might not make it if my body temperature doesn't rise. They were talking about *me*!"

## Donor Girl

It was no surprise that anesthesia would cause me to get physically ill. It has the same effect on both my mom and my sister. What was a surprise to me was my body temperature had dropped to 93 degrees. This put me into hypothermia. I remember feeling extremely hot, which is a side effect of hypothermia. The body is actually so cold that it thinks it's hot. I had been wrapped in hot blankets to try and raise my temperature.

I later asked about hearing the woman say the comment about me possibly not surviving. It was hotly denied by everyone I asked, but oddly enough, everything else I remembered hearing they agreed I'd heard. So I believe that it was said. At the very least, I *thought* I heard it being said.

I remember my mom and dad coming back to recovery. My dad was apparently quite disturbed by my condition and had to be escorted out of recovery. I tried to open my eyes and was not able to. I did manage to say, "I'm ok, Daddy, I'm ok," which I think upset him more. Dad didn't like being kicked out of surgery and tried to sneak around and come back in, only to get kicked out a second time. Kelly, mom and Randy had come in earlier, but I wasn't coherent. Randy said I was mumbling but not really conscious.

Meanwhile ... down the hall ... Dave was wide awake and feeling great. He told Kelly that his aches and pains and itching were immediately gone. He woke up hungry and swore his ice chips were the best he'd ever had. Dave also wanted to know when he could eat real food, while any real food I'd eaten recently was returning with a vengeance. Dave was Chatty Cathy; feeling great while I was doing my best Linda Blair imitation. Apparently, I gave him the better of the two kidneys. I needed a do-over. I started ripping off my hot blanket and heard a voice say, "You're exposing yourself." I didn't care. I was happy to go naked if it

Donor Girl

would help me feel cool. I was absolutely miserable. I was throwing up, wrapped in horrible hot blankets and thrashing around like a scene out of *The Exorcist*. I'm not sure how long I was in there while they raised my body temperature, but I was finally being moved and taken to my room.

Unfortunately, they had to take me past "The Great Cookie" on the way. Prior to this day, "The Great Cookie" was one of my favorite stops. There's nothing like a big ol' chocolate cookie except when it is about to make me throw my guts up. I thought, "I'm never going to eat another chocolate chip cookie for the rest of my life."

"I'm going to get sick!" I yelled.

"Just breathe through your mouth," the person pushing my bed said.

"I really think I'm going to be sick."

"No, you aren't. Just keep breathing through your mouth."

How did she know if I was going to get sick? The smell from "The Great Cookie" was wafting past me, filling my senses with the need to get sick. I was holding my breath.

"Breathe through your mouth,'" she repeated. She was determined not to give me a pan and to keep me from vomiting.

I breathed through my mouth and managed to not vomit on my way past "The Great Cookie." I don't remember much about the rest of the day. I was moved into a gorgeous donor suite on the 8th floor, Room C864, as promised. There was a stocked fridge and a "Welcome" fruit tray." I didn't notice any of it.

Around 7:30 P.M. or so, I remember my sister and Randy coming in and Randy saying they were going to dinner. I managed to open

Donor Girl

my eyes and acknowledge them. While they were gone, Dr. Cooper came in. I'm not sure of the time, but it was sometime while Randy and Kelly were at dinner. I tried really hard to focus. He was in his blue scrubs. How do I remember that? I managed to open my eyes for roughly 1.5 seconds and all I saw were blue scrubs and blue eyes. So I was able to register that it was Dr. Cooper. Past that, I couldn't open my eyes again. I remember thinking, "Open your eyes and look at the nice man. Be polite. Focus on him. You're being rude."

"How are you feeling?" he asked.

"Nauseous," I answered.

"I know," he said. After that, I just couldn't focus enough to say anything. Dr. Cooper was very kind and comforting. I couldn't remember communicating with him, but I did hear him say, "Your surgery was very boring; just how we like it." That was kind of his catch phrase. In his line of work, boring is good ... actually great!

I tried to respond with a laugh but don't know if it came out. I was hooked to a machine that was monitoring my vitals. It was giving me my temperature, blood pressure and heart rate. Any time one of my vitals dropped below the acceptable range, an alarm went off. It wasn't a very pleasant sound. Due to the hypothermia, my vitals were a bit erratic. I'm not sure which vital dropped, but the alarm went off.

"That's a horrific sound," I heard Dr. Cooper say. I couldn't respond, but I remember him saying it. He turned the alarm off and adjusted the clip on my finger. He sat there with me for a while in silence. I'm not sure he knew I was awake since I was in such a state that I couldn't talk or respond. If anything else was said, I don't remember it. The next thing I remember, Randy was returning from dinner.

# Donor Girl

I finally started to come around at 11:00 P.M. That was roughly 17 hours after they had first put me under. I was groggy but able to focus on the TV. Randy was able to stay in my room on a pull-out chair. It wasn't very comfortable, and it was a very long night.

Looking back at what the expectations were, I realized I didn't quite make the goals. I was supposed to be sitting up in a chair by that evening. Ha! Not even close. I did have some ice chips as allowed and a few family visitors, but that was about it.

The doctor who checked on me throughout the night had absolutely no bedside manner. He was quite cold and didn't do anything to make me feel comfortable or safe. My vitals continued to be off. My heart rate was high, my blood pressure was low and my temperature still wasn't normal. On top of that, I apparently wasn't passing enough urine. That possibly meant my remaining kidney wasn't functioning correctly. This was making for a very long evening.

Somewhere around 2:00 A.M., the same doctor came in and we discussed my situation. "Your heart rate is high and your blood pressure is low. It's about eighty over fifty. If it gets down into the forties, we're going to have to do something," Dr. Cold said.

"Well, I am going to be ok, right?" I asked, feeling scared.

"I can't guarantee that," he said.

Oh dear God. Was he serious?? He couldn't "guarantee" that I'd be ok. Here I was -- one less kidney -- scarred, scared, and apparently, possibly dying. Ok, I didn't really believe I was dying, but when a doctor can't guarantee I'm going to be ok, certainly my first thought at 2:00 A.M. was: "I'm dying." Randy was half asleep, half awake, but not really able to help. I spent the next 4 hours until 6:00 A.M. watching my vitals, making sure I didn't die.

Donor Girl

Randy actually made the comment, "You are your own worst enemy." That pretty much pissed me off. I knew he was right and that my paranoia wasn't helping my recovery. Randy and I always differed in our approach to life. Randy was an optimist, assuming everything would always be fine. I was a realist that bordered on pessimist. However, I didn't need a statement like that at 2:00 A.M.

It used to drive my dad crazy that I was a hypochondriac as a kid. So if I got sick, I'd ask, "Daddy, am I going to be ok?" He always said, "Nope, you'll be dead by morning." He was saying it as a joke hoping to make me relax. But I'd take it seriously and try to stay awake all night hoping not to die. This took me right back to childhood.

I dozed uncomfortably throughout the night as they continued to monitor my vitals. Finally, it was morning. Poor Kelly had slept off and on in the lobby, and Randy was quite cramped after sleeping on his little pull-out chair.

I had inflatable pillow-like things around my legs that inflated every 15 minutes to keep me from getting blood clots. And the absolute worst thing was the catheter. I didn't need to worry about my panties anymore because I had some sort of tube going into my bladder. This was the worst thing I'd ever experienced. Every time I moved the slightest bit, I felt this thing in my bladder and had the urge to urinate. Of course, this is what they wanted me to do so they could measure the output in a bag and make sure my lone kidney was functioning correctly. Apparently, the tubing had gotten twisted around and hung up so the urine was not flowing into the bag. I was being told that my body was not producing the correct amount of urine and that was a concern.

"Lovely. Dave's down the hall peeing like a racehorse, and I got the kidney that doesn't want to produce urine. I want my left kidney back!"

## Donor Girl

So, along with worrying about my temperature being low; my blood pressure being low; my heart rate being high; I now wasn't peeing properly. Oh happy day! (As mom would say, "No good deed ever goes unpunished.") Finally, they realized that the urine bag tubing was hung up. The nurse, who was aware of my concerns, pulled the tube. A beautiful flow of healthy yellow urine streamed into the bag.

"Oh look," the nurse said, "you have plenty of urine." Usually not words that make you elated but next to "You won the million dollar lottery," they may have been the best words I could have heard.

I used to joke about older people being obsessed with their bodily functions. I've heard more than I ever needed to know about the fecal habits of my father-in-law, mother-in-law, grandparents, etc. But I now understand. The very basics of the body are what show us if we're functioning correctly. If you're passing gas, peeing and pooping, you're pretty much good to go.

Needless to say, I didn't die that first night. The next morning, the nurses were very nice and tried to be helpful. They had given me morphine for the pain, but that caused me to get sick and vomit more. I was getting very tired of feeling nauseous. I have a fairly high threshold for pain, but my tolerance for vomiting is zero. I had probably thrown up a total of 3 times in my 18 years of marriage. The first time, we had only been married a couple of years when Randy came in to try and offer his assistance. He told people about my reaction when he asked if there was anything he could do to help.

"Lee transformed into this scene out of *The Excorcist*. Her head spun around, and she spoke in this horrible voice that said, 'Get me a wet washcloth and get the hell out of here!'" Yes, that is my tolerance for nausea.

# Donor Girl

I requested that they stop the morphine. Even though they were giving me the strongest anti-nausea drugs possible, nothing was working. I'd rather have the pain than the nausea. Hospitals tend to use Tylenol versus other forms of painkillers, but for kidney donors, it's what they insist on. Ibuprofen-type painkillers (which I prefer) break down in the kidneys, where Tylenol breaks down in the liver. I would now have to use Tylenol for all pain. For me, that's barely a step above a sugar pill.

I was experiencing horrible shoulder and neck pain, probably from the position I was in on the cold operating table. The most I could handle were ice packs and Tylenol. The only thing good about surgery was supposed to be the drugs. I was told about this wonderful little thing that, if you push a button, you get a morphine high. In fact, most people said that the body part hurting the most after surgery is your thumb from pushing that button. Not me! No sir. My body didn't want morphine; my mind wanted morphine. My mind was craving morphine. But like my craving for George Clooney, it was not to be. C'est la vie. I was having moments of "What have I done?" Morphine would have helped with that.

Dr. Cooper came in to check on me. Bless his heart! I was not very nice to him. "You did this to me," I said accusingly. "This is your fault." That could not have been something he wanted to hear. Here the man had saved Dave's life and had certainly not forced me to donate my kidney. Yet I was blaming him for my pain. Sort of like a pregnant woman in labor angry with her husband.

"And I hate this catheter. It's awful."

"I know it is, and we'll get that taken out soon, I promise." He assured me I'd get feeling better and to just give it time. He patted my knee reassuringly and promised to check on me soon.

# Donor Girl

I hated the catheter more than anything. It was awful. When the nurses would come in and ask, "Is there anything we can do for you?" I'd respond, "Yes, get this thing out of me!" Finally, they came in to say they were doing just that. All I could visualize was them taking it out and me spraying the room with urine. Of course, women don't spray. We are more like a waterfall, dribbling down and hitting everything in our path. But I felt like I would spray the room. The catheter just gave you a constant feeling like you needed to go. I asked them to bring me a towel just in case that happened. They offered a bedpan ..."Uh, no." They told me to breathe deep and let my breath out. I did and they removed it. I had visions of me running to the bathroom. I was running nowhere. I had a 3 inch incision in my lower abdomen and three .5 to 1 inch incisions on my stomach. I was hooked up to machines and had a hospital gown on that hid nothing. I managed to sit up in the most painful and awkward of ways, put a towel between my legs like a surfboard and pulled my IV cart into the bathroom. Despite the feeling of incontinence, nothing came out until I got to the bathroom, and then it was not as satisfying as I expected. They told me it would take a while for my bladder to get back to normal after the cath. Lovely.

Prior to surgery, I had e-mailed other donors, and many were happy to tell me their stories and communicate their support. One guy not only shared his experience but let me know that he would be in the Maryland area the day after my surgery and wanted to visit me. I didn't see any reason not to let him so I said, "Sure."

Thursday turned out to be my big visitor day. By everything I'd been told, I should have gone home on Friday as that would be two days after surgery. My best friend, Jodi, was flying in Thursday evening and had planned to spend the weekend helping me at home. That way, Randy would be able to do the things he needed to without having to babysit me. Once Jodi left on Monday, it would be all up to Randy again.

Donor Girl

Everyone seemed to want me to get up and walk. They didn't understand that it felt like an impossible task. I'd come into the hospital the picture of health -- able to run, work out, ski, play -- and here I was, on my back in pain, filled with worry and unable to even walk the halls. I remember just a week ago making my mom walk the hallway in the hospital and then sit in a chair. She had said, "You're lucky you've never had surgery. You just don't understand." I do now, Ma! If I could take it back and not make her walk, causing her more anguish and pain, I would have! I *thought* I was doing a good thing.

During the day, I had visits from my pastor, Phyllis, my father and my cousin, Amy. Amy was the big surprise. I hadn't expected a cousin to come by, and it meant a lot. She also went down to visit Dave, who wasn't getting nearly as many visitors as I was. Flowers were also arriving in droves. Kelly had brought me flowers and a stuffed kitty from the kids. My parents brought flowers. Craig Morgan sent flowers as did his manager. Erik sent flowers as well as my boss and my company, Broken Bow Records. It looked like a florist shop in my room -- or a funeral home during a viewing -- one of the two.

My mom had come down the day of my surgery, but she was still recuperating from her own surgery and ended up quite ill. Her doctor scolded her and told her to go home and not return to the UMMC. My dad visited for a while, and then went to see Dave. He then headed home to check on Sandi and the kids.

Phyllis came in early that day, and what I expected to be a rather quick half-hour visit turned into all day private nursing for me. Along with having had her own surgeries and childbirths, she's an RN. I was having trouble getting out of bed, and Phyllis asked, "Hasn't anyone shown you the proper way to get out of bed?"

"Not that I recall, but there are some fuzzy spots." She showed me how to roll over on my side and use the bed and handrails to sit up with minimum pain.  She then helped me into the bathroom and insisted I walk down the hall.  I made it about halfway and needed to turn around.  As I was walking back, I had an extreme feeling of shooting pain through my chest and up my shoulders.

"Oh dear God! My heart can't handle it.  I'm having a heart attack! Get the crash cart; hit the code blue button; someone help me!" Ok, I didn't say that, but I *thought* it.  What I think I said was, "AAAAAAAAhhhhh."

Phyllis asked, "What's wrong?"  I described the pain, and she said it was the carbon dioxide gas that hadn't managed to expel itself. When I stood up, it raised into my shoulders and chest.  It was excruciating.

"Lie down, lie down.  It will dissipate through your body and won't hurt as badly."  So she helped me into the bed, and we lowered it down so it laid flat.  It did help.

Thank God she was there!  The pain was so bad that it was the first and only time through the whole ordeal that I actually screamed. I've always heard people in the hospitals screaming in pain and thought, "Oh please, quit your screaming."  Ha!  "Oh please" my tush.  Scream if it helps.

I hit the nurse call button and begged for Percocet.  They brought me some, and slowly the pain went away.  Little did I know how much I'd regret that decision?

There's always a bright spot in any situation.  While I'm in the throes of pain and misery, in walks Curtis.  Curtis is a med student at the University of Maryland and couldn't be cuter.  Not in an "Oh my gosh, you're hot" kind of way.  Even though he was at the ripe old age of 21, I'd have felt like a pedophile even going there in my mind.  But Curtis was cute in an "Aren't you adorable" kind of way.  He had beautiful blue eyes, a perfect set of teeth that smiled

Donor Girl

often and a wonderful bedside manner. He was in the operating room during my surgery, and I'm assuming he was assigned to me. Lucky him. I'm a catch. And I assure you, as he was looking at my face with no makeup; the dark circles under my eyes; the unwashed hair and the swollen abdomen, he was thinking just that very thing. Bet his first thought was, "She's hot." Yea, right.

Curtis came in that first day post-op to check on me. After introducing himself, he smiled and said, "I was in the OR during your surgery. Everything went great. Doctor Cooper spent extra time double stitching your incision so it wouldn't herniate. He kept the scar low and small. How are you feeling?"

I gave him my best smile and tried to look as attractive as possible. Photos I'd later see of myself show that this was not possible, but considering I was still drugged, I thought it was possible at the time. I explained about some of my pain, but tried not to elaborate. This cute young boy did not have to hear about embarrassing things like my catheter or vomiting. I did have some pride.

"They'll try to manage your pain, just rest. Now tell me, have you passed gas today?" He asked, calm as could be. He did **NOT** just ask me if I passed gas. Did I hear correctly? Save me from this humiliation. When I didn't answer it got worse.

"Are you urinating? Have you had a bowel movement?" **MAKE IT STOP!** Tell me he did not just ask me about my poop experiences.

"Get me out of here!" my head screamed. "There's a cute boy asking me about body functions. So what if he has a white coat and stethoscope? They're a dime a dozen in this place. I think the janitorial staff wears them. Everyone seems to be in one except me, who has some sort of gown where my butt hangs out. The indignities are staggering. Young boys asking such questions; clothing that doesn't flatter or cover; need I go on?"

## Donor Girl

I regained some modicum of composure and said, "I appreciate your concern, but if you really want me to answer those questions, you'll need to bring in the sixty- year-old nurse out in the hallway. I'll be happy to let her know." He smiled that charming boy smile and said he'd check on me later. Wonderful; can't wait for the next set of questions.

In the meantime, my pastor came to see me. He later said that it was obvious I wasn't in a great mood. Not exactly what you want to be told, but the truth was, I was not in a great mood. Dave was running the halls like a teenager, feeling like a million bucks, and I couldn't get out of bed. Dave looked like a scene out of *Chariots of Fire* while I was the walking wounded. I had been warned that donation is harder on the donor than the recipient, but I thought, "Not me! I'm going to amaze them all." I managed to amaze no one, including myself.

I kept thinking about what the girl from McCormick had said about the surgery being a "nonevent." When would it become a "nonevent" for me? Right now, it was feeling very eventful. She had said, "If I'd had two to give, I'd do it again." SERIOUSLY? Again?? I kept getting asked, "Would you do it again?" You really want me to answer that right now?? No! Hell no! But then again, I said, "It might be better to ask me in a couple of months."

Of course, every time Dave called or stopped in and called me his "Angel" and said how great he felt, I had a fleeting moment of: "Ok, it was worth it."

One of the former donors I had been e-mailing wanted to come visit me in the hospital. Our e-mails had gone like this:

Sent: Saturday, June 09, 2007 9:19 PM
Subject: Kidney Donation

Donor Girl

Hi. I'm a 42 year old female about to donate a kidney to my brother in law and Nina Schroder was kind enough to put me in touch with you. I appreciate your being willing to share your experience as the unknown is quite scary. If you get the chance to reply, I'd appreciate your sharing all you can about surgery and recovery up to this point. Whatever you're comfortable with will mean a lot. Many thanks. Congratulations on making what I know is a very difficult, yet rewarding decision. I hope you are doing well. Lee

In a message dated 6/17/2007 he writes:

Lee,
First, let me say I am sorry for not checking my E-mail sooner and you have had to wait for a reply. I will tell that surgery was the easy part. All the work ups to the surgery date was the tough part. The team did every test they could to make sure that I was Health enough to even give to my bother. The surgery day went very well for me we were the first two scheduled for surgery of course I went in first and came out before my bother did. I did very well, and they took my right kidney because it had a small stone (what a way to pass a stone). Therefore, the surgery for Jim was longer since they had to do more work. The surgeons like to take the left kidney. I was in the donor room before 4:00 pm, and they had actual stocked the room so I could entertain my family. There is some pain with it and they will assist in the pain management. I was off any pain pills in one week. I will say if you have to travel any distance say the extra day in the hospital or local hotel, and ask for an abdominal support wrap. My bother Jim is doing very well and I'm doing just fine. Please give me a call if you need to talk. Will keep you and your bother-in-law in my Prayers.

Sent: Tuesday, June 19, 2007 10:30 PM
Subject: Re: Kidney Donation

**Were you scared? I'm finding that with 3 weeks left before surgery, I'm feeling rather anxious. Did you go through that at all? Thanks, Lee**

In a message dated 6/25/2007 he writes:

**Lee,**
**You and your Bother-in-law are still in our prayers. I hope everything is going well. Also, my brother's girl friend found this neat web site: www.status.com It allows you to register on the site and you give out the pass word to all your friends and family and then they can post you and your bothers status while the surgery is going on, and during recovery time. There is a computer in the donor room, so you could see the prayers and well wishes that everyone gives to you. I was able to update while in the hospital. The site is free. Check it out. Good luck and you are in our prayers.**

Sent: Monday, June 25, 2007 10:15 PM
Subject: Re: Kidney Donation

**Thank you for all of that information! You have been wonderful! It's truly appreciated. Lee**

In a message he writes;

**Lee, Please keep me informed on how everything goes. What date is your surgery scheduled?**

Sent: Tuesday, June 26, 2007 10:05 AM
Subject: Re: Kidney Donation

Donor Girl

If the final blood test/mix goes well on July 5th, it's set for July 11th. Thanks for your thoughts and prayers. Lee

In a message dated 7/6/2007 he writes;

Lee,
I hope everything went well yesterday, by now you are ready to just get it done. Good luck, you, and your bother-in-law are in our prayers.

From: LAdams
Sent: Friday, July 06, 2007 12:23 PM
Subject: Re: Kidney Donation

The tests went well for me. Not so much for Dave. He'll have to go on dialysis prior to next Wed. It does look like it will still happen on the 11th. I'm VERY ready for it to be the 12th!! Thanks for your prayers.

In a message dated 7/8/2007 he writes;

Lee,
I now have to be in DC on the 13th for a meeting at the Navy Annex and will travel up on the 12tth I will be staying with my bother, could you use a visitor on the 12th? If you feel funny about it I will understand and will continue to keep you in my Prayers.

Sent: July 7th, 2007 Subject: Re: Kidney Donation

Sure! You are more than welcome to visit. I can't guarantee I'll be at my best!! haha But that would be very nice of you. I'll probably be under Lilli Adams

**Kuhn. It would be a pleasure to meet you. Travel safely.**

I appreciated those e-mails and his care and concern. Of course, I was visualizing myself coming out of surgery and being up and about and ready for visitors. He did visit. Randy was with me when he shared his story. He gave me a coin, which was a gesture from his military background I had learned from Craig Morgan who had spent over 10 years in the Army. Divisions of the military get coins, and they share them with others. There's a lot of significance in receiving a coin, but there's also an unwritten rule that if someone "coins" you, the next time they see you, they can ask to see the coin. If you don't have it, you owe them a drink. I was honored to receive a coin from Steven.

There was a part of the visit that was disconcerting, however, and left me feeling quite nervous for about two weeks. After his release from the hospital following surgery, he got into a bit of a coughing fit on his 5 hour drive home. Apparently, the coughing fit caused his incision to herniate. He had to come back to the hospital and be opened up again and have yet another surgery.

So he warned me against sneezing and coughing while I was healing. Naturally, the minute he left, I felt the need to start coughing and sneezing. I went into a total panic as I was sure my incision was herniating. It wasn't, but trying to convince me of that wasn't possible. I was in full panic mode. My sister was beside herself and went out into the hall. As she later describes it, she was praying for a miracle and in walk Nina and Meg; shortly thereafter, she ran into Dr. Cooper. She explained to them my panic and the reason for it. Meg assured me that I had nothing to worry about and told me that, while she couldn't say for sure what had caused his incision to herniate, she was certain that basic sneezing and coughing wouldn't do it. She reassured me again and again. My sister also told Dr. Cooper what happened and that I was a bit freaked out. Dr. Cooper stopped in to tell me that my

Donor Girl

stitches would hold through normal coughing and sneezing. He was very reassuring and told me not to worry.

I was starting to feel better, and they gave me another Percocet to help with the shoulder pain. Eventually, my guests left and Randy went down to the airport to pick up Jodi. Originally, Jodi was going to spend the night and Randy was going to head home to take care of the pets and get a good night's rest. I was worried about Kelly who was staying 24/7 at the hospital and had actually slept in the lobby on two chairs pushed together. With Dave not having a private room like I did, there was nowhere for her to stay in his room. I was getting to the point where I just wanted some time alone. I was irritable and frustrated and didn't want to be mean to anyone. Kell and I have the kind of relationship where I could get mad, be mean, be totally me, and she'd be fine with it. Plus, Kelly needed a place to sleep that was more comfortable. She had left the hospital long enough to go home and reassure the kids that everyone was doing well. The whole time she was gone, I wanted her to come back. She's my big sis, and I just needed her there. We had suffered through so much together with regards to this surgery and I needed her to know that I was ok, and to reassure me that both Dave and I were ok.

When Jodi and Randy got back, I knew they had to be tired. Randy had barely slept. Jodi had been getting kids ready for a weekend without her; a job ready for a day without her; and she had traveled far. I encouraged them to go home, get a good night's sleep and come back the next day. They visited awhile and protested, but eventually they left. Another reason I didn't want Jodi to stay was I was worried about Randy driving the 100 miles home by himself. He was tired and it was late. I wanted someone to help him stay awake. I needed Jodi taking care of Randy as much as I needed her taking care of me. She couldn't be in two places at once so I sent her home with Randy since he was alone.

Donor Girl

Kell was staying on the pull out chair and I said, "The whole time you were gone, I just wanted you to come back. I really needed my big sis here."

Kelly was so touched. "I didn't think you felt that way. I watched Phyllis helping you, and I know how close you and Jodi are. It means a lot to me that I'm the one you wanted here." I wanted all my people with me and Kelly, Jodi and Sandi are my people. Having them there and having Sandi in town was a comfort beyond words.

Kelly was very patient with me. Every time I sneezed or coughed or laughed and was worried I'd done something to my incision, she'd come over and lift my gown and look at the bandage and say, "No bleeding and no oozing. You're fine." Kell wanted to spend some time with Dave, so she went down to his room for about an hour or so and then came back up and made herself a bed on the little pull-out chair.

The nurses came in at various times, and one happened to come in around 2:00 A.M. while I was wide awake. She talked to me and asked what was wrong. I explained that I was scared. I was worried about so many things, and she was such a beautiful nurse. She spent the longest time talking to me. Kelly woke up, and we both listened to her talk about her pregnancy, the five kids she already had and how she had remarried her first husband after they both realized they were each other's true love. She was hardworking, Christian and so reassuring. I just adored her. She got me through another tough evening.

I realized around 5:30 A.M. that I was once again nauseous. The Percocet! Ugh! I laid there in bed, not moving, afraid that the slightest movement would cause me to vomit. I breathed through my mouth like they told me to do when they first brought me to my room. I literally lay still for hours. Kelly woke up, and I told

Donor Girl

her I was feeling nauseous. She wanted me to get up and walk, move around, and ... oh my God ... **EAT!** The thought of food was awful, absolutely awful. It was the ride past "The Great Cookie" all over again.

While Kelly was gone -- unbeknownst to me -- she was calling Randy and Jodi to tell them I was not doing well and needed to be encouraged and "pushed." I assure you that was not what I felt like I needed. Dr. Cooper came in around 9:30 and asked how I was. "Horrible. I'm nauseous again. I guess it's the Percocet. I know if I don't get up and move around and eat, you're not going to let me go home today. But I don't think I can move, and I don't want to eat." I was all but whining.

"Lee, you aren't going anywhere today. I'm keeping you here at least through tomorrow."

"Oh, thank you, Doctor Cooper." The thought of a long drive home was overwhelming, and I couldn't even fathom it. He patted my knee and told me it would be better by the next day. "I did manage to roll over and sleep on my side," I said, happy with my small accomplishment.

"It's the little steps that help," he said.

I hate sleeping on my back. People have asked me if David took on any of my characteristics with my DNA in him. Kelly told me that the second day in the hospital Dave was having dreams about wanting to sleep on his stomach. Dave *never* sleeps on his stomach and couldn't understand why he was having the dreams. *Weird!* The only other thing that happened is Dave's eyebrows and hair went from gray to brown, my color.

After Dr. Cooper left, Randy called and was full of energy to get me up and going. He had been working out for about 6 weeks in a program called "Boot Camp," where the leader teaches the workout by pushing the students hard, military style. They ran hard, did massive push-ups, sit-ups and crunches. Randy is a very competitive person. He was determined to win whether it was racing, doing the most calisthenics, or running the farthest. All of this led to his hurting his knee to the point of limping. He was limping all over the hospital and almost having a harder time getting around the hallways than I was.

So when I answered the phone, the first thing Randy said was, "Get ready for Boot Camp. We're going to get you up and moving, walking the halls and eating."

"You just don't understand," I said. "It's not that I don't want to, I can't! I'm sick, I'm going to throw up, and I just don't want to eat."

"Well, we're going to get you doing all of that. We're on our way and will see you in a few minutes." He hung up, and I was dreading what was coming.

Kelly came back in and reported on Dave. Dave was doing much better than I was. He was eating, walking around, and was doing well enough to be released. In fact, without my knowing it, his doctor wanted to release him on Friday. Dave didn't feel ready to be released because he actually had to pass a test proving that he knew how and when to take all of his pills. It was a lot to learn, and he was nervous about it. There is a certain comfort that comes with being in a hospital and getting round the clock care. I'm not sure who eventually talked to whom, but Dave didn't go home Friday night.

When Randy and Jodi got to the room, Kelly and Randy were full of encouragement to get me out of bed. Jodi hung back a bit, realizing how much I didn't want it. We had made an agreement years before that when everyone else told us what we *should* hear, we'd tell each other what we *wanted* to hear. She was keeping her

Donor Girl

promise. I just kept telling Kell and Dave, "You just don't understand."

Finally, Randy reached over to my breakfast tray, took off the lid, and waved it under my nose saying, "Look, just have some eggs." That was all it took to open the floodgates. After 5 hours of lying there, not moving so I wouldn't get sick, the smell of eggs did it.

I yelled, "Get the bucket." What came next was nothing shy of the Three Stooges. Jodi, who is a sympathetic vomiter, fled the room for the bathroom to get a wet washcloth. Kelly and Randy both thought the bucket was on the opposite side of the room, and they literally collided in the middle. I was laughing while trying to contain the rising bile and finally pointed to the bucket. Randy reached it just in time, and I hurled for the next few minutes. The nurse came in to help and cleaned me up. I, of course, went into a panic and was sure I'd broken my stitches wide open and had herniated my incision. I asked the nurse, "Could throwing up make me herniate my incision?

The pretty, petite nurse was so sweet, but she said, "Well, yes it could." Of course, that put me right into a frenzy. Kelly immediately came over to check my bandage while Randy followed the nurse into the hallway. I could hear him yelling at her, so I was yelling at him to stop. I begged Jodi and Kelly to go stop him. Basically, he was telling everyone that they needed to be more positive with me and stop freaking me out. Between the doctor who told me I might not survive the night; the donor who told me that coughing could herniate the incision; and now the nurse telling me that vomiting could also cause me to herniate, I was pretty freaked. Randy had had enough. He never wanted me to have the surgery, and he was tired of the staff upsetting me. I didn't blame the staff at all; they were just answering my questions. They didn't realize how my mind worked and that everything they said negative I figured would happen to me. It went back to my "worst case scenario" personality. Finally,

# Donor Girl

everyone calmed down, and the nurse came in to tell me I'd be fine.

People with hangovers always say that once you throw up, you get feeling better. This was true. I was tired and stayed in bed a lot, but I was feeling better and able to get up and walk around. At one point, I looked around the room and noticed Randy asleep on one chair, Jodi on another chair. I had dozed off in the bed. Jodi had her laptop and was catching up on work. I thought we'd be home watching movies and sitting in our hammocks by Friday afternoon, not hanging in a hospital room. I apologized numerous times to Jodi, but she seemed quite happy.

"Lee, I never have time to just catch up on work, read a book, talk to my friends and have no interruptions. I'm quite happy."

We took some walks down the hall and had some lunch, which I managed to keep down. In the evening, we walked down to Dave's room. It was the longest walk I'd taken. While we were there, Dr. Cooper walked in.

"Well, it's nice to see you down here." Randy, Kelly, and Jodi were there with me.

"I hear they almost released David before me," I said. "That would have been depressing."

"Yea, I knew you wouldn't handle that well." He replied. And he was right!

I felt kind of guilty that Dave and Kelly could be home but weren't because of me. Dave, however, said,"I wasn't ready to go home today. I needed one more day." Dr. Cooper said a few more words and left.

Donor Girl

Earlier that day, a man who had also donated a kidney on Wednesday, was able to go home. He was up and walking around, looking great like nothing had happened to him. What the heck was wrong with me? Why did I look and feel like a train wreck? I'd always felt like a strong person, but boy did I feel wimpy. I kept reminding myself that the rest of them had some awesome painkillers while, lucky me, I got Tylenol. I assure you I'd have been much livelier if I was on morphine!

Randy and Jodi headed back home shortly afterward, and Kelly once again slept in my room. All signs were pointing toward me going home on Saturday. The other donor was on his way home and stopped in to wish me luck. He had bounced back much faster than I had, but he hadn't gotten sick off the pain meds either. That was a big part of my problem. I couldn't heal as quickly while vomiting. At least that's what I kept telling myself.

Sure enough, the next morning, I was told that I'd be going home. Randy and Jodi were on their way as a team of doctors walked in. Curtis was among them, and I said hi to him. I wasn't feeling great, and I was looking worse. There were three female med students and two guys, including Curtis and the doctor. It wasn't Dr. Cooper this time but Benjamin Philosophe, who is Chief of the Division of Transplantation and Director of Liver Transplantation. He holds an MD and a PhD.

One of the blond female med students was trying to hand Dr. Philosophe a pen and apparently, she had a small roll of toilet paper in her pocket. It attached itself to the pen causing her to break into a fit of giggles which prompted the other girls to fall into a fit of giggles. This made me pissed off. Here I was; looking horrible; feeling even worse; having just given up a working body organ and these girls were giggling like a bunch of cheerleaders. Thankfully, the male med students and Dr. Philosophe didn't join in. In that moment, I learned to respect and appreciate the character on *Grey's Anatomy* that Sandra Oh plays. Give me someone serious and focused on my health when I'm sick. I didn't need giggles. I needed Christina!

Dr. Philosophe asked if I wanted to go home and I said yes. He looked over my chart and announced that he'd be releasing me that day. I thanked him, and after they left, I requested a shower. I hadn't had one since I got there and desperately needed one. In fact, I think everyone on the hall was requesting that I take one. I noticed my number of visitors was slowing down and figured the lack of a shower might be the #1 reason. Kelly came in and helped me with some logistics, and I finally felt clean. I didn't look any better, but I was clean.

I was finally going to get released from the hospital. I was ready to go, although the drive home was looming ahead of me. It's never fast getting released from a hospital, and we had some time remaining. Kelly and Dave walked down, and we decided to take on the stairs. We wandered down the hall and went down a flight of stairs. Dave actually made it down two flights, but one was all I could do.

My opinion hadn't changed. He received the stronger of the two kidneys. When we got back up to the 8th floor, we stopped in front of the Wall of Fame where they list all the living kidney donors. My name would one day be on that Wall. Kelly, always with her camera, took a picture of Dave and me in front of the Wall.

We made it back to my room as Randy and Jodi arrived. Eventually, my medications were ordered. Randy picked them up at the hospital pharmacy. My release papers were signed, and they came by to take out my ever present IV. The poor little sweet nurse that Randy had yelled at came by to wheel me out in the wheelchair while Randy, Jodi and Kelly took all my flowers and gifts out to the car and drove around to the front door. Kelly snapped photos the whole way, and Jodi surprised me with some treats from, yes, "The Great Cookie." Oh Lord. I explained that I might have to wait a bit to eat them but she and Randy were welcome to dive in.

I was supposed to get out and walk around en route to home since it was a 100 mile drive, and they don't recommend you travel that far without stopping and walking. So we stopped at a gas station and minimart where Randy gassed up the car while Jodi walked around the parking lot with me.

I was craving French Vanilla tea and begged Randy to stop at Martin's on the way home. Randy chose to stop somewhere else though, and I knew they wouldn't have French Vanilla tea. Randy came out and there was no French Vanilla tea and offered to go to Martin's. I really wanted some but I also really wanted to get home. Little did I know, it would be two weeks until I could drink French Vanilla Tea.

Once we got home, Jodi and I settled into the outdoor hammocks that are underneath the deck and shaded. I had built a little fish pond in the weeks prior to surgery and I had planted some nice flowering and tropical looking plants around it. We had a great view of the river. It was very quiet and serene. We had two chair hammocks and one swinging bench hammock. I had settled on the bigger one so I could lie down, and Jodi was on a chair hammock. She was happily reading while I rested. I had taken my Tylenol and had my ice packs.

My cousins, who live behind me, came down to visit and my parents stopped by. Mom and I compared our incisions; she was still recovering from her surgery 10 days prior to mine. We sat there looking rather pitiful. But at least I was home.

I had always joked that my one dog, a Puli named Eddie, would die lying beside my lifeless body before he'd move. Whereas, my Border Collie, Jacke, would nudge me a few times and run off to play. I was very surprised to find that both of them stayed right by my side. It was an odd comfort. My cat, Mick, was just happy I was home.

My family didn't stay long as both mom and I were fairly worn out. Randy got to work taking care of some things around the house, and Jodi and I continued to enjoy a beautiful day outside. My neighbor, Anne, who had her own emergency surgery over the summer, stopped by to assure me things do get better. Jodi relaxed and read while I napped.

We had a quiet evening; Jodi and I watched chick flicks. I had Xanax to help me sleep and was between sleeping on my back and my side, but still longing to sleep on my stomach. The Xanax helped me to relax and sleep, but I was getting migraines every afternoon. Since I couldn't take anything more helpful than Tylenol, Xanax was my saving white pill.

Doing the simple things was difficult: getting out of bed, using the bathroom, getting dressed, etc. None of my clothes fit since I was bloated in my abdomen. I looked about 3 months pregnant. I was not planning on coming out with a distended abdomen. I had lost about 9 pounds and was down to 102, but I had a bloated tummy. This left me looking like a child from a Third World country. I was all bony with my spine showing through, yet I couldn't get my jeans to button over my stomach. Everyone at the hospital had told me the swelling would go down in "a couple of weeks." Last I checked, a couple was two, so I was counting on it to be gone in two weeks.

I wasn't able to sleep for long since I hurt so badly, so I got out of bed, grabbed a blanket and some orange juice and went out on the deck. We have a recliner style deck chair that I sat on, wrapped up in my blanket. Sitting up, even just on a slight incline, helped with the pain. I don't know if it was the hot blanket ordeal or what

# Donor Girl

caused my sudden aversion to hot beverages, but I couldn't even stomach the thought of drinking a hot tea.

As the sun started to come up and warm the earth, I also realized I had no tolerance for heat and sun. Again, I believed this to be a side effect from those awful hot blankets, but it was a horrible side effect. I was worried that two of my favorite things would no longer be my favorite things. I love hot tea; and although I try to be careful in the sun, the truth is I spend a lot of time boating and doing water sports. This does require a certain amount of tolerance for heat and sun. Add that to the current loss of appetite for a chocolate chip cookie, and life wasn't looking nearly as happy as it had a week ago.

Jodi and Randy woke up not too long after I did, and Jodi and I returned to our spots under the deck. I did fine in the shade, and we were enjoying a Sunday morning, despite my pain. I kept apologizing to Jodi for the horrible time she had to have had. First, I had to spend an extra day in the hospital, which was fun for no one. Second, I couldn't do anything fun. She continuously reassured me that just having time to sit with a friend, read a book, look out over the Potomac River and have no real responsibility for a few days was heaven. It meant the world to me to have her there, so it all worked out for the best. She and Randy would need to leave early in the afternoon so she could catch her flight home.
I rested outside while Randy took Jodi to the airport. It was sad to see her go, but it meant so much that she was there. My cousin brought some dinner down, and my mother-in-law stopped by. Then Karen from Curves came by with a bottle of diet Mountain Dew and a plant. I managed to talk to everyone for about an hour and eat some dinner. But after an hour, I stood up and thanked everyone for coming and said that I had to go to bed.

After Randy returned, we were just hanging out and watching TV. Randy continued to have problems with his knee and was hobbling around worse than I was. At one point, he was lying on the

# Donor Girl

loveseat while I was lying on the sofa. I had an ice pack going and had taken some Tylenol. He was taking my much stronger Percocet. The phone rang from across the room. We looked at each other and neither of us exactly jumped up. Finally, I realized I would be able to get there easier than he would, so I got up and answered the phone. While I was up, I decided to refresh my ice pack. The hospital had sent me home with some ice packs. All I had to do was add ice.

"Do you have another of those?" Randy asked. "I could use one for my knee."

"You're kidding me, right?" I asked, incredulous. "I just had a kidney ripped out and I'm getting *you* an ice pack?"

"If you wouldn't mind ... while you're up and all," he said.

"Sure, let me hold my insides together while I grab you an ice pack. Thanks, Hon." MEN!

My friend had told me a story while I was in the hospital which made me laugh even more now. The day she had gotten home from her brain surgery she wanted to take a shower. There were no clean towels in the upstairs bathroom, so she asked her husband to go downstairs to the laundry and get some. She was only supposed to stand for short periods of time, and she got in the shower for a quick few minutes of warm water. She waited and waited and waited and waited. Finally, she got out of the shower and yelled for her husband. When he came upstairs with a towel, she asked, "What were you doing?" He explained that on the way to the laundry, the computer had caught his attention, and he stopped to play a video game. MEN!

And of course, my mom had her own story. Following her hysterectomy, she needed her prescriptions filled. They got home too late the first night, so my dad was to go to the pharmacy the next day. Dad woke up sick and didn't feel he could make it to the pharmacy. Mom still wasn't allowed to drive, so she had a friend from church come pick her up and take her to the drugstore. MEN! I was obviously in good company. The funny thing is all three of these men are very attentive, caring, loving husbands. This would later become quite a joke between Randy and me; that I had to take care of *him* following *my* surgery.

On Monday, I made it out to the deck by about 6:30 A.M. I wasn't sleeping much past about 5 to 6 hours, and that was with the help of Xanax. I made myself some toast and orange juice and curled up in a blanket, finally falling back asleep. When I woke up, I made my way to my computer and decided I might as well log on and do some work. Working out of the house makes it hard to take any real time off, and as long as I was just sitting there, it made sense to work.

This was an e-mail I sent to the entire BBR staff on Monday, July 16, five days after surgery. It summed it up pretty well.

**For those of you who don't like graphic details, suffice it to say I'm doing better today although I have a long way to go. I get tired very easily. David (the recipient) has felt great since he got the kidney and is running laps around me. That was what it was all about so I'm grateful.**

**For those of you who like graphic details (and I know Mark is saying "Oh yea") feel free to read on.**

**<u>Wednesday:</u> Admission at 6 AM, 7:30 knocked out by IV and wheeled into surgery. Somewhere around 10:30 AM I recall someone saying (although everyone at the hospital denies it) "If we don't get her temperature up, she's not going to survive this." Apparently, my temp had dropped to 93 degrees. Hypothermia sets in around**

94. They wrapped me up in hot blankets which I kept trying desperately to rip off, all the while I'm hurling my guts out...very comfortable with a recent incision. My dad came back to see me, freaked out at my Exorcist like existence and had to be escorted out of recovery. Lovely.

Meanwhile, down the hall at 11 AM, my recipient was wide awake, feeling great, exclaiming he's never tasted better ice chips in his life. His cramps were gone. His chills were gone. His itching was gone. All his scores were great. All signs of kidney failure had immediately reversed. Please pray that it continues!!

1:00 PM - finally have my temp to 96 and wheeled me to my room. Sadly it was past the "Big Cookie." No need to get graphic but I may never eat another chocolate chip cookie in my life.

11:00 PM - I FINALLY get coherent enough to realize I'm alive. Throughout the night they are worrying about my blood pressure which dropped to 87/53. My heart rate which was spiking in the 90's...my temp which was still in the 96 range. When I asked the know it all intern/doctor if I'd "be ok", he replied "I can't guarantee it." Had I felt better, I'd have cold cocked him. I stayed up all night watching my vitals to make sure I didn't die. Long night.

Thursday: Introduction to morphine. Morphine is not my friend. Bucket was. Ugh.

Thursday afternoon - VERY cute 23 year old med student came to check on me. He was in on my surgery and assured my it had all gone well. He proceeded to

Donor Girl

ask if I'd "passed gas or had a bowel movement." Oh dear God, let me die now.

Friday:  Introduction to Percoset. See above. I spent from 3:30 AM - 11:30 AM afraid to move due to nausea. Enter my husband, friend and sister trying to get me to "walk, eat and dress in real clothes so I could go home." Then my husband opens up the breakfast tray and says "try some eggs." No need to explain what came next. Finally told my surgeon "I have an extremely high threshold for pain...I'M A RECORD PROMOTER! I have NO threshold for nausea. Lay off the drugs." So I'm doing this the old fashioned way with Tylenol (no codeine) and ice packs. Randy however is enjoying the percoset they gave me anyway. Continued nausea set me back from going home on Friday as I couldn't eat or drink.

Saturday: Finally came home. More discomfort than outright pain. Bloated and looking like I'm 3 months pregnant and bruised beyond recognition. I told my surgeon that the next time he wanted to inflate a body part, I could use C cups!

Overall, God has blessed me that I was able to do this. David called me Thursday when I was coherent and said "I don't know what to say to the person who gave me my life back." Not much more you can say. Would I do it again? Ask in about 3 months. Too soon to make that call.  ;-)

THANKS for the beautiful flowers from BBR. They are beyond gorgeous. The e-mails, phone calls, texts, etc. It's great to work with people who care so much.

Donor Girl

While he still wasn't feeling great, Randy was going to work during the day but coming home at night and helping me as best he could. There wasn't much he could do, and I had my cousins living right behind me to help if necessary. Church friends were right down the road and mom and dad would drive down if necessary. I was covered.

Meg checked in on me the Monday following surgery to see how I was doing. I replied to her e-mail:

July 16th, 2007: To Meg Baker from Lee Adams:

**Other than the shoulder pain which has been horrible and the headaches, the rest of it is just discomfort. Of course, without taking any pain meds and handling it with ice packs and Tylenol, I'm sure it's different for me. But I'd rather have some pain than nausea ANY day!**

**Body functions seem to be working. I still look 3 months pregnant and am bruised like you wouldn't believe...or maybe you would. Too bad it didn't inflate other areas. I would like C cups. Overall, today has been the best day which gives me hope that every day will continue to be on the upswing. Thanks for asking!**

July 16th 2007: To Lee Adams from Meg Baker:

**You are way ahead of the program, believe me. The bruising is common, and often you don't notice it until after you get home. Sorry about the puffiness, I promise it will go away, but takes a little time. I'm glad you are managing w/o narcotics...are you at least taking Tylenol XS every 4-6 hrs or so?**

Donor Girl

July 16<sup>th</sup>: To Meg Baker from Lee Adams:

I am taking Tylenol and it's knocking the edge off. My "drug of choice" has always been Ibuprofen and Tylenol has never really done much for me...but I'm strictly staying to it as told. And taking a zanax at night to help me sleep.

Otherwise, the pain in my shoulders, neck and back are just too overbearing to sleep for long. Overall, today has shown me a light at the end of the tunnel which has been good. Thanks!

July 16<sup>th</sup>: To Lee Adams from Meg Baker:

The neck and back complaints are no doubt from being on the unforgiving OR table for so long. If you're miserable, I could see if we could call in some Toradol, which is non-narcotic.....it's an anti inflammatory that can be helpful w/post-op pain. Let me know.

I jumped at the chance to have a non-narcotic pain killer and Meg called it in to my pharmacy. I called Randy who was on his way home from work and he picked it up. I was ready for anything to stop the pain and was happy to have something else to try.

Donor Girl

# **The ER**

Tuesday morning was almost one week to the date from my surgery. I got up, similar to every other morning, showered and looked in the mirror. I looked like I was wearing boy shorts even when naked. I had blue and purple bruising going from around my left hip to around my right hip. It was probably 3 to 4 inches wide. I grabbed my digital camera and took a self-portrait of my nether regions, showing my extreme bruising. I e-mailed it to my caseworker, Meg, begging her not to show it to anyone. Of course, "anyone" meant the handsome Dr. Cooper, the cute Curtis or any other male who might happen by.

The e-mail exchange went like this:

7/17/2007 8:37 AM I wrote:

**Hey Meg. Is this amount of bruising normal? Everyone I've felt close enough to show my bruising to has said "I've never seen anything like that." It looks like I'm wearing shorts when I'm not. Kind of scary but if it's normal, I'm ok with it. Not a picture I want shared around the office though.**

**Also, am I able to take off the band aids from the smaller incisions? Not the large one...I know the strips have to fall off naturally. But I worry about what's happening under the band aids. 'Cause that's what I do...I worry. Haha Thanks for the prescription. I had some wild nightmares but woke up without a headache after 7 hours of having one. It was a fair trade off. Lee Adams**

7/17 From Meg Baker;

Donor Girl

Hi Lee, I certainly have had patients with impressive amounts of bruising post-op, even worse than this, but to be safe I would like to have you go to LabCorp today and get labs done just to make sure. I would also, unfortunately hold off on taking any more Toradol until we get the labs back. Am I correct that you go to the Hagerstown Lab Corp?  Meg Baker

7/17/2007 9:01 AM to Meg Baker:

Yes, that's the one. What procedure do I need to follow? Lee

7/17  From Meg Baker;

I'll fax lab slip to Hagerstown and call to confirm that it was received. Then you just show up and hold out your arm :)  Don't want you to worry at all, this is just me being overly cautious. I also think it would be a good idea to move your appointment with Dr. Cooper to this week. Pictures are good, but I'd rather him see you live, up close, and in person. Would Thursday at 1:30 or 2:30 work? Could also do Friday between 10 and 2 if that's better, just let me know.

I tried to call my cousin's house but didn't get an answer. I called her cell; they were on the golf course, just starting their game. I explained that I needed someone to take me to get my blood drawn, but she asked if it could wait until after their game. Meg seemed like she wanted me to get it drawn right away. My cousin offered to leave the golf course, but I didn't want to impose on her, so I called Magda. She was happy to take me. She gently put me in her car and took me to the lab. It didn't take but an hour to go up, get the blood drawn, and get back.

7/17/2007 I wrote:

Donor Girl

**I got the blood drawn about an hour ago. She said it should be ready in about 4 hours. Let me know if I need to dial 911. ;-)**

**Unless you feel like it has to be Thurs, I just set up an apt. to have my masseuse come to my house on Thurs to help me through this shoulder and neck pain. I think I'd rather come down there on Fri. I'll have to find someone to drive me...**

**My temp is staying normal. What is it you're looking for with the labs? Anything I should be aware of that I could be looking for? Lee**

I was worn out by the time I got back, so I took a Xanax and went to sleep. I figured a nap would be good before Randy got home. I was having a dream about being in the hospital. I was talking to a doctor and his cell phone started ringing.

He said, "Excuse me, I need to answer this." However, the phone wasn't ringing in my dream it was ringing in my house. I had brought the cordless phone into bed with me. I reached over in my Xanax haze and answered the phone. It was Dr. Cooper.

"Lee, it's Doctor Cooper."

"Hey, Doctor Cooper, I was just having a dream about being in the hospital."

"I see. Well, I need you to come in to the hospital," he continued, without skipping a beat.

"I know, I talked to Meg," I said through slurred speech. "She wants me to come in on Friday."

"I need you in earlier than that," he said.

# Donor Girl

"Well, I can come in tomorrow," I said.    Again, my speech was quite thick. I was, after all, drugged.

"I need you to come in now if you can. You'll need to go straight to the emergency room," he insisted. "Will you do that for me?"

"Will you be there?" I asked.

"If it will make you come in tonight, yes, I'll be there," he replied. Then he began to explain where I had to drive to and where to park, and it all got very confusing as I was still in my Xanax-induced haze. I wasn't really getting it at all.

Randy walked in at that moment. "Hey honey, I have to go to the ER." I said with no explanation.

"What? Why?" Randy asked.

I was still on the phone with Dr. Cooper, and I heard him ask, "Is that your husband? May I talk to him?" I passed the phone to Randy, and Dr. Cooper explained everything to him.    Within minutes, we were in the car headed to the UMMC ER. I was still pretty relaxed on the Xanax, so I wasn't freaking out too much. I'm not sure I really understood what was going on but had gathered that my blood count had gone down and due to the extreme bruising, they thought I might have internal bleeding.

Randy and I followed the directions to the ER and signed in. An emergency room in Baltimore is a fun time in the evening. I was pretty sure there was a gang member in there.    While he was wearing his hospital issued "Johnny," he had a T-shirt with his "colors" over top.

When I signed in, the administrator said, "Your sister is here and is asking about you."

## Donor Girl

"That's not possible. I didn't tell her I was coming back in."

"Well, she's here." I looked at Randy and he shook his head. He mouthed the words, "She's confused."

She took my information and sent me in to have my blood pressure and temperature taken. My blood pressure had always been very low, but tonight it was 128/85; very high for me. The nurse assured me it wasn't too high, but I told her my normal blood pressure was around 110/60 or lower. So this was high for me, and I was worried. I went back out to sit with Randy and sure enough, my sister walked out.

"How did you know I was going to be here?" I asked Kelly.

"Doctor Cooper mentioned you were on your way in."

"But why would he call you? Why'd you come in?"

"Well, we were already here. Dave is showing minor signs of rejection, so he had to come back in today." Dave had a fever and some of his numbers were off. So they were giving him IVs of anti-rejection medication. Great. One week in and Dave was rejecting my kidney, and I was having internal bleeding. Tell me this is a joke!

I called Dr. Cooper as he had told me to. I couldn't really hear what he was saying too well, but I let him know my blood pressure was up. He tried to reassure me as he always does. I had to move on for more testing. They wanted me off the phone, so we hung up. He promised to check in later.

They called me in for further testing and put me in one of the ER rooms. Some doctors came through the room and introduced themselves. I was giving them a rundown of my current time in the hospital when one of the doctors said, "So, on a scale of A to

C, you're an A plus personality."

I replied, "So, you're a smart ass doctor." And I smiled. Luckily, so did he. There's power in being a kidney donor. You remain on top of the food chain, and they have to treat you well.

A third doctor came in to start running options with me and explained that depending on what the tests said, they may have to open me back up and operate. I said, "Nothing happens to me without Doctor Cooper's approval."

"I don't really care what Doctor Cooper has to say," he said, but with a smile. He was a young, cute redhead, and I could tell he was only teasing.

But I told him, "I do care what Doctor Cooper says, and nothing happens to me without him OK'ing it!" The doctor assured me he'd only been joking and Dr. Cooper would be informed of everything, especially another operation. I felt better. In his defense, he was trying to be nice and joke with me to put me at ease. At that point, there was nothing that was going to put me at ease.

They were going to come and get me later to take me for further testing and at that point, I encouraged Kelly and Randy to go home. They were both exhausted and had long drives home. There was nothing they could do for either Dave or me, and it was best for them to get some rest. They left around 10:00 P.M.; I was alone. I was worried for me and even more worried for Dave. The thought of rejection was one of my biggest fears. How would I feel if I went through all of this and within days, his body rejected my kidney? He'd feel like he had let me down. I'd feel like my kidney had let him down, and we'd both mourn the loss of my kidney.

# Donor Girl

I had a male nurse who kept checking on me. I didn't have a pillow, and I was cold. He brought me in a heated sheet and a pillow. He kept coming in to see if I needed more pillows. At one point, I could hear a man screaming in pain. Through the curtain I could tell he was bleeding. It also looked like he was handcuffed with a police officer nearby. The policeman kept asking, "Could we get some help here? He's bleeding."

I looked at the nurse and said, "Don't worry about my pillows; you need to help that guy who is bleeding."

When the nurse left, I broke down crying. It was the first time I'd cried during the whole episode. And I didn't just cry, I did the whole body shaking bawl. The nurse came back in and asked if I was ok. I just hid my head in the covers and nodded yes.

"Are you hurting?" he asked.

"No."

"Are you scared?" he asked.

"Yes," I replied.

"I'll stay with you. There's nothing to be afraid of." But there was. Dave was in for a possible rejection. I might need another surgery. It was all too much.

He put a rush on my test, and they sent me down to another room for an MRI to see if I had internal bleeding. As promised, he stayed with me the entire time. The hospital was filled to capacity, and they didn't have a room for either Dave or me.

Another doctor came in to check on me, and who was it but the good-looking yet *rude* doctor from the week before. The same one who told me he couldn't guarantee I'd be ok. Lovely. He was

## Donor Girl

about as nice as he'd been the last time, but at least he didn't tell me he couldn't guarantee I'd be ok. Thank God for small favors. Finally, the redheaded doctor came back in and told me the tests showed that I did not have internal bleeding and they were just waiting to get me a room. He turned the light out because the fluorescents were rather annoying.

At about 1:00 A.M., they came to get me. I had repeatedly told them that it didn't matter what room they put me in; I didn't need a private room. I begged them not to move some poor patient out of the donor room. When they were wheeling me upstairs, they explained that I'd be back in the same room as I was in before. I worried about the person who'd been moved, but they assured me the patient hadn't been a donor, and it was hospital rule that I be put in a donor suite.

I had a splitting headache, but they wouldn't give me anything but a Tylenol. I had pressed my hands against either side of my head like a vise and walked out to the nurses' station. "***Please*** give me a Xanax."

"We can't do that without doctor's orders," they answered.

I was still holding my head. "I'm in severe pain, and I need something to help me. Look at my records from last week. I'm allowed to have Xanax."

"That was last week. Without a new order, we can't give you anything but Tylenol," they repeated.
"Please bring me an ice pack then," I requested and walked back to my room still holding my head.

At 1:30 A.M., my cell phone rang. It was Dr. Cooper.

"Hello," I answered.

## Donor Girl

"Lee, it's Matt Cooper." I'd never heard Dr. Cooper use his first name when talking to me before. It's like a child with a teacher. Dr. Cooper has a first name other than Doctor? Really??

"Hi, Doctor Cooper."

"I just got a copy of your CT, and you don't have internal bleeding. I'm sorry I made you come all the way down here but, especially with donors, I want to err on the side of caution and make sure you were ok."

"I understand. I'd rather you do that than just assume everything is ok."

"Do you need anything?" he asked.

"I need either a vise or a Xanax. I don't care which one, but I need one immediately. I have a massive migraine."

"Well, vises are a bit archaic. We don't keep those around anymore."

"Wal Mart is open. They carry them in the tool department," I replied.

"How about I get you a Xanax?"

"That would be great. And I'd like to apologize for our conversation when you called the house earlier. I know I was really out of it. I was a little high on Xanax."

He laughed. "Don't worry about it. I'll come by and see you tomorrow. You should be able to go home then. Get some rest."

"Thanks, Doctor Cooper."

# Donor Girl

It wasn't but a few minutes until they came in with a Xanax, and that was a big help. I was able to fall asleep shortly thereafter.

While I was getting settled into a room, so was Dave. They were going to put him on a run of IV anti-rejection medication that would last over a couple of days. This may have been an even more difficult evening than the one after surgery. While that one was definitely more painful, this was filled with fear of rejection. As a donor, the concern over your own health is nothing compared to the fear that your kidney will be rejected. While I often said, "Even if my kidney is rejected, I will still feel like I did the right thing," the truth is immediate rejection would have been devastating. You want to believe that your sacrifice is not for naught, and to have your lifesaving surgery fail in a short period of time would be horrible.

The next morning, I was told I could be released. I really didn't want to ask Randy to take another day off work, and Kelly was coming in to visit Dave. So we had decided I would go home with Kelly. Of course, we didn't realize we'd be on "hospital time." Ugh!

Meg and Nina, my angels of mercy, once again came to see me. Kelly and I were in my room, and they came in with beautiful smiles. They couldn't believe this had happened to *me,* their hypochondriac patient. Of all people, I was the last one they wanted to see come back in with fears of more surgery, internal bleeding, etc. Luckily, it was a false alarm. We all agreed, however, that we'd rather have a surgeon who was concerned enough to make sure I was ok than one who let it go until there were serious issues.

Kelly talked to Nina about Dave's issues and his mild signs of rejection. Nina was very good for Kelly and helped talk her through it. While I definitely believe that donors need counseling, the wives, husbands and significant others of the recipients could also use some help. My sister had so much on her plate. At this point, Sandi had gone back to Maine and my mom was still recuperating. Kelly had worked it out to put her kids in the church day care that day. Will was actually too old to officially be there, but they'd agreed to help out, and he was a "helper" for the day. Kayla still attended, so it was natural for her to be with friends. Nina stayed for a while, and we told some stories and laughed about various things. It felt good to laugh!

Later that day, Dr. Cooper came in. He had just finished a surgery which he told us about. It was different than a normal transplant in that the person's kidneys were so bloated and diseased that they had to be removed. With most transplants, you don't remove the person's kidneys to put in the new one; they just have three. Eventually, the two bad ones will dry up and allow the new one to take over. This man needed his kidneys removed before he got a new one. It was interesting to hear Dr. Cooper describe the surgery, and you could tell that it was different and more challenging than the normal "boring" surgeries.

I needed to have one more blood test taken, and Dr. Cooper assured me he was going to order that and have it rushed so we could get home. Kelly had to pick up Will and Kayla by 5:00 P.M., and we were starting to push it to get there on time.

I didn't make it down to visit Dave that day. I'm not sure why, but I didn't really want to go. Although I didn't admit it to Kelly, I think the fact that Dave was dealing with rejection was something I didn't want to face. Everyone was reassuring us that this was common and the treatment would halt the rejection, but I still felt the need to stay separate from it. I'm not sure why I felt that way, but I did.

Kelly had talked to a woman whose son was back in the hospital after his transplant. Apparently, he had experienced a similar rejection back when he first received his kidney, and his mother swore by the treatment Dave was getting. She told Kelly that it had done the trick and he hadn't had any more problems. We found that very reassuring.

Time was passing rapidly, and things at the hospital were happening slowly. I finally had my blood drawn, but we were not getting any quick results. We became the complaint sisters. We were definitely the squeaky wheels. I kept calling Meg, telling her we had to leave. She kept calling to try and find out what had happened. Finally, we discovered they had forgotten to test my blood and lost it. Then they found it, but it still hadn't been tested. Poor Dr. Cooper was wearing out the residents' pagers, telling them to get this done so I could leave. I think he felt badly that I was there in the first place and now couldn't get out on time. My concern wasn't for me; it was for my sister, who was on the phone trying to find people who could pick up her kids if we didn't make it back in time. The whole thing became very stressful. All the while, I'm only 7 days post surgery and still not feeling great and still in a good amount of pain.

I had a male nurse, Francis, who was working his tail off to get us answers. I'm not sure what heads he was trying to roll, but he was doing his best. And I think most of that was because he really wanted to be rid of me. Finally, I said I was leaving with or without their ok. So they brought me paperwork to sign. It was a form that I was supposed to sign saying I was leaving against doctor's orders.

"But I'm not leaving against doctor's orders. The doctor said I could go."

"But we don't have the final signature on the tests to allow you to go," they said.

Donor Girl

"But I'm not leaving against doctor's orders, so I won't sign the papers," I replied.

"Then you can't leave," they said.

It was a dumb off. When I worked with the country artist Gary Allan, he coined that phrase and I love it. Whenever two people keep arguing with neither side coming up with a reasonable answer, he'd say, "We're having a *dumb off*." We were definitely having one that day.

While a hospital is not a prison, and there were no cells or clanging doors to keep me inside, I realized that there is a conspiracy to keep you in place until they're ready to let you go. It's the "IV Conspiracy." They have the IV in your arm taped in place. Someone less squeamish than me would just simply rip the IV out, like they do in movies when they're really pissed. Randy would do something like that, but not me. The minute I actually touched the IV, I'd probably faint. I couldn't look at the IV line under my skin without getting the stomach willies. The idea of just pulling it out all by myself seemed beyond something I could do, as I just *knew* I'd accidently puncture a main artery as I was bringing it out and bleed to death while Francis was looking for my blood work.

I looked hopefully at Kelly, who said, "I'm not doing it." So, I could either leave the hospital with an IV stuck in my arm or wait for the nurse to take it out.

The nurse would only do that when a doctor had signed the paperwork. Thus, it was a conspiracy to keep me there.

The doctor on duty came in and his beeper went off. He said, "That's the fifth message I've had from Doctor Cooper telling me to release you."

## Donor Girl

Duh, that should tell you I am ready to be released."Then release me!"

Finally, after hours and hours -- and that's no exaggeration -- they released me, and Kelly and I sped off to go get her kids. But with rush hour traffic, there was no way we'd get there on time. We were in the height of it at 4:30 P.M. So, a church friend picked up the kids and took them back to her house to go swimming. All were happy, except Kelly and me.

Randy picked me up at Kelly's house when we finally arrived, and we headed home. I was exhausted but happy to be home. I was now 7 days post surgery. I knew I'd have another visit to the hospital the following week for my 2 week follow-up. I was actually looking forward to it. The last couple of times everyone had seen me, I'd looked hideous. Lying in a hospital bed without makeup or your hair done was not the way to be remembered. I had visions of me going back after two weeks; hair done, makeup on and wearing a pretty dress. It was one of the few things that fit over my distended abdomen. I'd be the perfect picture of post donation. I could actually visualize my floating through the halls and greeting everyone with a smile. I may not have done well with surgery, but I would be a poster child for post surgery!

## **<u>Kicked From The Nest</u>**

The next day, I was sitting on my couch when the phone rang. I picked it up and Dr. Cooper said, "How's my favorite patient?" Considering my demanding behavior the day before, I wondered if there was a hint of sarcasm in this. I didn't detect any, but I couldn't be sure.

"Fine," I said, glad he was calling to check up on me.

"I just wanted to let you know that all your tests came back fine, and we can use this blood test as your follow-up. I won't need to see you again.'" I could actually hear my stomach drop to my feet. It made a weird thudding sound. If you've never heard it, you won't understand.

"Ok," I said, not sure what else to say. I honestly don't remember what else was discussed, but I'm sure it was along the lines of, "If you have any problems, let us know ... blah, blah, blah." It was recommended I get tested with my family physician at 6 months, 1 year and 2 years.

When I hung up, I felt like a bird that had been kicked out of the nest before it was ready. For months, I'd been made to feel like my health was the most important thing in the world. I'd been poked and prodded and tested and bled and X-rayed to the point of perfect health. Now that I was minus a kidney and not feeling so healthy, I was no longer getting tested. I felt alone and scared.

I'm not sure how most people go through their recovery. Randy was home in the evenings and mornings, but wasn't by my side 'round the clock. Kelly had the kids and Dave to worry about. Mom was recuperating from her own surgery. Dad and I would have lasted 5 minutes in the house together before one of us would

Donor Girl

have said something stupid. I was all alone in the house and had just been told I was no longer needed. My health was now my concern. It didn't seem right but it was the procedure.

As I sat there feeling sorry for myself, I thought of all the people who had helped me through this process: my team, Dr. Cooper, Meg and Nina, and the nurses. I went online and found gift baskets to send to everyone as a way of thanking them. I think it might have also been a way for me to say, "Don't just forget me! I'm still here, but with one less kidney." I think most people are happy to get that phone call. All is good, and you don't have to come to the hospital anymore. But for some reason, I didn't see it that way. Luckily, the feeling wouldn't last long as I'd start to heal and become more positive that I was healthy and would recover.

The truth was, I was scared. I wanted to say, "What about me? What about the donor?" I was actually, in an odd way, jealous of Dave! He was still receiving attention; he'd be receiving follow-up care for the rest of his life. Everyone still *cared* about Dave! I wanted them to *care about me*! I was frightened of what I had done, even though I believed in it. But what if mine was the body that needed two kidneys? What if mine was the body where one kidney couldn't do the job of two? What if I was the one person who needed more follow-up than one week post surgery? It seemed to me that follow-up should be a little more intense than this.

Back in high school, my sister had dated a guy named Brian, who had a younger brother, Andrew. When the family would all be around the dinner table, poor Andrew would try to join in the conversation, but he'd be ignored. Finally, their mom would say, "Quiet everyone, Andrew has something to say," and all focus would go on Andrew. Twenty-five years later, my family will still try to help the person out who is trying to talk, but can't be heard by saying, "Let Andrew speak." Well, *Andrew was speaking,* but no one was listening. I felt very small that day, sitting on the

## Donor Girl

couch, still in pain, bloated and without a kidney. I think I even missed my kidney.

The one thing that would bring me out of my self-imposed pity party was talking to Dave. He continuously called me his "angel." He told me how I had saved his life; how he hadn't even realized how sick he was until he became well. Dr. Bartlett had actually said that to him on our last appointment before surgery. "Dave, you've been sick for so long, you don't remember what it's like to feel well." Dave now felt well, and he called me a few times each day to thank me. **THAT** made it all worthwhile. When I heard how well Dave was doing, I felt less scared and less alone. The healing process helped me get past those feelings as well.

And the truth was, my hospital team had not "left" me. Anytime I had a concern or question, they were just a phone call or email away. Once I realized that, it made the mental process much easier as the physical healing was happening.

Donor Girl

## **Meanwhile, Back at the Hospital**

Dave was finishing up his anti-rejection medication and Kelly was standing by; nervous, praying that he get past the minor rejection episode.

How would I feel if he actually rejected my kidney? I felt like I was calling for constant updates and reassurances, but Kelly only knew so much. She did inform me that she ran into Dr. Cooper, who gave her a hug, inquired about me and told her they were taking good care of Dave.

So what is rejection and what causes it? The following was explained in fairly layman's terms on the Internet site **www.wisegeeks.com.**

**Transplant rejection is caused by the body's immune response to foreign material. The body naturally tends to attempt to destroy encountered foreign matter. As a result, those who receive transplants are given transplant rejection medications that reduce the body's immune response.**

**In most cases, the white cells of the blood, called leukocytes, serve our bodies very well. They identify viruses and bacteria that have entered our bloodstream and begin to assiduously eliminate them. Leukocytes help us recover from illnesses and also keep us from getting some illnesses because we have already become immune to them from previous white blood cell action.**

**However, when someone receives a transplant, leukocytes work against the new organ. They**

immediately recognize the organ as foreign, and set about to destroy it. More leukocytes are produced to rid the body of the organ, setting up a battle between the new organ and the white blood cells.

When the white blood cells are effective, this causes transplant rejection. Usually transplanted organs are tested for the presence of leukocytes to gauge amount of rejection. The answer to this problem is problematic itself. The leukocytes have to be reduced in order to allow the new organ to do its job.

As such, those who receive an organ take immunosuppressant medications that can prevent transplant rejection. This results in a weakened immune system, because leukocytes are not available to fight off the normal diseases one might encounter. Those receiving a transplant are then more vulnerable to both viruses and infections. In addition to transplant rejection medications, most who receive a transplant frequently must take antibiotics, or are on consistent doses of prophylactic antibiotics to prevent infections.

The long-term use of antibiotics creates another issue. Germs tend to become resistant to antibiotics over time, thus fighting bacteria means switching to newer and stronger antibiotics. As well, patients can be allergic to certain classes of antibiotics, limiting the kinds of medications patients can take. A stronger antibiotic also translates to more side effects like frequent fungal or yeast infections, stomach upset, and skin rashes.

Thus, attempting to avoid transplant rejection requires a very delicate pharmaceutical balance. One must have eliminated enough leukocytes to avoid transplant rejection, but not so many that viruses will claim the life

Donor Girl

of the patient. Antibiotics must be given to stop infection; yet antibiotics must not be so strong that the patient will die from antibiotic resistant illnesses.

With anti-rejection medications, transplant rejection is now reduced to about 10-15%. Closely matching blood types and blood factors help, but the body still "knows" the organ is not of the body. Only transplants from identical twins, and cornea transplants seem to go unrecognized by leukocytes. As well, valves for the heart taken from pigs, cows and from cadavers seem not to be considered "foreign." Often transplant rejection is not the cause of death in patients with transplants. Fighting transplant rejection is. Complications from immunosuppressants are more likely to cause death than transplant rejection.

The field of transplant science is, however, continually evolving. At one time, almost all transplants were rejected. Now, continual research into anti-rejection medications is turning the tide on transplant rejection and complications from transplant medications.

The goal of transplant specialists is to reduce rejection, and also to create medications that will not cause those receiving a transplant to suffer life-threatening complications. When this goal is reached, the medical field can certainly claim victory.

So, the goal of the Medical Center was clearly to stop the rejection as quickly as possible.

Typical signs of rejection are a rising creatinine level, decreased urine output, pain at the transplant site, fever, elevated BP, etc. He may have needed a kidney biopsy to evaluate for rejection. The usual treatment is

Donor Girl

**Thymoglobulin, which is given by IV infusion and it's not a terribly pleasant drug. The first few days can cause flu-like symptoms. The most frequently reported adverse effects (> 25% of patients) are fever, chills, headache, abdominal pain, diarrhea, nausea, low white count and platelet count, edema, infection, high potassium, and rapid heart rate. Thymoglobulin passed FDA tests in 1999.**

Source: www.wisegeeks.com

Dave stayed in the hospital for 5 days while undergoing the treatment.

My sister was there every day, acting positive and putting on a brave face. She ran into Dr. Cooper in the hall one day and felt reassured by his positive attitude as well. One day, she was sitting on the stairwell looking sad and forlorn when a woman asked her what was wrong. She explained her situation and the woman told her about her son who had a kidney transplant 15 years before. She said he'd also experienced rejection early on and they put him on the same intravenous anti rejection drugs and he went on to keep the kidney for the last 15 years. That's what Kelly needed to hear to perk her up and give had additional hope. Yet another one of God's angels on Earth!

David was finally released to return home. We were warned the first year would be the hardest, and in the very beginning, every hospital visit, doctor visit or slight rise in temperature would be cause to wonder if rejection was starting. Eventually, we'd realize that's no way to live and we'd just need to remain positive. Dave always stayed positive. From moment one, Dave was sure my kidney was going to last 20 years. I figured I'd be content with 5; happy with 10; ecstatic with 15 or more. Dave was resolute that he would walk Kayla down the aisle with my kidney still working well within him. From Dave's lips to God's ears.

Donor Girl

# **<u>Recovery</u>**

The first two weeks were by far the most difficult. I worked for about 4 to 5 hours each day when I wasn't in the hospital. I would get migraines every afternoon around three, turn off the computer, take a Xanax, grab an ice pack and climb into bed. I would get up a few hours later when Randy returned home and spend part of the evening with him. I would once again get tired and go to bed. I was sleeping so much and in such uncomfortable positions, I would wake up around 6:00 A.M. I was craving orange juice more so than my favorite hot tea. I'd pour a glass of juice, make some toast and bundle myself up to sit on the deck on the reclining lounge chair, which hurt less than laying down flat.

Once I returned from the ER visit, each day got better, and suddenly, it was two weeks after surgery and I was feeling well enough to get dressed in regular clothes, grab a book and sit on the back of the pontoon boat

Sandi had given me the book, *The Kite Runner*, and I was sitting on the back of the pontoon reading it when Randy took a photo. Since the last photo I had sent to my "team" was a picture of my horrible bruising with a subject line, "Is this normal?" I decided to send them another picture. This time I put in the subject line, "Is this normal after two weeks?" I knew Meg would open it with some concern and then find a photo of me sitting on the back of the boat happily reading a book. Meg loved that picture and would mention it many times in the coming months.

I needed to drive and inquired about the rule of waiting two weeks. I was told that that was mainly for people on Percocet, but since I wasn't, I could drive. They did warn me not to have any sudden stops and to try and avoid accidents (like I usually go looking for them) as any impact could cause my stitches to rupture. That

Donor Girl

weekend, two weeks after surgery, I was feeling so good I got it in mind that I should weed my garden. I actually spent about 10 minutes weeding. **WOW!** Was that a mistake? Yes! It was a huge mistake. I actually thought I could do it, but I definitely pushed before I was ready. I hurt for a while afterward. I wouldn't be weeding anytime soon. I don't even like weeding! If I was going to go out of my way to hurt myself, why weed? Who likes weeding? Feeling like an idiot (a very in pain idiot), I vowed not to weed again. Ever! For the rest of my life this would be my no weeding excuse!

Jodi sent me an email that week asking how I was doing and I replied:

To JWhitman from LAdams:

**Every day is definitely better. I even went out on the pontoon boat this weekend. Probably a bit of overdoing it as even gentle rocking still hurt a bit, but there was no "slamming" on the wake like we get in the other boats. And mentally, it was wonderful.**

**Still a bit of lump where the incision is. I got on the scale and had dropped to 102. Now that's a home scale so it's probably different than the hospital scale. But normally I'm between 107 and 110 on it so I had definitely lost weight. I was all bone with a distended stomach. Weird.**

**Hopefully, Dave will get released today. He's been back in since last Tues and going stir crazy. Mainly they can't get his blood pressure and sugar regulated. But I think it's slowly coming around. At least I hope so. Overall he feels great and the nurses are going crazy trying to keep track of him. He's constantly walking up and down**

Donor Girl

**the halls and stairs trying to stay in shape and gain energy. Gotta love the guy's enthusiasm and optimism.**

Each day for me continued to get a little easier. I was in less pain and found that I was getting out of bed faster, walking up the hill easier, and overall healing. I was also handling steps much better. As I entered my 3$^{rd}$ week post surgery, I was putting full-time hours in at work, although I still wasn't traveling. The fact that I worked out of the house using a phone and computer made it much easier for me to return so quickly. Many people wait 4 to 6 weeks before returning to work, but I figured I'd probably be on the computer anyway so it was easier not to fall behind.

Time began to pass more quickly, and on day 21, I headed back out on the road. I had to go to Springfield, Massachusetts with Megan Mullins and Crossin Dixon to do a show with WPKX Radio. I packed as lightly as possible and wore a pair of chinos that had an elastic waistband. I was still a bit bloated and jeans hurt my incision. Megan and her brother, Marcus, as well as Crossin Dixon, were great about helping me. The station sent an RV to pick us up so I wouldn't have to do any driving. Everyone went out of their way to make sure things ran smoothly for me. It was my first meeting with WPKX's assistant program director, Marc Spencer, and he couldn't have been kinder in helping things run smoothly.

We finally returned to the hotel and retired to our rooms. I was sharing a room with Megan, and we stayed up talking until we were too tired to talk and fell asleep. I was home the next day. I was tired and drained from my one-day trip, but I survived it well. I was on my way to a full recovery.

My cousin, Tommy, was due to get married at the 4 week post surgery date, August 11$^{th}$. His mom, Phyllis, was my mom's first cousin and also my Godmother. I knew her as Aunt Phyllis and my sister and I were very close to her and her 4 sons. My mom is

## Donor Girl

Godmother to Phyllis' youngest son, Pat. Phyllis had passed away nearly 10 years prior to Tommy's wedding and he had asked me if I would step in and take her role. I was beyond honored. In 1993, when I was going to my 10 year high school reunion, Kelly and I had visited with Aunt Phyllis in Raleigh NC and gone shopping for a dress that I could wear to the reunion. I still had that dress and asked Tommy if it would be appropriate to wear it in her honor at his wedding. He and his fiance' felt it would be perfect.

Dave and I were both somewhat anxious that we could make it to Raleigh, a 5 hour drive, and attend the wedding and reception. However, by week 4 I was feeling great and made it through the rehearsal, wedding and reception with no problems. It was a proud moment for both Dave and me and an honor to be a part of the wedding. I was still somewhat sore, and didn't move extremely quickly, but was about 75% recovered.

I had been told that I couldn't work out or do any lifting for the first six weeks. So when six weeks were up, I immediately emailed Meg to ask if I could work out and do sit ups. I was still trying to get rid of the persistent lump. Meg said she felt certain I could but encouraged me to contact Dr. Cooper to be sure.

August 22, 2007; From MCooper to Lee Adams:

**Exercise is fine including sit ups but please, please take it slowly and let your body tell you when you're doing too much too fast. You'll get back to where you want but I'd like you to get there without any complications.**

**Matthew Cooper, MD Associate Professor of Surgery**

So I began to work out, making sure to take it easy on the sit ups or anything that could cause trauma to my incisions. At the six week mark, I felt 90% and practically back to normal.

Donor Girl

I really wanted to water ski again before the end of season. The month of September can be good skiing, but it can also start to get quite chilly. I was nearing the end of the skiing season. I finally asked Meg and Dr. Cooper if I could go water skiing at the 8 week mark. When I received the OK from them, I enjoyed a wonderful day on the river boating and skiing. I hadn't thought I'd get to ski until the next season, so it was such a blessing. This is when I remember thinking "wow, I'm 100% recovered." The pain was gone, the bloating had finally gone down, and I didn't feel any different than I had prior to surgery. The only minor issue that remained was tenderness and numbness in the 3 inch incision below my naval. It would remain slightly numb for many more months. But it didn't hurt and in no way bothered me. I was healed! What a great milestone that was.

Donor Girl

# **More Life Changes**

Psychologists say not to change more than one major thing in your life at a time. I was about to do numerous major things at once. Needless to say, the most major change had taken place during my surgery. My boss resigned to go to another label weeks after my surgery. Rumor was strong Craig Morgan would be leaving the label as well. In fact, when our boss resigned, Craig also sent his letter stating he was exercising his contract option to leave the label. It would be 7 months before he actually left, but this was all happening at the same time. These are the two guys with whom I had joined BBR 6 years ago to help make this fledgling label work after all three of us had lost our jobs in the Atlantic Records closing. And now our 6 years together were falling apart. It was sad but everyone must do what's right for them. For me, it was to stay at BBR. For them, it was to try another label.

I called Brad, my general manager and gave him my opinion of the situation. I said, "Decisions made in haste are often the wrong ones. Let's take our time and make the right decision for our next VP of Promotions." He agreed that we should take time over the next few weeks. He and I could hold things together and keep it moving. We had three singles due to come out: Jason Aldean's "Laughed Until We Cried," Craig Morgan's "International Harvester" and Crossin Dixon's "Make You Mine." We were most likely losing two members of our promotions team. But all we had to do was make it until mid-December, just 4½ months away, and we'd get a few weeks' break.

I started sending Brad my ideas for who would make a good VP. He kept giving me his reasons for why they wouldn't make good VPs. Finally, he asked if I'd be willing to consider taking the job. "Me?" I was rather shocked. "I don't think I can. I'm not willing to move to Nashville." It was a rather well-known fact that to rise

Donor Girl

above National or VP, you had to relocate to Nashville. It was one of the reasons I'd never accepted a promotion. I was currently the National, but I was a Regional/National, so I was able to stay in the field.

"Maybe you won't have to," Brad said. "Maybe we can work something out. Just think about it." I promised to think about what he had said. He wanted me to talk to the VP of the Company and the owner and see what they thought. They agreed to consider me. My "soon-to-be-former" boss was supposed to stay until Labor Day weekend, but due to some issues that had arisen, he left earlier. The next week, my GM was due to be on vacation, so he asked me to fly in to Nashville for the week. It would be the first week of many. This was right around week 6 in my recovery and I wasn't sure I could take it on, but I did and felt fine.

After doing the job for 6 weeks on an interim basis while flying back and forth to Nashville, I was offered a job by another label. The catch was: they needed an answer within two days. I hadn't been formally offered the new job at BBR, so I had to force everyone's hand. Plus, I had to make sure it was right for me.

Randy and I had discussed the offer, and he believed I should take it. His opinion had always been that owning his business in PA held me back from going to Nashville and moving up the corporate label ladder. I never felt that way, but he did. He encouraged me to take the job. I thought about it and prayed about it. More than anything, I felt a loyalty to the artists at BBR. We were losing the Head of Promotions and probably losing two of our best regionals. Our artists deserved someone who would stay and work their music. I had put a lot of time and effort into the careers of Jason Aldean, Craig Morgan, Megan Mullins and Crossin Dixon and felt I owed it to them and myself to continue working with their careers and allow them some stability in the staff that they trusted.

## Donor Girl

I had been staying with one of my coworkers when I was in Nashville, but she and I were both getting a bit tired of that. She was in her late 30s and I was in my early 40s, so neither of us was eager to have a roommate like back in college.

After talking to Brad and Randy, I decided to go for the job with BBR. I put together 3 options for what I was willing to do the job for moneywise. I called the owner of our company, Benny Brown, and explained that I had another job offer on the table. I told Benny that I'd be faxing 3 different options. If he was interested in me staying with the company as the Head of Promotions, he could sign the one of his choice. If not, I'd be putting in my two-week notice as the other offer was very good. I wasn't trying to play hardball at all. It's not my style. I was simply put in a situation where I had to make a quick decision, and I had some excellent options.

I spoke to the label owner, Benny Brown, and the VP Jim Yerger, and we reached an agreement that night. It was agreed that BBR would provide me with an apartment and fly me in on Monday mornings and back out on Thursday nights. I would have to travel to all the regions throughout the country as well. It was a wonderful opportunity and I was happy to take it. Benny has always been good to me, honest with me, and I was happy at BBR. In the next couple of months, two more regionals would leave for other labels; Craig would still be in the process of looking for another label while still working with us on his single, "International Harvester"; and Brad and I would be trying to put together a new staff while working music with basically half a staff. It was a crazy, difficult time, but within months, we had a full staff of some incredibly talented promotions people.

We had a battle ahead of us until the chart freeze in December. We were working an incredible song on Jason called "Laughed Until We Cried," however, it was moving much slower than we'd have liked. It became a weekly battle to make sure the song remained bulleted and moving up the chart. We spent 6 weeks at #28! Finally, after much battling and convincing radio this song *was* a hit, we finally made it to Top 25 and the chart freeze. YAY! We now had 3 weeks where we wouldn't have to watch the daily charts for our report card.

Donor Girl

# <u>Well Deserved Vacation</u>

During the months before my surgery, Dr. Cooper would always tell me to focus on a happy place; somewhere that would take my mind off what was going on and give me some peace. I was very focused on my upcoming sailboat cruise to Tortola and the surrounding islands. It was the same cruise we had taken the year before, when kidney donation was just a thought, not a reality.

Years before, when Jodi's daughter was born, I had promised her that no matter what, I'd attend her daughter's bat mitzvah. Ironically, it fell on the same day we were due in Tortola. Randy and I agreed that he would fly ahead with the luggage and have everything unloaded and on the sailboat by the time I would arrive late Saturday night. I left Nashville and flew to Long Island, arriving at 11:00 P.M. on Thursday. Jodi and I stayed up for as long as we could, finally going to bed with the big morning ahead of us.

I love Jodi's family; they have this wonderfully chaotic way about them. While watching the flurry of everyone running around and Jodi's husband heading out to get bagels while Jodi and Amanda's hair and makeup person got them ready, I marveled at this family I had known for 20 years. As much as I wanted to be on the way to Tortola, *this* was the same girl who had dropped everything months earlier to be by my side during one of the most difficult times of my life. I was so glad to be there that day. Jodi's father had passed away back in 2000, and his absence on this big day was felt. Jodi's mom was there as well as her in-laws.

It was icy outside, and we all carefully made our way to the car. Jodi and I shared the front seat, and Amanda, Brock and Jodi's mom, Ruth, were in the back. Ken was driving. Everyone was worried about being late, but it was noted that nothing was going to start without Amanda there. When I saw Jodi's brother, Stuart,

he hugged me and said, "Thanks for always being there for Jodi."
I said it was my pleasure and she was always there for me.

Unfortunately, the airline had moved my flight up from 5:30 to
1:30, which would greatly reduce my time at the bat mitzvah. I'd
get to see most of the ceremony, although I'd miss the reception.
After watching Ken and his brothers, Stu, Jodi and Amanda all go
through the ritual of the bat mitzvah (which was quite amazing),
the car service showed up to take me to the airport. The good
news was, with the change in flight times, I'd make it all the way
to Tortola that night and not have to stay by myself in Puerto Rico.
I arrived, checked in, and went to the gate. Everything was on
time; right up until 1:00 when they announced the flight was
delayed until 4:30. **ARE YOU KIDDING ME?** I called Randy
who was at the San Juan Airport, and he told me to get on the last
flight out of San Juan into Tortola. So I called and got my flight
changed. We finally boarded around 4:30, and then sat on the
plane for an hour while the world's slowest baggage handlers
loaded our luggage. We finally took off at 5:30 which was the
original time of the original flight. I could have enjoyed at least 4
more hours of the bat mitzvah.

All the Tortola connectors were assured the flight would wait for
us. We all got off the plane and ran to our next gate, only to be
told the flight had just left. I was now an English-speaking
American alone in Puerto Rico. Lovely. I called Randy who
assured me it wasn't a problem; he was having a blast without me.
Lovely. Luckily, I was put up in a nice Crowne Plaza hotel with
an ocean view. I was given a minimal dinner voucher and went
down to the beachside restaurant to eat by myself. I ran into one
of the guys from the plane who was also stuck. He was an
adorable young guy who had been raised in Tortola and attended a
university in England. He was coming home for Christmas. We
agreed to meet in the morning and grab a cab. As devastated as I
was to miss the flight, he was more disconsolate. He and his
friends were due to go to a huge concert on Tortola that night, and

## Donor Girl

he was very excited about it.   He would end up missing the concert.

Finally, the next morning came, and we flew the puddle jumper to Tortola. I caught a cab to the marina and joined the revelers on the sailboat for what would be an amazingly wonderful week in the islands.  I had purposely bought one piece bathing suits to hide my scars and Randy had said "Don't you dare hide those beautiful scars.  You wear them with pride."  By December, my scars were already fading, I was feeling great and a week on a sailboat was just what the doctor ordered.  I was truly looking back and saying, "That was a nonevent."  *Now* I understood what she meant.

Donor Girl

## <u>And Life Flies By</u>

July 11, 2008 came faster than I ever would have thought. It was now a year post surgery. To commemorate the moment, I met Kelly, Dave and the kids at the hospital. We walked up to Floor 8 and relived the experience, yet in a more positive way. We posed for pictures in front of the Wall of Fame which has my name printed as a donor in 2007. It was a proud moment, and I thanked God that my kidney had served Dave well for a year.

I'd been flying back and forth to Nashville every week, sometimes not seeing home for 2 weeks at a time. It was tough but rewarding. "Laughed Until We Cried" kicked in and reached Top 5; "International Harvester" went Top 10; and in February 2008, Craig did leave for another label. Months later, we signed country music icon Randy Owen who was lead singer for Alabama for over 25 years.

Being out on the road with Randy Owen was a whole different experience. As a teenager, I had spent 3 hours waiting in line to meet him. I had done it again two more times in my 20s. Being on a bus with him was surreal. In fact, at one point, he was in the process of writing a song and asked me to give him my opinion of it. Randy Owen; writer of so many hit songs like "Lady Down On Love" and "Feels So Right"; seller of 57 million albums; singer of 30 some #1 hits. He was asking *me* to be the first person to ever hear his song. It was truly a high point in my career. Being with Randy Owen is being around a true star. Everywhere we go, people know him. Whether they are in their 20s or 60s; they all know Randy Owen. If we still had Craig on the label, would we have signed Randy? I don't know. But things happen for a reason and as sad as it was to lose Craig as an artist, working with Randy became equally enjoyable. And luckily, my friendship with Craig remained very strong.

Donor Girl

And being a living organ donor changed my life. Nina now calls me and asks me to talk to other potential donors. I'm always happy to do it and remember what it meant to me that people were willing to talk me through my fears. Now I try to be there for them. I've talked to both Dr. Cooper and Nina numerous times about my feelings concerning the donor getting left out the cold after donating. And in talking with other donors, I realized I was not alone. There had already been talks about a living organ donor clinic, and when I met Nina for lunch in the spring, she told me it was going to happen. Now, after someone donates an organ, they not only have tests 2 weeks after surgery, but can come back to the clinic for a 6 month, one year and two year follow up! What a wonderful service to offer donors.

I wanted to do a benefit to help them raise the initial funds and decided to throw a concert at my church with Crossin Dixon and Megan Mullins. The University of Maryland Medical Center was very supportive and loved the idea of the benefit. I set it for August 7th, which happened to be Dr. Cooper's birthday. That was by chance because I had to plan it when the artists were in my area for cost effective reasons. Unfortunately, Dr. Cooper would be out of town vacationing with his family at the time of the benefit. I was hoping he'd be able to speak at the benefit. Nina had planned on being there and was willing to speak, but at the last minute, she was unable to attend. They promised to get a replacement.

A couple of weeks before the benefit, our church hosted the Emmaus picnic. I met a man whose daughter had donated her kidney to a friend. He put us in touch, and she had such a wonderful story that I asked her to speak. She and her twin sister were both a match for their friend; however, they made the decision that she would donate if they were both a match because her sister had children. This way, if something ever happened to her kidney or the recipient's kidney, there was yet another backup plan. Deb Evans from the Medical Center also drove up from Baltimore with 2 other women and agreed to speak on behalf of donors and the clinic. A woman named Stefanie whom I'd worked with from the University of Maryland Foundation was there. She'd been a huge help in organizing the actual monetary donation part of the benefit.

My friends, Randy, my church and my family all pulled together to sell tickets and get the word out and on August 7, 2008, we had about 150+ people show up and donate money. I had asked all my friends at other labels to donate items for a silent auction. We had items signed by Faith Hill, Jewel, Martina McBride and many others. My own artists had signed guitars, and we even had a Limited Edition Alabama Farewell electric guitar signed by the members of Alabama. My dad bid up everyone on that one just so he could give it back to me! He did make me put a plaque on it, though that read, "This item on loan by Bill Adams." We were able to raise $5000. Hopefully the first of many benefits for donors!

Donor Girl

# **One Year Later**

I was a couple of months late scheduling my one-year follow-up testing and was delighted that I could do it at the University of Maryland Medical Center Living Organ Donor Clinic. A year ago, that wouldn't have been an option. The Medical Center wanted to do a check presentation for the $5000, so we planned to do it all on the same day; Sept. 4, 2008.

I showed up in the conference room of the office building across the street from the Medical Center. As people started to come in, I recognized some of them as those that had attended the benefit. They stopped to give me a hug and tell me how much they'd enjoyed the evening. Then beautiful Nina came in and gave me a big hug and said how sorry she was that she missed the benefit concert. I had brought some photo books from the benefit and passed them around.

Dr. Cooper came in a few minutes later and asked everyone to sit down. He spent a few minutes talking about the kidney donor clinic and kidney donation in general, and then expressed his gratitude to me for all I had done. I was actually starting to get embarrassed by the praise and finally said something stupid like, "Well, it's not all altruistic. Being a kidney donor, I *will* benefit from a kidney donor clinic." Afterward, Dr. Cooper and I posed for pictures, holding the oversized check Randy had made that showed $5000 being given to the Kidney Donor Clinic.

Next, I was off to get my follow-up tests. I had blood drawn (a process I still hated but had learned not to freak out over) and a urine test ... which begs the question, "Why a cup?" Have they not figured out yet that women cannot properly hold a cup down there and aim without gross things happening? A FUNNEL is what women need. Come on people, figure this one out!

# Donor Girl

Dr. Cooper came in the room and asked overall questions about my health, exercise, eating, drinking, etc. He then examined my scars, exclaiming that I "heal very well." I can't imagine he'd say, "Oh geez, these scars look horrible." No matter what they looked like, he'd probably say, "You heal well," but it was nice to hear.

I then went to Nina for a follow-up discussion on how I was handling things emotionally. I spent the most amount of time with Nina and as always, it was a pleasure. She's such an interesting woman that the time flew by.

A week later, I had my results. My creatinine had gone down since my 2 week and 6 month follow-up. My pre-surgery number had been .8. My post surgery at 2 weeks was 1.2 and my 6 month was 1.2. I didn't like that it had gone up but was told that was normal. Dr. Cooper encouraged more water drinking which I hate but did, and my 1 year test was a 1.03. **YAY!** My proteins had also risen from pre-surgery but were in healthy parameters.

"I won't know until I know" is what I say when people ask, "How will this affect you long term?" But I recently talked briefly with Meg, who has since left the hospital to move to South Carolina, and she told me about meeting a man who donated to his father 25 years ago. The donor and recipient are both still doing well, and the kidney has lasted all 25 years and is still going strong. I pray for that outcome for Dave and me. I won't know until I know, but each and every day is a gift, and I thank God for it.

People often ask, "Would you do it again?" And the answer is, "Yes, I would." It's been an amazing journey of self-discovery that I wouldn't trade. Women at my church tell me I'm different. I know I feel it inside. I don't walk around with my head in the clouds and a smile on my face. I still give the occasional one finger wave to annoying people on the highway. I didn't become the saint I was called. But I am different for having made the decision to be a living kidney donor. I now have a sense of peace

## Donor Girl

about who I am and what my purpose is. The rest of life's little stuff has lost some of its importance. And now, I try to focus more on what is really important.

I read an article in which Dr. Cooper was quoted as saying, "When living people agree to donate a kidney, the gift of life is especially powerful because of the message it sends. For an individual to selflessly, and through no apparent gain of their own, go into an operating room and put themselves in harm's way to do something for another person is no small thing." I once asked him why he became a transplant surgeon and part of his answer was, "Usually, you have to take something out of a person to save their life. It's rewarding to put something into someone in order to save their life." When I reminded him he took "out" my kidney, he laughed and said, "Yes, but look at what it gave you."

So while there is no apparent health benefit, there is a gain; a gain you can't even imagine until being there yourself. The summer of 2008, our family went to Ocean City, Maryland. Dave was in the water with Randy and the kids; playing, riding waves and acting like a kid himself. When he came out of the water he said, "Wow, thank you, Lee. A year ago, I wouldn't have even been able to make this trip. Now I'm in the ocean playing with my children and riding waves. Thank you." **WOW!** Dave is back to work; he's back to running; he's back to being a husband and father. And I was able to help him do those things. **WOW!**

If it took giving up a kidney and saving a life to learn what's really important in my life, then it was a small price to pay. And while this choice might not be for everyone, I would encourage you to please check "yes" on your driver's license to be an organ donor. You will save lives, and I'm hard pressed to think of anything more miraculous than that of giving and saving a life.

Donor Girl

# **<u>Dedications</u>**

I have had the honor and privilege to meet other kidney donors who have given the gift of life to save people they loved and cared about. Marla Zielinski donated her kidney to her mom, and both are doing great over a year later. Ruth donated to her friend. Teri George donated her kidney to her boss of 20 years, and both are doing great nearly a year later. And Ryan Griffin donated his kidney to his cousin. All are doing great.

To all of them, and everyone who donates blood, bone marrow, and organs, this is dedicated to you. Those of you that went before me helped to make the surgery easier, safer and more successful. Those of you who were practically cut in half to donate a part of yourself so others would live. It was you who allowed medicine and surgery to grow to where it is now. A one small cut incision! You are the true heroes.

**Front and back cover art by Laura Wilson Champion.**

Made in the USA
Lexington, KY
28 October 2013